John G. Gunnell

AMERICAN POLITY
POLITICAL SCIENCE
AND THE DISCOURSE OF DEMOCRACY

THE PENNSYLVANIA STATE UNIVERSITY PRESS
UNIVERSITY PARK, PENNSYLVANIA

Library of Congress Cataloging-in-Publication Data

Gunnell, John G.

   Imagining the American polity :

     political science and the discourse of democracy /

     John G. Gunnell.

   p. cm.

   Includes bibliographical references and index.

   ISBN 0-271-02352-X (cloth : alk. paper)

   ISBN 0-271-02353-8 (pbk. : alk. paper)

   1. Political science—United States—History.

   2. Democracy—United States—History.

   I. Title.

JA84.U5 G783 2004

320'.0973—dc21

2003008774

IMAGINING THE AMERICAN POLITY

IMAGINING THE

For Jane Frances and Ariel Aldisa,
may they live in democratic times.

For since we are, after all, products of earlier generations, we are also the products of their aberrations, passions, and mis-understandings—indeed, of their crimes; it is impossible to free ourselves completely from this chain. If we condemn these aberrations, and regard ourselves free of them, this does not alter the fact that we are descended from them.

—FRIEDRICH NIETZSCHE

CONTENTS

PREFACE

This work is grounded in the belief, and argument, that there is a symbiotic relationship between objective historical research and critical analysis. Historical study is not only an important form and dimension of disciplinary self-reflection; we have reached a point at which rhetorical images of the past, such as those that have typically characterized accounts of academic fields, are less persuasive than methodologically and substantively defensible scholarship. I have long been involved with what I have called "encounters of the third kind," that is, the theory and practice of the philosophy and history of the social sciences. This book is the culmination of two decades of research on the history of American political science. An earlier book (*The Descent of Political Theory: The Genealogy of an American Vocation,* 1993) was devoted to describing, explaining, and assessing the history and contemporary status of academic political theory. While that work focused on images of and concerns about the relationship between political science (and political theory) and politics, the present volume is primarily a study of the evolution of the vision of democracy in American political science. These two themes are in many ways closely related, and in both cases I have followed what I call an internalist approach to intellectual history, an approach that is more fully described and applied in the present project. Although there is some overlap between these works, as well as a complementary relationship, with respect to both the argument and the content of the narrative, I have attempted to avoid unnecessary duplication. The initial stage of the research for both books was supported by a fellowship from the National Endowment for the Humanities, and the final portion, including much of the research and final drafting of this volume, has been sponsored by a grant from the National Science Foundation. The State University of New York at Albany and its Rockefeller College of Public Affairs and Policy and Department of Political Science have been generous in providing material support and leave. My work has benefited from the contributions of, and conversations with, a small but growing group of scholars who have been devoted to innovative work on the history of political and social science. In particular, David Easton, James Farr, and Gene Poschman have, in their individual ways, consistently sustained and contributed to my search for the past of political science, and Peter Breiner and Henrik Bang have enhanced significantly my encounter with, and understanding of, contemporary democratic theory. James Farr and Stephen Leonard provided helpful, careful, detailed, and knowledgeable comments and suggestions on an earlier version of the manuscript.

INTRODUCTION

They constantly try to escape
From the darkness outside and within
By dreaming of systems so perfect
That no one will need to be good.

                    —*T. S. Eliot*

Although today it is commonly assumed that the American political system is the epitome of a democratic regime, Americans from the late eighteenth century to the present have had difficulty determining exactly what kind of political society they had created and what form of government they possessed—or by which they were possessed. This situation has inspired many attempts both to give an account of the nature of popular government, self-rule, or democracy and to judge the extent to which the United States conforms to such an account. John Adams mounted a *Defense of the Constitutions of America* before the creation of the United States Constitution, and from the time of the debates about the ratification of the Constitution to the present, Americans have continued to *imagine* their nation's polity. American political science, from its conception and inception, has been a central and unique part of this dialogue, and this book traces, in detail, central dimensions of the evolution of the discourse of democracy in this academic practice. However we may judge that discourse and its vision of democracy, the discipline has consistently defined itself as a science devoted to the understanding and propagation of democracy, and it has played a large role in valorizing that concept and equating it with the American political system.

   The study of the history of political science, and particularly American political science, has evolved to a point where it would be hubristic to attempt to write a history of the field as a whole or even to describe fully its participation in constructing the American democratic vision. Consequently, this volume represents a selection. This study is organized around three closely related and historically overlapping indigenous concepts that, I argue, have been pivotal in demarcating paradigmatic transformations in the meaning of the word "democracy" and the conversations in which it has been featured: *state, pluralism,* and *liberalism.* My principal concern is with the manner in which each of these concepts has represented and entailed a theory of democracy. Since much of the focus is on the decline of the nineteenth-century theory of state and the evolution of pluralist theory, this study could be construed as a history of the latter, but while this transition in the field may be the only one to which Thomas Kuhn's criteria for designating a scientific revolution could be applied, my concerns are more broadly with democratic theory in the context of American political science.

One correlate of this endeavor is to rethink what we mean by American political thought. The study of American political ideas has come under the spell of its own "myth of the tradition."[1] Just as the "great tradition" of political theory, from Plato to Marx, was less an actual historical tradition than an analytical and retrospective construction created by political scientists, political theorists, and other commentators, many of the dominant images of the history of American political theory, as well as of subsidiary traditions, such as that of liberalism, are canonical fictions that have been reified and presented as if they were genealogies that in some way explained contemporary configurations of political thought and action. A pantheon of authors and texts, representing diverse genres and realms of discourse from the Puritans onward, has been selected by various criteria adduced in the present, the components of which have been arranged chronologically and presented as if they were participants in a conversation over time about matters such as democracy. While there may be many reasons and justifications for *constructing* traditions of this sort, problems are created by the failure to distinguish between such constructions and *reconstructions* of preconstituted traditions. It is, in this light, indeed appropriate and necessary to reconsider what we mean when we speak of the history of American political thought, and part of that reconsideration must involve recovering the identity and contours of actual traditions, both first-order (in political life) and second-order (such as those in social science), considering the relationship between them, and assessing their explanatory and normative significance for the present. One such preconstituted

1. See John G. Gunnell, *Political Theory: Tradition and Interpretation* (Cambridge, Mass.: Winthrop, 1979); *Between Philosophy and Politics: The Alienation of Political Theory* (Amherst: University of Massachusetts Press, 1986); "Annals of Political Theory: Replies and Reflections," in *Tradition, Interpretation, and Science,* ed. John S. Nelson (Albany: State University of New York Press, 1986).

tradition is that of democratic theory in American political science.

Although this literature may not be considered as philosophically and literarily complex and intriguing as the texts of the classic canon of political philosophy or as romantic as some of the textual icons characteristically designated as exemplars of American political thought, it has often been neglected and prematurely depreciated. It is less that this literature has been demonstrated to be theoretically deficient than that it has fallen out of style. But the visions of democracy conjured up by American political science, whether judged to be banal or profound, have, on the whole, exercised a far greater and more direct influence on contemporary political perceptions and forms of life than, for example, the work of either John Locke or Ralph Waldo Emerson. Yet, even within the discipline of political science, the history of this literature has received insufficient and less than careful attention.

Describing, explaining, and evaluating the United States as a democratic society has, in many respects, been the defining mission of political science, yet contemporary political scientists seldom step back to reflect, in any thorough and objective manner, on past accounts of American politics and government. Even less often do they scrutinize the received images of their history. Both mainstream political scientists and those who seek separate personae as political theorists have been prone, for a variety of reasons, to forget, suppress, or falsify their past—and to deny or fail to recognize that it is a past that they share. Consequently, they understand adequately neither their contemporary intellectual identity nor the manner and the extent to which the structure and content of the conversations in which they are now immersed are a legacy from that past. This suppression of the past also leads to a neglect of the relevance of the dreams and insights about American politics that were produced by earlier generations. Some of the persistent wariness about examining the history of the field can be attributed to a fear on the part of certain mainstream practitioners that such studies might undermine the belief in scientific progress that they wish to foster and sustain, but many political theorists and disciplinary dissidents also often tend to trivialize that history and disassociate themselves from it. There are many reasons why we should peer into the past of political science, but one specific and salient reason that extends beyond disciplinary issues is that the history of the field has significance both for thinking about contemporary democratic theory and for understanding the pedigree of the issues that today animate discussion.

Although contemporary empirical political science remains concerned about democracy, the principal focus, at least in recent years, has been

primarily on what are taken to be various democratic processes and indi-
cators, rather than on the theory of democracy and on the general character of the United States as a democratic polity. Since the early 1970s, or
the beginning of what is commonly referred to as the postbehavioral era,
democratic theory has largely been the domain of the subfield of political
theory, which, although professionally attached to political science, has
become intellectually estranged and discursively separate from the discipline as a whole. The interdisciplinary enclave of political theory has forged
a quite distinct intellectual identity and even constructed a separate history for itself. Although both mainstream political science and political
theory are prone to seek their roots, and validate themselves, in terms of
springing from Aristotle, the story of political theory as presented by someone such as Sheldon Wolin is very different from the narrative of scientific
achievement told by someone such as Gabriel Almond. One consequence
of this alienation has been that democratic theory has tended to become a
somewhat abstract, decontextualized philosophical endeavor, while the
empirical study of democracy has attenuated theoretical grounding and
import. Much of contemporary democratic theory speaks only obliquely
to issues in American politics, and many of the traditional democratic concerns of political science have become latent.

Despite recent advances in the historiography of social science, "telling
the story" of American political science often continues to be a rhetorically
motivated endeavor. The critical and legitimating functions that historical narratives may serve need not, however, nullify their scholarly integrity,
and, in fact, we have reached a point at which convincing criticism and
historical credibility can no longer be easily disjoined. Engaging in the
serious study of disciplinary history, however, inevitably raises a number
of complex methodological problems, as well as the issue of the relationship between the study of the history of political science and contemporary disciplinary practice. This book, most generically construed, is an
exercise in the history of social science, but since such research is still a
less than clearly defined scholarly genre, I will specify and emphasize the
particular historiographical assumptions that inform this work.

As Bernard Crick and other scholars have stressed, political science has
been a distinctly and uniquely *American* social science. Notwithstanding
its universal scientific aspirations, emigration, and export to other countries, especially subsequent to World War II, and the waves of foreign influence that have contributed to shaping it, political science bears a unique
relationship to American political life and ideology. And its concerns have
been practical as well as scholarly. While political science has sought to

give a descriptive and explanatory account of the nature of the American democratic polity, affecting democratic thought and behavior was, from the beginning, a principal goal of the discipline. It was committed to creating a truly scientific study of politics, but despite changing images of science, there has been a persistent search for a discipline that would have an end in action and that would contribute to realizing and enhancing democratic values and institutions. There has been, nevertheless, considerable ambivalence about the discipline's actual and proper relationship to politics, and it has often been suggested that the simultaneous commitments to science and democracy have not always been in harmony with one another.

This tension between theory and practice has in part involved the problem of reconciling scientific and political criteria of judgment, but it has also been the consequence of a longstanding assumption that only by remaining aloof from politics could the discipline gain the scientific authority that would, in the end, give it political purchase. Consequently, although the American science of politics emerged from, and has remained tied to, American political culture, it has in various ways sought to distance itself, both conceptually and institutionally. The social sciences in general have tended to conceive of their subject matter in an abstract manner, and political science has been no exception. Anthropology chose, and we might even say invented, culture; sociology studied the vague entity, society; and economists turned away from economic issues to examine an analytical image called the economy. Although politics was a more concrete and prefigured phenomenon and less subject to such theoretical displacement, political scientists, through concepts such as the state, have sublimated their object of inquiry and created intellectual and practical distance. Such detachment was viewed as necessary in part because, as many in the nineteenth century who attempted to speak in a partisan manner from the podium discovered, politics in its actual manifestations was a dangerous object of inquiry—much as in the case of anthropologists studying cannibals. And the real task was often conceived to be one of purifying or "converting" it into something such as administration. But a degree of remoteness was also pursued, because science seemed to hold the key to practical authority, and science demanded objectivity and distance. Thus while it is often assumed that American political science can be understood as a reflection of American society and that it has, in turn, reinforced and legitimated the values of that society, it has also often been suggested that the discipline is quite alienated from the particularities of public life.

Self-consciousness and concern about its relationship to politics has

significantly informed political science's successive crises of identity, and
the issue of this relationship has, from the beginning, been an important
theme in the discourse of the field as well as in historical accounts of the
discipline. But despite diverse, and sometimes contradictory, claims about
the extent to which the images of politics and government produced by
political science influence political ideas and behavior, about how these
images have been a product of their political context, and about the discipline's apolitical character and lack of political relevance, we possess little in the way of detailed knowledge about the actual character of this
relationship. Yet notwithstanding the paucity of distinct evidentiary support, it is undeniable that the imaginings produced by the discipline have,
in various ways such as through diverse levels and vehicles of pedagogy
and their influence on a variety of media, been sedimented in the perceptions and practices of citizens and political actors as well as in the vision
of other denizens of the academy. The discourse of democracy in the discipline represents the most persistent, articulate, focused, and self-conscious tradition of democratic thought in American life. Although
American political science has never fulfilled the dreams of practical effect
that have extended from its nineteenth-century founders to modern policy analysts, the discipline has, both formally and informally, played a significant role in shaping political education and in forging popular
conceptions of American democracy. But what is involved is a complicated
relationship between two orders of practice and their accompanying modes
of discourse.

Political participants and citizens embrace and disseminate representa-
tions and idealizations of politics and government, however inchoate and
inconsistent, or in some cases simplified and simplistic. Embedded in or
entwined with these constructions are a variety of validating and embel-
lishing historical and normative metapolitical claims, which are articulated with varying degrees of explicitness and reflectiveness. In the United
States, the image of democracy and the story of its origin and development
constitute such a metanarrative and have been a significant element of
American political identity and the language of politics. From the time of
the American founding, however, there have been parallel accounts of political identity along with complementary metanarratives that have been more
critically informed and relatively autonomous. These *re*-constructions, such
as those located in the scholarly practices of history and social science,
despite their eventual home in the academy, often sprung from practical
concerns, but even if they have sometimes repenetrated everyday political
life, they constitute a different realm of discourse. Various and complex

attitudes and perspectives have informed these formal metapractices, but the supervenient accounts and ideal typifications produced by such institutionalized forms of inquiry represent a language *about* politics, which, despite similarities, overlap, and relationships with political discourse, is distinct from the language *of* politics.

The existence of such discourses about politics, whatever their intention and purpose, not only raises questions about the verisimilitude of their claims but, at least implicitly, presents a challenge to the form and content of political life and entails the issue of the relationship between politics and political science. The claims of political science not only often constitute a rival description and evaluation of the polity but also may reflect a different theory of social reality than that embedded in the activity of politics itself. While, for example, the practices of science and religion may compete with each other with respect to rendering an account of nature, nature is not, literally, a party to the dialogue. Different renditions within and between the social sciences may also compete with one another, but, in an important sense, they also often compete with their subject matter. Sometimes these metapractical accounts represent an attempt to make explicit what is merely tacit in the activity and self-image of their subject matter, and sometimes they serve to justify those self-images. At other times, however, they contain pointed contradictions of received wisdom and constitute theoretical, factual, and ethical challenges to the social construction of political reality, challenges that often seem rather hollow if disjoined from political reform. Both attitudes have been part of the story of democratic theory in political science.

While I engage certain dimensions of the relationship between the language of politics and the language of political science, my purpose is not primarily to trace empirically the interaction between these realms of discourse. My focus is essentially on the internal constitution and development of political science's vision of the American polity and on its attending beliefs, hopes, and fears regarding its relationship to that polity. I assume, however, that this reveals something about the character both of American politics and American political science themselves as well as the connections between them, and I also assume that understanding the history of political science is a necessary prolegomenon to any informed investigation and evaluation of this relationship. It is impossible to study the history of the field without recognizing the degree to which the discourse has been propelled by a concern about the discipline's practical relationship to its subject matter. Although I have adopted an approach that I label "internal history," which stresses the dynamics of conceptual change within

the discourse of political science, this approach does not imply a depreciation of the political setting in which political science evolved. It does,
however, assume that it is the political scientists' *perceptions* of that setting
and of the discipline's relationship to it that is crucial. Although this book
is limited to the discipline of political science, the study is pursued against
the background of the more general issues of the relationship between social
science and American public life, the nature of American democracy, and
democratic theory in general.

To speak, as this volume does, about the past of American political science
and the images of the American polity that it has evoked is to enter a third
realm of discourse that is neither that of the first-order universe of politics
nor the second-order practice of political science. Such third-order studies
involve not only exploring the discursive constitution of the social sciences
and their relationship to their subject matter, but also confronting what
might be considered fourth-order issues regarding the nature of this enterprise, how it has been conducted, and its relationship to the fields that
constitute its subject matter. The study of the history of social science raises
a number of epistemological issues that are structurally parallel to those
involved in the relationship between social science and its subject matter
and that cannot be disjoined from substantive claims about the past of the
discipline. My concern in distinguishing these various orders of discourse
and practice is not to suggest that they are insulated from one another but,
on the contrary, to demonstrate that while they are not the same, there are
significant relationships between them that must be grasped and confronted. Accounts of the history of political science, whether informal or
the product of a distinct research domain and whether authored by political scientists or professional historians, have become part of the self-images
of the discipline and its search for identity. It is necessary, however, to raise
the question of whether what has often largely been part of what might be
called a rhetoric of inquiry can become a practice of knowledge, that is, to
what extent claims about the history of a discipline can be judged by criteria of historicity. The major portion of this volume represents, so to speak,
an effort to practice methodologically what I have, over a number of years,
professed about the conduct of intellectual history, textual interpretation,
and the study of concepts and conceptual change. Although I do not want
to "frontload" and overload this study with complex methodological arguments and critiques, it is necessary to clarify the presuppositions inform-
ing its research and writing.

The internalist approach represented in *The Descent of Political Theory* has consistently and consciously informed this volume.[2] By referring to my project as *internal history*, I first of all signal my wish to move beyond the kind of externalism characteristic of rhetorical or "presentist" histories, whether of the Whiggish or polemical variety, which have tended to dominate accounts of the history of the discipline and that have told the story of political science in terms of some a priori image of progress or decline. Second, much of the history of the political science, and intellectual history in general, has rendered its subject in terms of analytical concepts and constructed traditions that have, in many instances, effectively obscured important aspects of the character of indigenous conversations and transformations within these conversations. Third, I want to alter somewhat the distribution of emphasis characteristic of much of recent historical scholarship which has employed a variety of contextualist approaches, and to avoid some of the problems involved in such approaches. Although I do not want to suggest that I am modeling this study on Thomas Kuhn's account of the history of scientific revolutions, there is a similarity in that the emphasis in both cases is on the internal dynamics of scientific discussions rather than on explaining the content and evolution of such discussions in terms of some broad account of their social and political ambience. One might reasonably argue that in the case of *political* science ambience is more salient, but my assumption and claim is that the discipline itself and its university setting, as in the case of natural science, is the most relevant context. My focus, for both pragmatic and epistemological reasons, is on the internal structure and content of the discourse that is investigated rather than what might be characterized as the wider social and political context in which it arose and evolved. A third major concern is to give more careful attention to what might be called the longitudinal dimension of historical analysis, to the archaeology and genealogy of conversations, and to the principal concepts and conceptual changes that have defined those conversations.

The approach in this work, then, focuses on understanding *concepts* and *conceptual change* in the context of the evolution of *conversations* in academic *discourses* and *practices*. Most of the discussion in historical studies and social science, and in the philosophies of history and social science, about understanding and explaining social and historical phenomena has been conducted in terms of competing but theoretically unanchored epistemologies and methodologies. These claims about the nature of social and historical

---

2. Gunnell, *The Descent of Political Theory: The Genealogy of an American Vocation* (Chicago: University of Chicago Press, 1993).

knowledge and the manner of its acquisition have not been redeemed by a fully explicated theory of the phenomena in question. Although in this setting I can neither elaborate fully such a theory and the tenets of interpretation and the theory of concepts predicated upon it, nor describe in detail my framework of analysis based on the "orders of discourse" and the *cognitive* and *practical* relationships between them,[3] my concern is to make the basic elements of such a theory and the entailed approach clear and explicit.

In the following chapters, the basic object of analysis is neither particular books, journal articles, and other discursive artifacts nor their authors, but the conversations in which they were involved and the concepts and arguments that were the nuclei of those conversations. Although the term "conversation" is frequently, and often loosely, employed, my usage is neither metaphorical nor analytical, that is, it does not refer simply to a selection of certain things that, from some perspective and in terms of some criteria adduced by the interpreter, possess a family resemblance. Although the participants in a conversation may not always have recognized or articulated what I specify as its identity and parameters, my specification is a corrigible claim about the existence and character of a certain configuration of discourse. I am not suggesting that participants were lacking consciousness of their situation but only that, while in process, a conversation may not have been easily circumscribed and acknowledged. Such a conversation is admittedly a kind of phenomenon that is more readily perceivable within the relatively determinate confines of an academic discipline than in more general and amorphous dimensions of human activity, but the concept is not necessarily confined to the former venue. My assumption is that the principal explanation for transformations in the concepts that define a conversation must be internal to that conversation no matter how important some broader context might be as far as limiting, allowing, and instigating certain conceptual formations and modes of discourse. Just as in the case of evolutionary biology, it is the genetic capacities of organic forms that largely govern development rather than the random role of environment. There is neither any a priori means of determining how forms will respond nor a definitive explanation of why they responded in the manner that they did. But we can *describe* the character of the transformation. The chapter divisions in this volume represent what I take to be natural or indigenous stages in the conversation about democ-

---

3. For a fuller discussion of a theory of conventional objects, practices and discourses, and interpretation, see Gunnell, *The Orders of Discourse: Philosophy, Social Science, and Politics* (Lanham, Md.: Rowman & Littlefield, 1998), chapters 1, 2, 5; "Time and Interpretation: Understanding Conceptual Change," *History of Political Thought* 19 (1998).

racy in political science, and, in order to capture the integrity and flow of the conversation, I have not imposed analytical subdivisions within the chapters. While much of intellectual history categorizes, characterizes, and describes arguments and ideas, and supports those descriptions with a few apposite quotations, I seek to render more fully the structure and content of the arguments that constitute this conversation. This approach admittedly makes the narrative somewhat dense at times, particularly since the original arguments may have been less than perfectly articulated, but my goal is to render the arguments as they emerged rather than to rationalize them in terms of some contemporary framework. In order to factor out my interpretation from other historical claims and to maintain a separation between the interpretation and the subject matter, I have, except where immediately related to a specific claim, largely eliminated references to secondary literature in the body of work, and have instead included an Appendix devoted to the subject of "telling the story of political science."

While my brand of internalism involves theoretical claims regarding the nature of social or conventional phenomena and the cognitive and practical relationship between the practice of interpretation and its object, there are also, in the case of the history of political science, some more circumstantial reasons for adopting an internalist approach. No matter what quarrels I may have with past attempts to recount the history of political science, most commentaries, as I have already noted, have focused on the manner in which the problem of the relationship between academic and public discourse has structured the development of the field. Many commentators have also stressed the extent to which professionalism, the commitment to science, and the habitat of the university have served to create a gulf between the field and public life—even while the goal of social science has consistently been to affect public life. As a consequence, the discipline and profession of political science have developed, as has much of the American academy, quite independent of what might be viewed as the general social and political context. This is not to say that there have not, at various junctures, been important connections and relationships, both perceived and real; however, the situation in the United States has not, for example, been like that of Germany and other European countries where there have been much more complex and intimate interactions between the university and the structure of political power. Despite the common tendency to attempt to explain what has taken place in the history of political science by referring to its general sociopolitical setting, there is reason to emphasis explanatory factors that are internal to disciplinary practice. This in no way implies that the discourse of political science has not been driven by its concerns about the political world and about its relationship to that world, but only that in the end it has been that discourse's understanding of that world and of its relationship to it that has been most decisive, and that the understanding has been through the lens of disciplinary constructions.

This volume is, to repeat, for the most part a third-order interpretive study of a second-order practice and its discourse, that is, a discourse about the first-order world of politics. The conversations revolving around the *word* "democracy" and the *concepts* to which the word has referred constitute the basic subject matter. I stress this difference between words and concepts because while historians often claim to be writing the history of a concept, such as the state, they are actually writing histories of words that, in the course of their use, have referred to quite different concepts. The continuity of a word often does not represent the continuity of a concept, as I will demonstrate with regard to the "state"; likewise, a concept may persist with different words assigned to it, as I will argue in the case of "liberalism" and "pluralism." Although much of contemporary intellectual history reflects the impact of the late-twentieth-century "linguistic turn" in its approach to conceiving and interpreting social phenomena, much of it is still bound to the assumption that what it is uncovering are the thoughts, beliefs, and other mentalistic entities expressed in words and actions. I often persist in using the term "idea," but that use is simply a convenience of speech. I am not referring to anything that lies behind language. The conversations I identify are reconstructions, one might say even hypothetical claims, drawn from an examination of books, articles, and various other primary documents. These conversations are presented as the primary, or "natural," *context* for understanding these concepts. A secondary context is the evolving disciplinary matrix of political science, and its place in the university can be understood as a tertiary context. The types of putative contexts about which I am wary are abstractions such as "modernity" or "crisis of authority," but also more detailed constructions of the historian that are often derived from diverse bodies of secondary literature and often more juxtaposed as independent variables than concretely connected to the concepts that are the object of interpretation. I do not dismiss authors as historically situated agents, but since the principal objects of analysis are conversations and concepts, I treat authors primarily as participants in a conversation. While I attempt to identify adequately often now forgotten or obscure individuals, I do not offer an extended account of their biography. Although I am valorizing conversations over the "ideas" of individuals, this reflects less some philosophical claim about the primacy of language vis-à-vis authors than my particular distribution of emphasis. Although there may be something to be said for the idea of authorial authority in terms of the identity and meaning of particular texts, the claim is less convincing with respect to conversations.

Finally, on a related note, something more must be said about the perennially vexing question of historical objectivity, particularly in the case of disciplinary history that has characteristically been so rhetorically motivated. If one should mean by "objective" some perspective that is theoretically neutral regarding the nature of social phenomena, then the concept of objectivity would be an empty abstraction. If one refers to a position that is devoid of political or ethical focus, concern, or motivation, or that is not embedded in a social setting or is in some manner translinguistic, it would be nearly as sterile. Objectivity, like other modal concepts, has a universal force, but its ultimate meaning requires context-dependent criteria of application whether in matters of historical interpretation or refereeing football. There are no substantive criteria of objectivity rooted in either the "facts" or the manner of their apprehension. So what can we mean when we ask, for example, whether a study of the history of political science could be objective? It does little good to suggest that it can never be entirely neutral when there are no criteria for, or even an image of, something such as complete neutrality. In the case of metapractices such as history, as with any practice of knowledge, objectivity entails basically the establishment of standards in a scholarly community, but there are attributes peculiar to metapractical endeavors.

While there is no position that is not informed by various theoretical premises, critical concerns, choices of subject matter, distributions of emphasis, and problem orientations, the discursive identity of what is interpreted, as I have already stressed, is not in the first instance a function of interpretation and interpretive communities. This claim should not be construed as a suggestion that there is some authoritative epistemological standard to which we can repair in order to settle differences between competing historical reconstructions; but a text, or any interpretive object, does have a physical and conventional constitution distinct from its interpretive reconstruction. An interpretation is another text, and the very concept of interpretation carries with it the assumption of a distinction between an interpretation and what is interpreted. To achieve objectivity in the case of the human sciences requires the recognition of a prior discursive entity upon which the reconstruction or interpretation presented by a metapractice is predicated. What is involved is not the postulation of some given realm of facticity but rather the existence of a conventional datum about which corrigible claims are made. What actually distinguishes natural science from social science is not the "givenness" of natural phenomena but the "givenness" of social phenomena. Although one might subscribe to some form of metaphysical realism regarding the existence of natural phenomena, they are accessible only in the language of natural science or some other first-order discourse, while social phenomena are conventionally constructed prior to second-order reconstructions or interpretations. It is precisely the kind of claims about the past that are in principle and practice incorrigible that we should label subjective and designate as lacking objectivity. When, for example, Leo Strauss claimed that Machiavelli was the founder of modern political thought, he made an observation that we can regard as meaningful at various levels, both philosophically and rhetorically, but we cannot seriously debate it as a potentially refutable historical proposition. Similarly, when Louis Hartz talked about the liberal tradition in America, he was, despite the subsequent reification of the concept of liberalism, talking about the persistence of certain attributes that he perceived as similar rather than about an actual and preconstituted tradition. In the following chapters, I have attempted to provide evidence for the claims that I have made about the existence and character of the conversations and concepts in question, but that very evidence leaves space for alternative renderings. My practical concerns are diverse. In part, I wish to provide a genealogy of some important strands of contemporary democratic theory, but my purpose is also to put to rest a great deal of mythology about the history of political science and political theory that continues to inhibit critical reflection.

Although one might contemplate reconstructing in its entirety the manner in which the American polity has been imagined in metapractical discourse, such an undertaking would far exceed the scope of my project. The literature that might be viewed as belonging to this general category, or even to that segment exemplifying the democratic imagination, would include not only political science but fields such as history and sociology and practices such as journalism and literature. Although the interaction between political science and these other enterprises must on occasion be confronted in this study, the conversations constituting the democratic discourse of political science represent a distinct historical tradition. One might also go about the task of recounting how the American polity has been imagined by focusing on iconistic authors such as James Madison and Alexis de Tocqueville. This ground has, however, been heavily trodden, and although I will discuss the *Federalist* and *Democracy in America* at some length, my concern is less to offer any original interpretation than to point to certain dimensions that relate, in various ways, to my principal narrative regarding the concepts of state, pluralism, and liberalism in the discourse of political science. These concepts have also been at the center of a persistent and defining problem in the discourse of democracy in the United States and in political science in particular, and this problem is a principal thematic focus of this volume. Since the narrative in the following chapters is at certain points necessarily complex, I will offer some prior thematic guidance to the reader.

There has been, from the time of the formation of the American republic, a theoretical paradox that has been a central axis in discussions of popular government. This paradox, which was bequeathed to and engaged by the field of political science, as well as by other forms of political commentary and political discourse itself, emerged with respect to validating American democracy—or validating America as a democracy. While it was assumed that a republican or democratic regime required an identifiable and autonomous people, it was at the same time difficult, after the Revolution, to specify any such entity in the American polity. The concept of democracy and the idea of the people were, however, difficult to disentangle, and even the critics of American politics were typically reform-minded individuals who did not so much suggest a root and branch transformation of political society as advise what they took to be the reestablishment of the public over private interest. This, however, assumed that the concept of the public could be given substantive meaning. This search for the public or "people," and for American democracy, has been confronted, and conducted, in two distinct ways. One approach has been to argue that, despite appearances to the contrary, there is, at least latently or potentially, an American people that is the author and subject of democratic government. The other approach has been to argue that a people as such, that is, an actual community as traditionally conceived, is not necessary to achieve, at least functionally, popular sovereignty. One persistent aspect of the democratic vision in American political science, represented in both of these approaches, has, however, been its *accomodationist* character. The tendency has been to adapt the concept of democracy to the perceived realities of American politics. And despite its sometimes radical pretensions, this continues to be the case in much of contemporary democratic theory.

This paradox of democracy was, as I elaborate in Chapter 1, distinctly exemplified in the *Federalist*. Although the authors maintained that the Constitution created a popular government that was republican, or representative, rather than strictly democratic, they had trouble clarifying and defending their continued allegiance to the basic idea of popular sovereignty. The idea of the people, which had been at the core of republican revolutionary theory and ideology as well as the arguments of certain Anti-Federalists, seemed to have an anomalous ring when juxtaposed to the political ontology advanced by Madison. One thing that the Federalists and Anti-Federalists had in common was the worry that there was not, as such, an American people, and from one perspective, the genius of the authors of the *Federalist* was to invent the very idea of a people that transcended more local constituencies, which was to be represented in and by the new national government. To the extent, however, that the oft-mentioned "people" had a concrete meaning in the *Federalist,* it seemed in the end to refer either to the sum of self-interested, and even antisocial, individuals or to diverse and divisive factions defined precisely by their attachment to their own, rather than the public, good. In place of the traditional republican notion of a people, Madison, we might say, conceived of a virtual people that would arise out of an institutional equilibrium and balance of conflicting social interests. He argued that the disease of republican, and now American, government was factionalism but that it could be transformed into its own cure through an intricate constitutional design combined with fortuitous social and geographical circumstances.

Political discourse, however, as well as certain commentaries such as that of former President Monroe, kept alive the civic republican image of a people, both capable of and the subject of popular government, which lay beneath the surface of American diversity. In the nineteenth century, academic publicists and the first and second generation of political scientists produced their own version of the people, which was represented in the concept of the state. While today many tend to look back on the nineteenth-century theory of the state as an archaic formalistic and legalistic doctrine or as an intellectual reflection of American state-building, it was, as I explain in Chapter 2, most essentially a theory of American democracy. Apart from a reference to the American states, the word "state" had, by the beginning of the nineteenth century, little currency in either political discourse or discussions of politics in the United States. The introduction of the concept of the state was largely through the work of the émigré Francis Lieber, beginning about the time that his acquaintance Tocqueville visited America. Lieber can reasonably be designated the founder of American political science as a distinct discursive endeavor, and his version of the theory of the state fundamentally determined the direction of political inquiry, and the conversation about democracy, in the United States for nearly a century. It may seem today that this concept of

the state, based on German idealist and historicist philosophy, and perpetuated and refined by second-generation theorists such as Theodore
Woolsey at Yale, Herbert Baxter Adams at The Johns Hopkins, and John
W. Burgess at Columbia, is little more than an antiquarian curiosity; but
what it represented, above all else, was a rather elaborate theory of popular government. Lieber grafted German, largely Kantian and Hegelian,
philosophy onto that part of the American university curriculum in moral
philosophy that was devoted to practical ethics and civic education, and
he adapted that philosophy to the circumstances and traditions of the
United States and to a solution to the perennial democratic paradox. What
Lieber and the later American state theorists who were educated abroad
and who imbibed the German paradigm created was the image of a democratic people, as well as a history of democratic institutions that sprung
from ancient Teutonic origins, passed through English government, and
culminated in the American polity. Although Americans were, in theory
and practice, at first wary of the word "democracy," it had, by the middle
of the nineteenth century, been largely divested of its radical overtones and
become a general term of approbation in the United States as well as in
many places abroad. Unlike some of his European counterparts and corre-
spondents such as Tocqueville and Edouard Laboulaye, as well as the
American historian George Bancroft, who all commented extensively on
American political society, Lieber, fearing democratic absolutism and
enthusiasm, still tended to eschew the word "democracy" in favor of phrases
such as "self-government" and "hamarchy." His vision of the state, however, was essentially that of an associationally and institutionally diverse
but organically unified people and its pedigree, which gave theoretical substance to the idea of democracy. Although the "state talk" of nineteenth-
century academic political inquiry, as well as that of public intellectuals
such as Orestes Brownson and Elisha Mulford, paralleled the discourse of
democracy in political life, it was, like many later constructions of political science, far removed from the language of politics in the United States
with respect to both the meaning of the concept and the frequency of its
application. The most essential feature of the concept of the state during
this long and formative period in the evolution of American political science was that it did *not* refer either to forms of government or to the institutions of government, but rather to a community whose voice expressed
a will that putatively stood not only behind government but preceded, in
time and importance, the Constitution, and that was manifest in the
processes and structures of American politics. This vision may have often
reflected and abetted the conservative ideology of theorists who wished to

propagate and justify limited government as well as to curtail democratic populism while still maintaining the idea of popular sovereignty, and it was in some ways both inspired by and functioned to legitimate the cause of the Union before and after the Civil War. But such contingent contextual factors are not sufficient to explain the origin of the concept of the state, the particular form that the theory manifested, and the manner in which it evolved in the language of political science. It was, in the end, a theory embraced by ideologically diverse individuals, and it served a variety of ends. It provided a scientific identity for the discipline and sublimity for its subject matter, but above all, it offered a distinct answer to the congenital paradox of American democratic theory, and it was an answer that, at its core, extended well into the Progressive era after the turn of the century.

The third generation of political theorists, which included Woodrow Wilson and W. W. Willoughby, continued to affirm the existence and supremacy of the state, but in part as a consequence of urging a more active administration, they began to blur the line between state and government. Although they were still bound by the language of state theory and continued to hold to the idea that a legitimate constitutional and democratic political order must be grounded in a national community, the term "state" increasingly became indistinguishable from the concept of government. In a country of such great complexity and multiplicity, the problem became one of specifying the locus of that community and, eventually, no one did more than Willoughby to empty the word "state" of its original theoretical meaning and transform it into an analytical or juristic category and synonym for government. This, however, precipitated a crisis in democratic theory that would not be resolved until the beginning of the 1930s. The decline of the concept of the state as the basis of a theory of democracy was paralleled by the origin and evolution of the theory of democratic pluralism, and Chapters 3 and 4, which represent the crux of this volume, examine this development in detail.

Although there is a persistent assumption that there was a fundamental break between the state theory of the nineteenth century and the conceptions of both political inquiry and politics embraced by early-twentieth-century social scientists such as Charles Merriam, which has become a piece of academic folklore, often supported by reference to works such as Morton White's *Social Thought in America: The Revolt Against Formalism* (1949), the continuities in many respects exceeded the innovations. One might very well ask how the largely conservative academic culture that dominated nineteenth-century universities, such as Columbia and Hopkins, produced the reformist scholars, such as Charles Beard and Merriam, who were often the students of individuals such as the archly conservative Burgess but who so significantly transformed American political science. In addition to retaining commitments both to the idea of scientific inquiry and to a political science with a practical purpose, one thread of continuity was a persistent belief in and dedication to the national state as encompassing both government and community. During the early part of the twentieth century, much of Progressive politics and political thought continued to be predicated on the belief that there was at least a dormant or incipient political community that could be mobilized and in whose name government could legitimately and authoritatively act. Or some, such as Herbert Croly, Walter Lippmann, and Merriam, argued that if such a community had disappeared, it must be created anew. It was eventually out of the ruins of both traditional state theory and Progressive dreams that a new account of democratic government in America emerged—the theory of democratic pluralism. As the theory of the state waned during the early years of the twentieth century, there was something of a theoretical hiatus in American political science. In addition to the increased difficulty of sustaining the idea of an invisible organic people amidst a society of such apparent diversity, the decline of the nineteenth-century theory of the state was in part a reaction, in the context of World War I, to its German, and allegedly authoritarian, origins. At the same time, the Progressive hope of awakening or reconstituting a democratic public slowly evaporated as social scientists became overwhelmed with evidence of social and cultural variety and contentiousness in America. There was an increased sense that there was no homogeneous American public, but rather only complex congeries of interests and groups that exceeded even Madison's account. It seemed as difficult to find the American people as it had in the period between the Revolution and the Constitution, and increasingly individuals such as Lippmann and A. Lawrence Lowell questioned the existence of a natural and identifiable public or even the reality of a public opinion that commentators such as James Bryce had emphasized as constituting the essence of democratic sovereignty in America. As the concept of the state gradually lost its theoretical import and gave way to becoming a synonym for government, there was a growing sense of the loss of a theory of democracy as well as the increasing difficulty of describing the United States as a democracy. When, in 1907, Albert Bushnell Hart claimed that the American theory of government was, paradoxically, not to theorize, like Tocqueville he stressed the unity of principle and practice and expressed the continuing faith that America was a democracy; but he could no longer, any more than most of his contemporaries, account for it theoretically. By the turn of the century, the term "pluralism" had not, in any substantial manner, entered the discourse of American political science, and it had no place in the language of American politics. Although Arthur Bentley's book, *The Process of Government* (1908), would become a central reference for later pluralist theory, it had very little immediate impact, and Bentley never employed the term "pluralism." It was during Harold Laski's brief sojourn in the United States subsequent to World War I, as well as through exposure to the work of other English theorists such as Ernest Barker and A. D. Lindsay, that the word was somewhat accidentally introduced into the conversation of political science. This was principally through Laski's attack on the idea of state sovereignty and centralized authority and his propagation of the notion that the state was merely one association among many in society. Laski's principal concern, as was the case for Tocqueville, was his own country, but just as Tocqueville posed questions for Americans about the nature of their democracy and the place of associations, Laski left behind him a debate about pluralism that focused on whether political reality consisted of anything more than an endless process of group inter-action with the government functioning as an arbiter, and whether this could add up, empirically and theoretically, to democracy. It was difficult for American political scientists to give up the idea that the state was more than government and that government was not the agent of a general pop-ular will. The problems attaching to images of a pluralist society were evi-dent in the work of Merriam, who, after Lieber and Burgess, exercised the most formative influence on American political science.

Merriam, like most members of his generation such as John Dewey, rec-ognized certain democratic values inherent in diversity and pluralism, but he was equally impressed with the divisiveness inherent in such difference and with the antidemocratic sentiments and practices of certain groups. He retained the assumption that democracy ultimately required unity, even if, in his view and that of his student Harold Lasswell, it was necessary to introduce it from the top down through social control and civic education. They transferred their hopes for a democratic society to the actions of gov-ernmental elites informed by social scientific knowledge, that is, to the pursuit of democratic values through less than what some might consider democratic means. But the exact nature of the American polity remained vague. No articulate image of American democracy and the American political system appeared, for example, in Merriam's principal early writ-ing. Progressive values persisted in the discipline and were exemplified in Merriam's arguments, but the idea that there was a people behind the com-plex universe of American politics seemed increasingly less credible.

Merriam's faith in the conjunction of state and democracy, however, was the beginning of one distinct theme in the democratic theory of political science that has reached forward to individuals who addressed the problem of democracy in the 1960s. They no longer believed that the state referred to the people, but they argued that the state, as government, could be the vehicle for realizing and expressing a democratic mandate. The irony of this argument was that it often accepted the pluralist vision of political reality, which called into question the very idea of an identifiable public and a democratic will.

The strongest riposte to the normative theory of pluralism associated with Laski, as well as to empirical political scientists and sociologists whose work increasingly lent support to the notion that political reality was irreducibly pluralistic, was executed by William Yandell Elliott. He spoke for many of his generation when he argued that to give up the concept of the state as a community was, in effect, to give up democracy, as well as the very idea of "the political" as a special realm upon which the autonomy of political science and political theory was predicated. He claimed to perceive, and suggested that it was at least necessary to believe in, what he called a "co-organic" community in American political life that was the basis of constitutional government. It was difficult, even for someone such as Dewey, who along with Laski was perceived by Elliott as a purveyor of relativistic pragmatism and other doctrines that had destructive implications for democracy, to sever the idea of popular government from the existence of a national community that transcended the diversity and complexity of modern society. The attack on the Austinian notion of law as the command of a sovereign, which was begun by individuals such as Dewey as early as the later part of the nineteenth century and which was pursued by thinkers as different as Bentley and Laski, had far-reaching implications for democratic theory, since it not only undercut Hobbesian notions but, often unwittingly, the idea of *popular* sovereignty as well.

By the end of the 1920s, however, the concept of pluralism had become the core of an empirical account of American politics, a new normative image of democratic practice, and a general theory of democracy as a form of government. For the first time since Madison, an empirical account of social conflict and of group pressures on government was slowly being transformed into a theory of popular government that would provide much of the content of a new and widely-embraced image of democratic identity. The group theory of political reality became deeply entrenched in political science, and it thoroughly infused the language of the field. It had little to do, however, with the medieval and Gierkean image of plural communities and dispersed authorities that defined Laski's concept. What emerged was a descriptive account of American politics as the pursuit of group interest, but eventually this was transformed into an argument about how this process constituted a form of both democratic interaction and representation. The beginnings of such an idea had surfaced in Bentley's work and other early literature, and it was also implied in the research of individuals such as Peter Odegard and even more explicitly suggested by Pendelton Herring. During the late 1920s and early 1930s, however, a number of individuals such as George Sabine, as well as many who have largely been forgotten, among whom John Dickinson was one of the most prominent, elaborated a detailed and complex theory of pluralist democracy. This theory challenged what they referred to as the traditional "democratic dogma" in both politics and political science, and it contained, and actually exceeded, the principal theoretical elements that would be rearticulated a generation later in the work of individuals such as David Truman and Robert Dahl.

Central to this theory was the claim that all societies consisted of groups seeking their self-interest and that this, at any stage of social evolution, required mechanisms for compromise and adjustment. In the context of modern society, such adjustment was achieved through the medium of government, which these thinkers now called the state and which functioned as an umpire acting pragmatically in response to the needs of the situation and with respect to matters of intervention and control. It was through participation in groups that individuals realized their goals and achieved identity, and it was through groups gaining access to influence, rather than through formal institutions, that democratic representation was most essentially effected. Stability in society was achieved, they argued, through a balance of conflicting social pressures constrained by appropriate enabling institutions and a fundamental consensus on the rules of the game. Majoritarian democracy was viewed as a myth that belied the fact that majorities were little more than indefinable aggregations of individual preference which were democratic only in the sense that they had the capacity, through elections, to effect a circulation of elites. The basic idea represented in Joseph Schumpeter's later account of democracy as a "method" had already been integrated into the theory of pluralist democracy.

During the later part of the 1930s, there was little in the way of a further explicit statement or elaboration of this theory, but Americans, in both politics and the academy, were seeking an account of democracy that would overcome some of the difficulties of earlier constructions as well as clearly identify the United States as democratic and distinguish it from the growing number of totalitarian regimes and foreign doctrines such as communism and fascism. The name for this new democratic identity was "liberalism," and the manner in which pluralism was transfigured as liberalism is a crucial part of the story of the evolution of democratic theory in American political science and the subject of Chapter 5.

Although it is today common to write the history of American political thought as a history of liberalism, this approach, and the very concept of liberalism as an American identity, was largely invented within a relatively short period during the 1930s. The term "liberalism" had seldom been used in either American politics or political science before that point. Liberalism became the name for American democracy in part because the term, widely used in Europe since the early part of the nineteenth century both in politics and in commentary on politics, had been applied, both positively and negatively, to the United States by foreign analysts. But there was a very distinct path of internal evolution. Politicians such as Woodrow Wilson, and later Franklin Roosevelt, began tentatively to court this concept as a label for a variety of policy initiatives, but everyone eventually seemed anxious to adopt this synonym for democracy. A variety of individuals, including Herbert Hoover, claimed to be the one "true" liberal and told the story of what they took to be authentic liberalism. In politics, Roosevelt finally won the title, and his opponents eventually accepted the name he had originally pejoratively bestowed upon them—conservatives. Meanwhile, the word "liberalism" gravitated into the language of political science, often via those sympathetic to the New Deal, but political theorists such as Sabine emptied the concept of its concrete political meaning and began writing the history of Western political thought and institutions as a story of the progress of liberalism culminating in the American democratic polity. Although in the work of individuals such as Dewey as well as a number of political scientists there continued to be a certain correspondence between the academic and political visions of liberalism, two quite distinct traditions of discourse began to evolve as liberalism in the language of political science was reified, provided with a philosophy and history, and reimposed as a description of American politics. To the extent that liberalism had a definite conceptual meaning in the literature of political science and political theory, other than a name for American government and society, it tended to mean pluralism and attending values such as social freedom, difference, bargaining, and compromise. Many political theorists and philosophers, such as T. V. Smith, took the position that what characterized democracy was less any absolutist doctrine and regime than a commitment to toleration and the propagation of diversity within a procedural framework for settling conflicts.

By the early 1940s, on the eve of the War, the basic elements of this vision were extracted from the riverbed of mainstream political science, systematized by individuals such as Herring, and once again presented as the "politics of democracy." Herring saw his task as taking all that was considered bad about politics—from pressure groups to bosses and soft money—and demonstrating that they were all, if understood scientifically, part of a democratic process. One reason for the rearticulation of pluralism qua liberalism was to provide a response to totalitarianism and a counterideal, but it was also, like behavioralism after it, which incorporated liberalism as its account of democracy, a response to a somewhat subterranean critique of liberal democracy that had begun to infiltrate the discipline. This critique, largely conceived and executed by émigré scholars, was gaining a place in the literature of political theory and was manifest in journals such as the *Review of Politics,* with its theological antiliberal perspective, as well as in the arguments of Robert Hutchins and those involved in the Committee on Social Thought at the University of Chicago. This critique gave rise to a new mode of political theory that would eventually lead a number of political scientists to make an identity choice with which they had never previously been confronted, that is, a choice between political science and political theory. The confrontation between this critique and the reconstituted pluralist account of liberal democracy in political science comprised the dialectic of democracy in the postwar generation and eventually gave rise to a fateful institutional and intellectual break between mainstream political science and the subfield of political theory.

Chapter 6, which presents a selective account of the conversation after mid-century, is in some respects more an epilogue than an attempt to reconstruct the conversation as fully as in the previous chapters. This is especially the case in the last portion of the chapter, where my purpose is neither to survey nor to delve deeply into the complexities of contemporary democratic theory, but rather to indicate the extent to which central themes in the discussions resemble, and in many ways are rooted in, the earlier history of political science. While I follow the conversation regarding pluralism quite closely up through the decade of the 1960s, my discussion of the subsequent years is more synoptic and interpretive, and probably contentious. I do not want to create the impression that the earlier chapters are simply background for defending these more tentative observations and judgments, since the latter are offered as only a gloss. I argue, however, that after the War, what most fundamentally separated behavioralists, or what was becoming the dominant persuasion in the discipline, from many political theorists and increasingly from the subfield of political theory as a whole, was less a dispute between "scientific" or "empirical" and "traditional" or "normative" theory than two quite different ethical positions revolving around the issue of democracy. Although the concept of science was a central part of the controversy, it was not a choice of science over democracy that defined mainstream political science by the 1970s, but rather a continuing dedication to a science that would describe and explain democracy in the manner in which it had been understood since the late 1920s. In fact, American political scientists were often quite at a loss with respect to analyzing regimes that were not, in their terms, democratic.

During the 1950s, historians and political theorists such as Daniel Boorstin and Louis Hartz set out to demonstrate that although there might not be an American public, there was, for better or worse, a liberal value consensus, and liberalism, pluralism, and democracy were treated as largely synonymous terms. This vision, however, was catalyzed and galvanized by the persistent but often still somewhat submerged attack on liberalism that had begun to influence what had been since the 1920s a thoroughly American political science. Liberalism, because of both doubts about interventionist government and events such as the McCarthy hearings, had become a highly contested concept in American politics during the 1950s, and often for quite different reasons, it was losing its positive valence in academic discourse. The predominantly German scholars who emigrated to the United States beginning in the 1930s were in many respects a philosophically and ideologically diverse lot, but what they had in common was the belief that liberalism as a political theory was philosophically flawed, and as a political form, inherently pathological and representative of political institutions that historically, as in the case of Weimar, were the threshold of totalitarianism. This form of antimodernism was a strange and difficult body of thought for Americans to absorb. These theorists, who rejected scientism and who were wedded to images of the decline of Western civilization, represented a profound challenge to the conception of democracy that had characterized American political science for half a century. This challenge, coupled with the continuing concern about presenting a coherent image of democracy as a counterpoint to communism, was the intellectual context of the postwar reconstitution of group theory and the pluralist theory of democracy in the work of individuals such as Truman and Dahl.

What is striking about this restatement was its failure to recognize or acknowledge that it was the redemption of an increasingly besieged theory, which had been very fully articulated by the previous generation. And many of the critics of this theory similarly failed to realize the extent to which their criticisms reflected and perpetuated the arguments of an earlier era. The intellectual and professional split between political theory and behavioral political science, which characterized the 1960s and evolved during the 1970s and 1980s, had profound consequences for the future of democratic theory in the United States as well as for the discipline of political science. It had the effect of relocating, or dislocating, the discussion of American political identity and democratic theory. While political science continued, in various ways and degrees, to validate the traditional liberal vision, even to the extent of viewing the discipline itself as distinguished by its pluralistic structure and attitudes, after the 1970s it tended to concede to political theory the role of normative theorizing and to relinquish its congenital mission of articulating a theory of democracy and assessing American politics in these terms.

During the 1970s, liberalism was rehabilitated in the work of individuals as diverse as John Rawls and Richard Rorty, but as these claims became the focus of discussions in political theory, the arguments became increasingly abstract, while at the same time, in mainstream political science, it was more difficult to find a coherent and shared image of the American polity as a democracy. Within the past decade there has been a subtle, but in some ways quite fundamental, shift in perspective in academic political theory. This can in part be attributed to perceptions of and reactions to various dimensions of the social and political environment, but it also springs from certain changes in the philosophical context. In the last decade of the twentieth century, the concept of pluralism once again appeared in the discourse of political theory as a centerpiece of democratic theory, but this, along with the resurgence of individualistic liberalism, evoked or provoked the resurrection of the traditional counterpoint and the equation of democracy with organic and communitarian images. Many of the theorists associated with these trends, often less than fully aware of the evolution of this dialectic, and of their own intellectual inheritance, seem condemned to confront once again the paradoxes that were at the heart of the conversation in American political science for more than a century. The philosophical and practical reconciliation of pluralism with democracy may be no easier than it was at the time of Madison, and the shadow of an invisible people continues to haunt the democratic vision.

THE DEMOCRATIC CONCEPT

No language is so copious as to supply
words and phrases for every complex idea,
or so correct as not to include many
equivocally denoting ideas.

—*James Madison*

Madison's remarks not only represent the quandary faced by the authors of the *Federalist* in attempting to find a word to designate what they imagined as the American form of government, but summarize the difficulty faced by succeeding generations in seeking such a specification. Madison and Alexander Hamilton wished to label the new regime "republican," and Benjamin Franklin, when asked what the Convention had created, quipped that it was a "republic, if you can keep it." John Adams, a few years later, however, exasperatedly claimed that "there is no more unintelligible word in the English Language than republicanism," and Thomas Jefferson and others of the founding period were equally vexed by its ambiguity. In recent years, there has been a great deal of controversy among scholars about how to characterize the intellectual and ideological foundations of the American polity, and the reassertion of the republican label has not only failed to produce any greater consensus but has raised significant issues about the "politics of history."

In the 1950s, it was claimed that the founding was, for better, the product of the immanent "genius" of American politics (Daniel Boorstin), or worse, the beginning of liberal absolutism (Louis Hartz),[1] but in any case, that the theory and practice of American politics had, from the point of the Revolution, been characterized by a consensual hegemony rooted in basically Lockean theory and ideology. By the 1960s, the "worse" scenario had gained momentum, but one difficulty with this whole range of literature that focused on retrieving the ideology of the founding was that the arguments, while historical in form, were often lacking in what many considered to be distinctly historical criteria. While, for example, C. B. Macpherson's image of liberalism as "possessive individualism," and of Thomas Hobbes and Locke as apologists for emerging bourgeois society, seemed for many to provide critical insight, it was vulnerable, as were conservative claims such as those of Leo Strauss about the pathology of a Lockean heritage, to the charge that it offered little in the way of actual historical evidence.[2]

Beginning in the late 1960s, particularly with the work of Bernard Bailyn and Gordon Wood,[3] a revisionist account of the founding period began to emerge that was based on more detailed scholarship. The ideas that informed and justified the Revolution were less, it was claimed, those of Locke, economic liberalism, and political individualism than an ideology adapted from the often inflammatory rhetoric of English publicists and opposition politicians and rooted in a kind of reactionary republican radicalism dedicated to restoring and reconstituting the principles of the British constitution. This image was further developed by J. G. A. Pocock, who argued that the basic line of American political thought was to be found in a classical republican tradition of civic humanism rooted in the work of Machiavelli, tied to notions of the priority of public virtue, and further exemplified in the English debate between town and country.[4] Others, also dedicated to what they claimed as a more truly "historical" approach to the history of political thought, joined in developing these

---

1. Daniel Boorstin, *The Genius of American Politics* (Chicago: University of Chicago Press, 1953); Louis Hartz, *The Liberal Tradition in America: An Interpretation of American Political Thought Since the Revolution* (New York: Harcourt Brace, 1955).

2. C. B. Macpherson, *The Political Theory of Possessive Individualism* (Oxford: Clarendon Press, 1962); Leo Strauss, *Natural Right and History* (Chicago: University of Chicago Press, 1953).

3. Bernard Bailyn, *The Ideological Origins of the American Revolution* (Cambridge, Mass.: Harvard University Press, 1967); Gordon Wood, *The Creation of the American Republic 1776–1887* (Chapel Hill: University of North Carolina Press, 1969).

4. J. G. A. Pocock, *The Machiavellian Moment: Florentine Political Thought and the Atlantic Republican Tradition* (Princeton: Princeton University Press, 1975).

themes. John Dunn, for example, suggested that there was little concrete evidence of Locke's influence in eighteenth-century America.[5] Garry Wills added to the depreciation of the influence of what intellectual historians called liberalism with his image of Jefferson as less a Lockean than a devotee of the ideas of Frances Hutcheson and the Scottish Enlightenment.[6] And, according to Donald Winch, even Adam Smith had been misread, by both celebrants and detractors, as the theorist of individualism and capitalism.[7] However, there soon set in an identifiable and considerable reaction to this new historical orthodoxy and its banishment of Locke and liberalism. Joyce Appleby, John Diggins, Isaac Kramnick, and others, although for diverse reasons, challenged this reading of the founding period and pressed the case for the impact of what they designated as liberal political and economic ideas in Anglo-American eighteenth-century ideology.[8]

What had seemed to be a nearly interminable controversy among intellectual historians and political theorists about whether the American founding was informed by a predominantly republican or liberal political philosophy finally, by the turn of century, disintegrated to the degree that it was difficult to hold on to the fragments of either position.[9] Although the literature of the last generation dealing with the origins of American political ideas was surely more grounded in careful research, it was increasingly caught up in scholastic and academic parapolitical debates. As I will demonstrate later in this study, what was called liberalism and associated with Locke was largely an analytical invention of political scientists and historians rather than an actual historical tradition, and what was referred to as republicanism was only slightly less a reification. Robert Shalhope, a historian who presented American democracy as rooted in a conflict between liberalism and republicanism, acknowledges that what he meant by "liberalism" was "an unarticulated behavioral pattern more than a sharply delineated mode of thought," and Appleby also notes that liberalism

---

5. John Dunn, "The Politics of Locke in England and America in the Eighteenth Century," in *John Locke: Problems and Perspectives,* ed. John Yolton (London: Cambridge University Press, 1969); Jerome Huyler, *Locke in America* (Lawrence: University Press of Kansas, 1995).

6. Garry Wills, *Inventing America: Jefferson's Declaration of Independence* (New York: Doubleday, 1978).

7. Donald Winch, *Adam Smith's Politics: An Essay in Historiographic Revisionism* (Cambridge: Cambridge University Press, 1978).

8. Joyce Appleby, *Economic Thought and Ideology in Seventeenth Century England* (Princeton: Princeton University Press, 1978); *Capitalism and a New Social Order: The Republican Vision of the 1790s* (New York: New York University Press, 1984); John Patrick Diggins, *The Lost Soul of American Politics: Virtue, Self-Interest, and the Foundation of Liberalism* (New York: Basic Books, 1984).

9. See Daniel T. Rogers, "Republicanism: The Career of a Concept," *Journal of American History* 79 (1992).

is less any preconstituted configuration than a "loose association of unex-amined assumptions" factored out by historians.[10] The most probable answer to the question at the heart of the controversy is that it was, in the end, a pseudo-question arising from the propensity of the academicians to impose conceptual single-mindedness on the complexity of politics and the often purposive ambiguity of practical political discourse and debate. The claims were often still wedded to the unlikely notion that a one-dimensional rendering of the political orientation of the period was possi-ble, and much of this literature was hostage to contemporary political concerns or, at least, academic versions of ideological positions. There has been a great deal of retrospective imposition of contemporary symbols of liberalism on Locke and others without sufficient attention to actual texts and their context,[11] but another problem has been that the arguments, even when they emphasized the influence of underlying economic and social conditions, tended to reflect and reinforce the general academic prejudice that ideas can be isolated as independent variables and viewed as the movers of actions and events. The image of human action that informed the work of Bailyn, for example, was in part a reflection of an emerging postposi-tivist account of social scientific explanation, but the form that it took was that of a rather naive inversion of the materialist accounts of the role of ideology that it was, in part, directed against.

The much contested issue of the philosophy of the founding is an exam-ple of the various dimensions of the politics of history, and it is best resolved by discarding the fundamental premise that has animated this debate, that is, that there was a distinct, or even dominant, philosophy. It may be quite true that people sometimes, such as in case of the authors of the *Federalist,* become prisoners of their own rhetoric and of the ideas on which they draw for justification, but political activity cannot, in any gen-eral way, be conceived as emanating from philosophical positions and explained by noting actors' references to the ideas of such individuals as Locke and Machiavelli. Like contemporary politicians, the political actors of the founding period, both for instrumental reasons and as a result of particular commitments, drew upon a diverse stock of available ideas and terminology in pursuing a variety of arguments and practical goals. Even what those who might be considered "true believers" embraced was often

10. Robert E. Shalhope, *The Roots of Democracy: American Thought and Culture, 1760–1800* (Boston: Twayne Publishers, 1990), 50; Appleby, *Liberalism and Republicanism in the Historical Imagination* (Cambridge, Mass.: Harvard University Press, 1992), 1.

11. See, however, Richard Ashcraft, *Revolutionary Politics and John Locke's Two Treatises of Government* (Princeton: Princeton University Press, 1986).

less something that lends itself to being identified easily in terms of labels such as republican or liberal than some much more narrowly circumscribed doctrine or program. This is not to say that the controversy has not, in various ways, fostered more than a generation of significant scholarship but only that, in history as well as in natural science, the production of knowledge is sometimes the consequence of ultimately defective assumptions. The lingering "presentism" in much of this literature led it, however, sometimes to overlook or quickly pass by some of the very things that it uncovered.

Whatever its deficiencies may be, recent scholarship has contributed to generating a new genre of historical literature that has illuminated the founding period. It is, for example, clear that there were some very significant transformations within and between many of the concepts involved in the rhetoric and ideology of the Revolution and those that were crucial in constructing and, more importantly, justifying or attacking the Constitution. The Revolution has often been construed as conservative, particularly if judged in comparison with the social and economic upheavals and subsequent chaos associated with the French and Russian revolutions, and characterized as a "political" revolution that was fought to sustain traditional republican values and even to reconstruct the Whig ideal of the British constitution. Wood has more recently argued that the Revolution, particularly if assessed in terms of the nature of the undertaking, what it finally accomplished, and its lasting social impact, was indeed a radical event;[12] but his earlier groundbreaking work demonstrated that the theory, ideology, and practice of American politics underwent some fundamental changes between the Revolution and the Convention with respect to the meaning of such key interrelated concepts as representation, the people, sovereignty, and the separation of powers. Perhaps most important was a continuing attempt to give meaning to the idea of popular government or the traditional republican idea of self-rule. One persistent and critical issue was that of finding the locus and character of the people who were, or could be, the subject of republican government, and this was an ever more significant issue as it became clear that one of the fundamental facts about the new political system was that it was, as the *Federalist* said, the first wholly popular and "unmixed" republican form of government. The "people," a term once considered as referring to a distinct element of an organic society or, particularly in the American setting, to the ruled, as opposed to the rulers,[13] was now difficult to identify as any concrete entity,

12. Gordon S. Wood, *The Radicalism of the American Revolution* (New York: Knopf, 1992).
13. See Richard Buel Jr., "Democracy and the American Revolution: A Frame of Reference," *William and Mary Quarterly* 21 (1964).

since it seemed coeval with the whole society. There also seemed to be dangers attending the mass or majority opinion that was taken to be the voice of people.

One general conclusion that was pressed by Wood and that has been supported by most of the recent scholarship on eighteenth-century American political thought is that, whatever the intellectual sources or rationale, the ideology of the American Revolution was infused with the assumption that there was a people that was capable of public virtue and of sustaining popular or republican government. This assumption had much to do with how Americans went about creating the first state constitutions and introducing, for example, limitations on the executive branch while enhancing the role of the legislature. By the time the debate about the ratification of the Constitution commenced, however, the idea of the people, as traditionally conceived, was in jeopardy. The Anti-Federalists, although also worried about the integrity of the people, held on to this conception, which formed an essential part of their argument against an extended republic and distant national government, as a possibility within the limits of a relatively circumscribed territory and population. Although it is necessary to be cautious about attributing "influence" to figures such as Hobbes and Locke, it is useful to note what might be considered Lockean and Hobbesian metaphors in the rhetoric of the Revolution and defenders of the Constitution respectively. The language of the revolution, like Locke's treatise, was focused on the problem of tyranny and the rights and sovereignty of a social and political community that created government as its representative, while the defense of the proposed Constitution assumed a context of fragmentation and conflict and the need for the restoration of order and authority. The Anti-Federalists could be construed as conservatives in that they wished to hold on to the decentralized federal form of government that was characterized by the Articles of Confederation and that implied the existence of several political wholes and peoples who were represented in the state legislatures. The basic assumption was that individual freedom and republican government were only possible in a small territory with a relatively economically, socially, and culturally homogenous population. Here there could be a close relationship, and mutual responsiveness and responsibility, between the people and government and trust between individuals. Representation under these circumstances, particularly in institutions such as the jury and popular branch of the legislature, could be virtual, that is, a surrogate for direct participation, and thus in effect could realize the ideal of self-government. In the Anti-Federalist view, the structure of government should be both simple and balanced by distinct institutional separation in order to limit despotic tendencies.[14] All of these assumptions were rearticulated in criticisms of the proposed Constitution, which, as it was described and defended by the Federalists, manifested in many respects a quite different and novel and, in its own way, radical conception of popular government.

The very idea of the people as a body politic and of how it can and should be represented by government has always been surrounded by mystery and paradox. It is probably roughly correct to say that the idea of the people, and of representing them (or it), was originally in part an invention of rulers as a device for legitimating their claim to authority. The "pointillistic" image of the sovereign in the frontispiece of Hobbes's *Leviathan,* as both embodying the people and embodied by them, was in some respects a reflection of the rhetoric of the time. It did imply virtual representation whereby the people gave rise to and constituted the government, and, at the same time, the existence of the government constituted the people. This idea persists in the view, for example, that the English Parliament is sovereign while assuming that there is nevertheless popular sovereignty. This concept of the people was, however, a dangerous invention in that others could claim to represent this entity, and eventually it was a fiction that was collectively internalized and adopted as a basis for rejecting the authority of kings, that is, the "people" began to believe they were, in fact, a people. As Edmund Morgan suggests, the "king's two bodies" eventually gave way to the equally problematic image of the "people's two bodies," which even further complicated the concept of representation and raised questions about how chosen or self-designated officials might represent a community or locality, let alone a whole nation.[15] Was government to be understood as virtually identical with the people, that is, authored by the people who were themselves created in the act of authorship, and the product of an irrevocable trust (Hobbes); an agent or proxy of a preexisting people or community (Locke); a mirror of the structure of society of which the people are a part (James Harrington); or some combination of these images?

In the context of the English experience during the seventeenth and eighteenth centuries, it was difficult to break with the idea of virtual representation and the notion that, at the most comprehensive level, there is no clear distinction between the sovereignty of the people and the

14. See Herbert J. Storing, ed., *The Anti-Federalist* (Chicago: University of Chicago Press, 1981); Storing, *What the Anti-Federalists were For* (Chicago: University of Chicago Press, 1981).

15. Edmund S. Morgan, *Inventing the People: The Rise of Popular Sovereignty in England and America* (New York: W. W. Norton, 1988).

government or, more particularly, between representatives and who or what they represented. The sovereignty of the government was, or was urged to be, acceptable because it *was* the people. Even when Locke imagined the government as a "trustee," and even though what was involved was presented as a distinctly revocable trust, he continued to imply that government, in the normal course of things, was virtually the people. As Locke wrote, a member of political society "authorizes the society or, which is all one, the legislative thereof, to make the laws." Only when they ceased to be virtually the people could the "people judge," a position that seems very close to much of the rhetoric of the American Revolution. The Americans were upset not because they did not have someone directly representing them but because there no longer seemed to be a shared identity between them and the English people. Either homogeneity had broken down or else English government had become corrupted. Despite Locke's emphasis, as opposed to Hobbes, on the people as an entity existing prior to government, he, like other and later Whigs, was cautious about implying a more radical view of popular sovereignty, and he did not fully let go of the notion that the dissolution of government was a threat to the integrity, and even existence, of the community that authored government. At times he suggested that when the government dissolves, "the people become a confused multitude."[16]

In Locke's argument, there was a distinct tension between the virtual character of government and the idea that government could be oppressive, a tension that would persist at least through the debates about the Bill of Rights. But those debates were carried on with only a partial grasp of how radical a theoretical transformation was portended in Madison's account of these matters in the *Federalist*. After all, when the Americans revolted against England on the basis of the failure to be represented, the basic assumption was, again, less that there was not an agency representing their case than that the American people and the British people were no longer identical. There was a suspicion that the English constitution had been so corrupted that the government no longer virtually represented the constitutive elements of an organic society. My concern in discussing the *Federalist* is less with the political philosophy of Madison, Hamilton, or any other individual than with the image of popular government that was invoked and evoked in that work, and with the manner in which, because of the authority consistently acceded to it in subsequent years in

16. John Locke, *Two Treatises of Government,* ed. Peter Laslett (Cambridge: Cambridge University Press, 1967), 343, 429, 445.

both popular perceptions and the discourse of political science, it presented a difficulty for, and was reflected in, subsequent attempts to delineate the nature of popular sovereignty and democracy in the United States. It represented the paradox of democracy, that is, that republican government seemed to require the existence of a people, but their account of society belied the existence of any such entity. This attempt to imagine the American polity was paradigmatic for subsequent commentators who, in the course of imaging the political system in the United States, were forced, at the very least, to confront it and often to either confirm or contradict it.

Whatever the exact pedigree of the *Federalist*'s projection of the American system may be and whatever similar images may have been floating about, a central theme was an unequivocal distinction between government and the people. There was much in the American colonial experience and the revolutionary and founding era that gave credence to the idea of separate government and the notion that the people and the government must be radically differentiated, and therefore that representation must be reconceived as something other than virtual. While some passages of the *Federalist* held on to the idea of virtual representation with respect to, for example, the manner in which elected officials might represent more than those who actually voted for them,[17] the notion that government as a whole was virtually the people, or even a mirror of society, was pointedly rejected. The separation of powers had little to do with assumptions about a correspondence between branches of government and fundamental natural divisions in an organic society, but rather was a technique for constructing an artificial self-correcting institutional mechanism. What would win out in post-founding political discourse and commentary was an idea of popular sovereignty that signified that the government was *not* sovereign and therefore that it could be limited—and should be feared. This implied, however, that there was an identifiable agency not only that had created or authorized the Constitution but, when necessary, that could materialize, express its will, and do such things as stand against its representatives. Maybe the concern in the *Federalist* was less to postulate a people and a popular sovereignty that could limit and counter a national government than to theorize one that could give the lie to a belief in sovereign states and embarrass the Anti-Federalists and their profession of faith in the people; but once created, this idea required substance. A "national sovereignty" implied a nation or a national people, and throughout

17. *The Federalist,* ed. Jacob Cooke (New York: Meridian Books, 1961), 219–223.

the *Federalist,* there is constant reference to the existence of such an entity even though it often appears as more a symbol than a reality.

It is a mistake, albeit a common one, to look for some perfectly coherent philosophy or theory in the *Federalist*. To a large extent, the distribution of emphasis followed the particular claims they wished to make at various junctures, and there is a great deal of apparent contradiction in the rhetoric. Yet, both in order to gain the favor of those with traditional republican sympathies and to break away from an identification of government with the people, the authors consistently pressed the idea that the people was an entity that was prior in time and logic to government, an idea that would be bequeathed to the nineteenth century. They maintained that the "Constitution is to be founded on the assent and ratification of the people of America," that the Convention represented the people to whom its product would be offered, that "this country and this people seem to have been made for one another," and that "we have uniformly been one people." They claimed that there was now "one united people" in which individuals were "knit together" by "many chords of affection" and that this people, as a whole, possessed general and objective "interests." The basic question, then, was one of the relationships between this entity and the government, and, to some extent, the answer was in terms of what role the people would *not* perform.[18]

The constant theme in the *Federalist* of contrasting a democracy and a republic may have served a number of purposes, but it was predicated on the claim that in the latter the people do not "exercise" the role of government, which includes both the making and the execution of law. Governance is by government, that is, by representatives and representative institutions. The authors imagined that, opposed to the British and European systems, which involved divided and shared sovereignty, the great novelty of the American system, which had "no model on the face of the globe," would be the fact that while the constitution and consequently the particular *institutions* of government may be "mixed" both vertically and horizontally, the *form* of government, that is, the type or kind, was "wholly popular" and "unmixed." They argued that "the true distinction between these and the American governments lies *in the total exclusion of the people in their collective capacity* from any share in the *latter*." The role of the government was presented as distinct from the role of the people, and once the government had been established, constitutional questions were to have been avoided because of "the danger of disturbing the public tranquility

18. Ibid., 9, 10, 13, 88, 254.

by interesting too strongly the public passions." There was, they argued, no need to worry about whether the federal or state governments were more sovereign, because government as such was not sovereign. Different levels and elements of government were just so many "agents and trustees of the people," and "ultimate authority . . . resides in the people alone," who ceded some of their "natural rights" in order to create the necessity of government and maintain order and security. The people, they claimed, created the constitution, and the constitution, in turn, established the government. "The fabric of the American Empire ought to rest on the solid basis of THE CONSENT OF THE PEOPLE. The streams of national power ought to flow immediately from that pure original fountain of all legitimate authority."[19]

The people, "the community," as the authors referred to it in *Federalist 28, 30,* and *33,* was projected as a separate and intelligible entity that, speaking with its majority voice, as Locke had depicted, both created and authorized government, and therefore could either withdraw its mandate or, when necessary and in a variety of ways, either throw its weight behind or constrain governmental actions. Although the authors repeatedly stressed that what was contemplated was not a government over states but "over individuals," such a government derived its authority "from the great body of the people" and sought the common or public good. It was precisely in part because the government was to be so distinct from the people that it was necessary to devise the institutions of government in such an intricate manner that the government internally controlled itself. The government and the public were consistently presented as logically distinct but comparable countervailing entities, which exercised mutual control over one another and compensated for their respective deficiencies—"public reason" regulated the government, and the government constrained public passions.[20]

The greatest difficulty with this conception of a people that stood separate from and comparable to the institutions of government specified in the Constitution was that it was joined to a social and political ontology that seemed, at every crucial juncture, to undermine it. The general characterization in the *Federalist* of both human nature as such and the particular circumstantial propensities and inclinations of individuals and groups was such that one might well ask how a people, in the sense of a political community or intelligible entity, was thinkable. There is no need to make a great mystery of this tension. It was in large part the consequence of

19. Ibid., e.g., 61–64, 83–85, 89, 146, 255, 258, 315, 339, 340, 428.
20. Ibid., 93, 129, 244, 251–52, 255, 340–51

diverse rhetorical strategies directed toward different audiences, and even at times the hopes and fears of the same audience, but it was also the residue of different and still contending conceptions of representation. Yet there was a problem in imagining the American polity when the idea of the "great body of the people" seemed to dissolve at the very moment that it was articulated. Political reality, the *Federalist* constantly asserted, consisted of individuals and groups seeking their own interest and domination over others and attempting to gain control of governmental machinery for the pursuit of those goals. Not only was a virtuous people lacking, in the traditional republican sense, but the "people" seemed, in the end, to be a term that referred either to the sum of discrete individuals or to the fluctuating collage of group interests around which individuals coalesced. The "people" seemed to be devoid of any substantive meaning and to function as a generic analytical or categorical concept that could be reified when necessary for assuaging traditional republican concerns. What emerged was an image of society in which there were various "classes" and "parties" professing "truth" and "right," while actually acting on the basis of "perverted ambition," "jealousies," "avarice, personal animosity," "angry and malignant passions," and similar motives that undercut reason and moderation. The *Federalist*'s authors contended that by nature "men are ambitious, vindictive and rapacious," but previous republics had not taken this sufficiently into account and realized that what most fundamentally drives social intercourse is "the love of power or the desire of preeminence and dominion" that had always led to "domestic factions and convulsions." Despite what naive visionaries, maybe such as Thomas Paine or Adam Smith, might have believed about republics and commercial societies, "has it not, on the contrary, invariably been found that momentary passions and immediate interests have a more active and imperious control over human conduct than general or remote considerations of policy, utility or justice?" And were not Americans "yet remote from the happy empire of perfect wisdom and perfect virtue?"[21]

What was to be expected, in the natural course of things, they maintained, was "faction and insurrection" and cycles of "tyranny and anarchy." While the maintenance of liberty and the protection of "the diversity of faculties from which property rights originate" were presented by the authors as the "first object of government," the characteristic downside of republican liberty was the "disease" of factions, which was, if unregulated, ultimately destructive of liberty. But just as it was self-defeating to con-

21. Ibid., 4–5, 28–29, 33–35.

trol factions by curtailing liberty, it was futile to seek to eliminate them, given the fact that man's "reason" was "fallible" and used in pursuit of "his self-love, his opinions, and his passions." The "latent causes of faction are thus sown in the nature of man" and in the "different and unequal faculties for acquiring property," which were in turn manifest in "the various and unequal distribution of property" and in "a division of society into different interests and parties." A variety of irreconcilable opinions and conflicts related to religion, politics, and other matters had "inflamed" individuals with "mutual animosity, and rendered them much more disposed to vex and oppress each other, than to cooperate for their common good." The Convention, they suggested, was a serendipitous, and probably unique, historical moment occupied by rare individuals who exceeded the common denominator of human kind, and it transcended the characteristic history of government, including republics, which heretofore had been a "history of factions."[22]

The authors, throughout, were sensitive to the fact that the very idea of a republic had presupposed the existence of a people and that their opponents were arguing there could not really be an adequately homogeneous and virtuous people in so large a sphere as that contemplated in the new polity. They were also aware that they themselves were presenting an account both of human beings in general and of a social, economic, and political situation in which one could only speak metaphorically of the people and the public good. There was a sense in which traditional republican theory, such as that of Montesquieu or Harrington, had always involved the idea of finding virtue in institutional arrangements rather than simply in the action of citizens, but it had never let go the idea of the people as an entity. And no matter how much the authors of the *Federalist* altered the concept of a republic to make it coincide with the proposed Constitution, to demonstrate *"the conformity of the proposed constitution to the true principles of republican government,"* as well as to the "fundamental principles of the revolution,"[23] they could not safely let go of either the general idea of popular sovereignty or the claim that there was a people beside and behind the government. Although there was no explicit solution to this basic paradox in the *Federalist,* what tended to emerge was an image of what might be called a *virtual* people—and virtual virtuousness—achieved through the institutional management of interests. The political system that they imagined was one in which the function of a people

22. Ibid., 58–59, 238–39.
23. Ibid., 7, 250.

was replaced by the organization of government, the fortuitous character of American society, and the relationship between them. Such a system would be imagined again in the course of the twentieth century.

While the checks and balances of mixed governmental institutions, "compound" government, representation, and other features of the Constitution were, on their face, coincidental with republican principles, "the ENLARGEMENT of the ORBIT" of the system seemed less so and appeared to exacerbate the danger of factions and undermine the traditional republican image of a people. The answer was, in effect, to cure this basic "disease" and "dangerous vice" of republican government by allowing the infection of "factious spirit" to become acute and thereby induce a proliferation of antibodies that would "break and control the violence" associated with factionalism. The basic idea of balance and harmony growing out of conflict was hardly novel, related as it was to arguments in the work of individuals such as Machiavelli, Bernard Mandeville, and Harrington, as well as to Montesquieu's celebration of republics and the character of the British constitution. It persisted in traditional Whig images of that constitution, but there was at least one fundamental difference between these conceptions and the formulation in the *Federalist*. Previous arguments had assumed that society was, in some sense, an organic whole within which the people, the "many," were a distinct element along with an aristocracy or some form of the "few." This was an image that some such as John Adams, in his *Thoughts on Government,* would not relinquish. Even though separation was viewed as a bar against tyranny, the principal reason for separation within government was to provide representation for these elements in a manner that would allow the government as a whole to represent each virtually, and thereby represent and reflect the structure of society. The balance within government would correspond to the balance within society, while government and society balanced each other. Checking and balancing was to be accomplished by this separation, but since separation was essentially a correlate of representation, the membranes were understood as impermeable, that is, interpenetration was, as it had been for the Whigs in England, the definition of corruption. The *Federalist,* on the contrary, as was the case for most post-revolutionary thought, equated the people with the entire society, and, consequently, the traditional rationale for the separation of powers made little sense. Although it was possible to make distinctions between the "few" and "many" on the basis of various criteria, both the boundaries and the contents of these categories were unstable. Society was basically viewed as lacking any distinct structure. It was still conceived as a natural entity as opposed to constructed and artificial government, but it was naturally amorphous.[24]

The *Federalist*'s invention of the oxymoronic concept of majority faction was indeed a radical rhetorical twist. While traditionally the majority was understood as a numerical indicator of the voice of the people, conceived as a community, it was now construed as the most troublesome and dangerous manifestation of faction, that is, an interest or passion that was "adverse to the rights of other citizens, or to the permanent aggregate interests of the community." Since it was necessary to avoid the paradoxical image of the people oppressing themselves, it was necessary that "majority" now stand for something other than the "great body of the people." The locus of the "community" to which a majority faction was a threat and the manner in which that community's "aggregate interests" and the "public good" were articulated was, however, not specified. Neither "moral nor religious motives," nor even the existence of "enlightened statesmen" at the helm of a strong and energetic national government, could be relied on as adequate to the task of dealing with the general problem of factions. Its *"causes"* could, and should, they argued, not be eliminated, and although the answer was ostensibly to ameliorate the *"effects"* of factions, even more was to be achieved. The positive goal was to transform by alchemy these effects into the artificial virtue of a virtual people. Even though the traditional image of the people seemed to fade as soon as it was articulated, the general argument regarding the conformity to republican principles as well as more specific claims about the relationship between the people and the government required that there be a surrogate. Since the principal concern was less with the dangers of social divisiveness and incoherence than with the possibility of a faction gaining access to and control over governmental machinery, the authors argued that minority factions would be curtailed by the simple "republican principle" of "majority vote." The real problem would be "if a majority is included in a faction." Even though there were, they claimed, manifold institutional safeguards, it was necessary to prevent this social and economic danger from arising and impinging on the sphere of governmental action where a majority interest could be translated into a majority vote.[25]

"Pure democracies," and the "Theoretic politicians" who champion them, offered, the authors claimed, no answer to the basic problem. A "Society" (and the word was capitalized to suggest that it named a distinct

24. Ibid., 51–52, 56–57.
25. Ibid., 57, 60.

entity) "consisting of a small number of citizens, who assemble and administer the Government in person" was susceptible to coming under the sway of a majority sentiment or interest and had eventually always become the scene of "spectacles of turbulence and contention." It was not simply the lack of separation between the government and the people that the authors condemned, that is, an identity between the government and the governed, but the very ideas of equality and homogeneity that attached to the traditional republican image of "Society." Rather than defending the notion that there could be such a "people" in a large territory, it was not only conceded that there could not be such a people but argued that there in fact should not be such a social configuration. One of the reasons that representative government, which they now equated with "Republic," was deemed better than a "Democracy" was that it did not create a conflict of interest by putting the government in the hands of the governed, and it served to filter out factional interests and passions as they sprung from the local level and sought a path to power. As always in the case of popular government, the people must at once be sovereign and subjects, but they should not also be the government. This more traditional argument for representative government, however, was supplemented, and somewhat displaced, by the claim that such a government made it possible "to refine and enlarge the public views." Representatives were likely, especially given the pool of possibilities in a populous and territorially extensive republic and the larger number of individuals involved in choosing them, to be wiser, more just, more patriotic, and more attuned to the public good than "the people themselves," and more likely to achieve a mean in numbers that allowed them to be both sufficiently close to and removed from their constituents. But, the authors argued, this could not be the basic line of defense, since it was just as likely that, in the end, general suffrage might elevate individuals who would "betray the interests of the people."[26]

The "circumstance" that, in the eyes of the authors, "principally" elevated "Republican" government over "Democratic" was that the former made it possible to encompass a larger citizenry and territory and thus give rise to a larger number of "parties and interests," which in turn would inhibit "a common motive" from arising and transforming itself into a majority faction. Should the seeds of such a motive begin to evolve at a lower level in this union of state and national governments, it would be unlikely to "spread a general conflagration" or even rise to the level of national politics. This dispersion within society was an essential element of their "Republican remedy for the diseases most incident to Republican

26. Ibid., 62–63.

Government," that is, "the antidote for diseases of faction" that had over the ages plagued popular governments, but it was not simply that it prevented majority factions from forming.[27] The more important and positive consequence would be that it would satisfy the functional requisites associated with the idea of the people. There would be a kind of balance and coherence in society, a kind of wholeness to the mass of individuals and group interests even if the exact character and contours of this body were somewhat ineffable due to the constant movement and changing form of its elements. But it was also necessary that the virtual people be represented by a virtual government, that is, a government that was neither the people nor simply their agent or proxy.

How, one might ask, did the *Federalist* conceive of the government representing the people given the fact that the people were not really identifiable and distinguishable? Unlike Hobbes's account, the government did not embody the people, and the people were not constituted by the government. It made no sense, in this theoretical context, to conceive government either as the trustee of the people or as a mirror image of the people. The rationale for "mixed" government was no longer that society was mixed, but rather that the mixture was exclusively a mechanism for internally constraining governmental action. The government basically performed the required functions of sovereignty, such as providing order and security, and by responding in various ways to the demands generated in society that, it was argued so pointedly, had not been accomplished, and in fact were impossible, under the conditions of confederacy. The government simply did not represent in a manner that fit any traditional notion of representation. While it was the very principle and mechanics of representation that, they argued, distinguished a republic from a democracy and made it possible to have government over a large territory, which in turn made it possible to overcome the disease of faction, representation, it turned out, amounted basically to the acts and procedures relating to the election of representatives. Although the authors presented election as playing an essential part in controlling government and giving it direction as well as in providing it with the necessary power and authority, the government, they argued, must in the end be contrived to be self-regulating and self-correcting. Although at times there were statements in the *Federalist* asserting that "a dependence on the people is no doubt the primary control on the government" and that other provisions are "auxiliary," the general thrust of the argument was quite to the contrary.[28]

27. Ibid., 64–65, 83.
28. Ibid., e.g., 146–47, 349.

What the *Federalist* claimed was most distinctive about "the particular structure of this government" was not that the legislative, executive, and judiciary elements were "separate and distinct" but that, despite the fact that they were to be different "departments," there was "a partial mixture" and in fact "not a single instance in which the several departments of power have been kept absolutely separate and distinct." What this indicated primarily, despite the pains taken to attribute the idea to Montesquieu and the British constitution, was that the separation of powers had less to do with matters of representation than with preventing governmental tyranny and preserving liberty. The basic rationale for two houses in the legislature was the danger of "legislative usurpation" that they claimed was inherent in republics. The popular legislative branch was characterized as "drawing all power into its impetuous vortex," and thus "it is against the enterprising ambition of this department, that the people ought to indulge all their jealousy and exhaust all their precautions" in order to prevent "an *elected despotism*." Since, however, this branch would gain its ambition and strength from its proximity to the people, there were "insuperable objections" against "recurrence to the people" as a way of "keeping the several departments of power within their constitutional limits."[29]

One danger was that of confounding the roles of people and government and diminishing the authority of the latter, which ultimately rested on "opinion," but the "greatest objection" was that it would upset the "constitutional equilibrium" and exacerbate "the tendency of republican governments" to produce "an aggrandizement of the legislative." The basic "expedient" for the constraint on government was that since all "exterior provisions" were insufficient, "the defect must be supplied, by so contriving the interior structure of the government, as that its several constituent parts may, by their mutual relations, be the means of keeping each other in their proper places." Their argument was that "you must first enable the government to controul the governed; and in the next place, oblige it to controul itself." What was proposed was a structured or artificial factionalism within the institutions of government, which would parallel, but not duplicate, the natural but random divisions in society, whereby "ambition must be made to counteract ambition" and "the interest of the man must be connected with the constitutional rights of the place."[30]

The government was once again to be a mirror of society but, according to their vision of a "science of politics," in a radically new manner.

---

29. Ibid, 324–25, 327, 333–34, 350.
30. Ibid., 339–41, 347–49.

"This policy of supplying by opposite and rival interest, the defect of better motives, might be traced through the whole system of human affairs,
private as well as public." The new republic would consist of a "compound"
of government institutions in that the federal and state levels would "controul each other," but each level would be divided within itself so that it
would be "controuled by itself." As a *form* or type of government, however,
it would be unmixed, because all of its "power" was simply that initially
and continually "surrendered by the people." Yet what constituted the people remained indefinable. What reemerged in *Federalist 51* was the
Federalist 10 image of a kaleidoscopic society. While the problem of how
to "guard society against the oppression of its rulers" was to be solved by
the proper architecture of government, rather than by virtual representation, the issue was once again how to "guard one part of society against
the injustice of the other part," and the principal danger postulated was
again that of a majority "united by a common interest." The idea of a "will
in the community independent of the majority" was rejected as a way of
"providing against this evil." This was associated with "hereditary or self
appointed authority," but, at least implicitly, the idea of a public that transcended "classes of citizens" was also ruled out. What would be exemplified in the republic of the United States was a "second method" based on
the existence of a "multiplicity of interests" deriving from an extensive territory and population. "Whilst all authority in it will be derived from and
dependent on society, the society will be broken up into so many parts,
interests and classes of citizens, that the rights of individuals or of the
minority, will be in little danger from interested combinations of the majority." Thus "in the extended republic of the United States, and among the
great variety of interests, parties and sects which it embraced, a coalition of
a majority of the whole of society could seldom take place on any other principles than those of justice and the general good." The authors, in the end,
rejected the idea that "there is not sufficient virtue among men for self-government," but distinct manifestations of natural virtue seemed rare and only
appeared in moments such as that represented in the Convention.[31]

The *Federalist,* if taken seriously as a theoretical document, presents a
conceptual conundrum, but it raises a fundamental and persistent issue
about the foundations of popular or democratic government. In the years
immediately following the adoption of the Constitution, there were few
attempts to explore the theoretical character of the new system, and the
Federalist imagination would exercise a consistent hold over the task of

31. Ibid., 349–51, 352–53, 378.

imaging it. In Nathaniel Chipman's exploration of the general principles of government, he gave special attention to the American case and stressed its republican character, but he offered a rather prosaic and pragmatic, and probably quite accurate, account of its inception. He noted that the colonies' struggle with England over a number of issues had created a situation in which "their common exertions had given them an opinion of their united importance" which carried them through the revolution. By the time that the "inefficiency of the federal government was discovered," there was, however, "no more a national sentiment, or the pursuit of a national interest," and there began a "state of civil and political retrogradation." In this situation, "the wisest and best citizens had conceived, that an energetic system of national government could alone give any reliable hope," and they developed a plan that was "adopted to the situation of the country." Chipman surveyed the basic aspects of the constitutional structure and concluded that it was "in theory, the most beautiful system, which has yet been devised by the wisdom of man," and that it also worked very well in practice. It was unique and although it had not at this point "pretended to have attained the acme of perfection," it did include distinct mechanisms for change and improvement that indicated that it would do better than past republics.[32]

The basic theoretical predicament generated by the *Federalist* is, however, easily stated: how to justify popular sovereignty without a people. This question would continue to haunt attempts to give an account of the American polity long after Americans were comfortable with designating the regime as a democracy. The basic arguments would involve either a renewed search for the people or a claim, like that of the *Federalist,* that there is a surrogate. It is necessary, however, to be cautious in viewing the *Federalist*'s negative attitude toward the term "democracy" as unusual. Whatever criteria historians may advance for arguing that the politics of the colonial and revolutionary period was democratic, the word and concept of democracy were not in common use. When employed, democracy represented a general category of popular government, and it was characteristic to note that democracy could be either "simple" or "mixed" and to prefer the latter.[33] It would be a long time before democracy would emerge as a general term of approbation in commentary on politics and as a model

32. Nathaniel Chipman, *Sketches of the Principles of Government* (Rutland, Vt.: J. Lyon, 1793), 243–47, 277.

33. Roy N. Lokken, "The Concept of Democracy in Colonial Political Thought," *The William and Mary Quarterly* 16 (1959).

for America.[34] When it was employed as anything more than part of the classical categorization of forms of government, it was often in a pejorative and derogatory sense, and seldom self-ascribed.[35] Even when the term was used by Paine in *The Rights of Man,* he took pains to emphasize, as did Robespierre after him, that he did not mean direct democracy but rather representative government. The evidence of the term's use, however, is varied. For example, a student at William and Mary in 1798 noted that the "political principles of the greater part of the Students are purely Democratic" and that, following Rousseau, "the government of the People is the great desideratum with us."[36] "Republic" or "democratic republic" was the more favored term, but there was a consensus regarding the assumption that America possessed popular government and manifested popular sovereignty even if the *Federalist* did not provide a clear or unequivocal image of what this entailed. By mid-century, political discourse had appropriated the word democracy even if exactly what it involved and referred to was still contentious, and foreign commentary consistently designated the United States a democracy.

My concern is not with the extent to which the United States, according to various contemporary criteria regarding political structures and processes, was, or had become, democratic. This is an interesting issue that has been addressed in detail by much historical literature.[37] My concern is with the extent to which, and the manner in which, the polity was perceived by commentators as a democracy. Despite the democratic and republican sentiments and strategies that are attributed to Jefferson, he did not offer any systematic account of American government as a democracy. He believed that the United States was a republic and that the citizens of the United States were "constitutionally and conscientiously democrats," but what this involved beyond conditions of equality and such characteristics as decentralized government, elections, and various modes of popular

34. For a discussion of attitudes toward democracy, see Ithiel de Sola Pool (with Harold Lasswell and Daniel Lerner), *Symbols of Democracy* (Stanford: Stanford University Press, 1952).

35. See Robert Palmer, "Notes on the Use of the Word 'Democracy' 1789–1799," *Political Science Quarterly* 68 (1953).

36. Quoted in Anna Haddow, *Political Science in American Colleges and Universities, 1636–1900* (New York: Appleton, 1939), 46.

37. See, for example, Robert Wiebe, *Self-Rule* (Chicago: University of Chicago Press, 1995); Andrew W. Robertson, *The Language of Democracy: Political Rhetoric in the United States and Britain, 1790–1900* (Ithaca: Cornell University Press, 1995); Sean Wilentz, *Chants Democratic: New York City and the Rise of the American Working Class, 1788–1850* (New York: Oxford University Press, 1984); George Reid Andrews and Herrick Chapman, eds., *The Social Construction of Democracy, 1870–1990* (New York: New York University Press, 1995).

control is difficult to say. When it came to the question of what constituted the people, Jefferson seemed to concur with his eventual ally,
Madison, that it was the "mass of individuals composing the society."[38]
One of the earliest direct attempts to confront the question of how to conceive of the people and their relationship to government in the new system was that of Jefferson's friend, former President James Monroe.

Monroe claimed that although the basic categories of government were
monarchy, aristocracy, and democracy, the "great distinction is between a
government in which the people rule, and one, in which they are ruled by
an absolute power," and he noted that "republic" was a "generic term,
applicable alike to all types of governments, in which the people hold the
sovereignty exclusively, or participate in it, and which are of a mixed character."[39] What was important, according to Monroe, as in the case of the
Federalist, was to determine what was truly unique about the United States
as a republic and what consequently would insulate it from the causes of
the "decadence and downfall" of "ancient republics." Even more pointedly
than Madison, he ascribed the failure of former republics to the fact that
the government and sovereignty were united. The union of these powers
in the people was as despotic as any other form of absolutism, and the failure to divide the government into separate branches was an invitation to
tyranny. Monroe argued that while "the terms Sovereignty and Government
have generally been considered as synonymous," even when the institutions of government have been divided, what made the American
Constitution unique was its assumption that "they convey very different
ideas." Monroe concluded that while there was much that was quite fine
in Locke's work, there was, in the end, little that "can be considered applicable to us."[40] He interpreted Locke, probably quite correctly, as well as
Blackstone and other English writers, not only as asserting legislative
supremacy but as providing no real check on parliamentary sovereignty
except when there was a popular uprising that dissolved government.

What is even more evident in Monroe's thinking than in Madison's is
the extent to which he found it necessary to give a distinct identity to the
idea of the people. "It is only in governments in which the people possess
the sovereignty that the two powers can be placed in distinct bodies."[41]

38. Thomas Jefferson, *Political Writings,* ed. Joyce Appleby and Terence Ball (New York:
Cambridge University Press, 1999), xxiii, 291.

39. James Monroe, *The People The Sovereigns,* ed. Samuel L. Gouverneur (Philadelphia: J.
Lippincott, 1867), 25–27.

40. Ibid., 30, 33, 146.

41. Ibid., 33.

Monroe eschewed the term democracy as characterizing the American system, and he claimed that the Constitution had overcome the designation of "Mac-oc-racy" (or "banditti of low Scotch Irish" indentured servants and their progeny) that a correspondent of his had seen fit to bestow, a decade before the ratification, on the typical governments of the American "Continent."[42] The problem articulated by Monroe, that is, untangling and determining the relationship between sovereignty and the people, would, for the succeeding century, constitute the theoretical nucleus of the conversation about democracy. And the same year that Monroe died, Alexis de Tocqueville arrived to declare not only that the United States was a democracy but that it was the world-historical paradigm case.

It has been widely noted that when Tocqueville came to America in April 1831 with Gustave de Beaumont, he was probably more concerned with his own country than with studying the United States, or even the future of democracy, as an end in itself.[43] Although his work could be construed, as John Stuart Mill suggested, as the first theoretical account of democracy, as well as of the United States as a democracy, and although it became part of the literature about politics in the American academy, it did not really speak directly to the issue of what constituted the American political system. The ambiguity of Tocqueville's use of the term "democracy," including his references to both a political form and a social condition, has often been recognized. For Tocqueville, democracy was, on the whole, more a type of society and a manner of acting than a kind of political system, and for the most part, he saw the former as more significant than the latter.[44] His work did little to amend the kind of abstract and ambivalent answer to the question of the location of popular sovereignty that the *Federalist* had advanced. Although he joined the growing consensus regarding the appellation democracy, his work suggested that what he believed he saw in America was more what took place in democracies generally than what took place in America as a specific democracy or how America measured up to the criteria of democracy. In many respects, Tocqueville's work evidenced the same kind of ambivalence as the *Federalist*, that is, while he did not hesitate to speak of an American people, much of

42. Ibid., 10.

43. For a recent and comprehensive treatment of Tocqueville, see Sheldon S. Wolin, *Tocqueville Between Two Worlds* (Princeton: Princeton University Press, 2001). See also Roger Boesche, *The Strange Liberalism of Alexis de Tocqueville* (Ithaca: Cornell University Press, 1987).

44. For a careful analysis of Tocqueville's uses of the word and concept of democracy, see Melvin Richter, "The Eclipse of the Political? Conceptualizations of Democracy in Tocqueville and Guizot," paper delivered at the International Meeting of the Conference for the Study of Political Thought and Canadian Political Science Association, Quebec City, July 29–31, 2000.

his description belied its existence. He noted that Americans were attached to the localities in which they lived and had little or no sense of belonging to or participating in a wider polity. He appeared to worry about this absence of the very characteristics that would constitute a people—tradition, social structure, national communal ties, and mutual interaction and trust. And while he valorized popular government, the shadow of the "terror" so much in his memory as well as the authoritarian aftermath hung over his discussion.

Although Tocqueville has been viewed as a prophet of American exceptionalism, something close to the opposite perspective may be a more accurate way to characterize his position. Democracy was, in his view, the future or fate of the world, and America was the precursor of that future. He wanted to convince the nobility in France that they should turn away from the extreme individualism and pursuit of economic freedom characteristic of middle-class bourgeois society, which threatened to lead to a new kind of majoritarian absolutism, and that they should embrace a different tradition, which was at least latent in the American paradigm. An American contemporary suggested that this "fluent but somewhat superficial writer" might have "shed more light upon the subject by turning his attention to the history of Europe,"[45] but Tocqueville did evoke, or invoke, images from the past. Although there was, he believed, no going back to a former historical period, his model, as for some of pluralist theory after the turn of the century, was in part the set of communes, guilds, and professional corporations of medieval society, which he saw both as a check on central government and as enclaves of free activity and protorepublican life which could, in the modern era, be realized in the "voluntary association of the citizens" and replace the authority of the nobility.[46] Here in America was where freedom, which he and his French contemporaries largely equated with various images of self-government, was nurtured and practiced through habit and custom and a form of political education that steeped citizens in virtue and responsibility but that also provided a sense of authority.

Tocqueville returned to France in 1832, and published the first volume of his work in 1835. His focus had been on local forms of political activity, and his initial worries about majoritarianism were also directed toward the situation in the various states. He was concerned about the divisive effects of parties and regionalism and even about the possibility of the dissolution of the Union. In the second volume, however, he began to con-

---

45. Richard Hildreth, *Theory of Politics* (New York: Harper & Brothers, 1854), 263.
46. Alexis de Tocqueville, *Democracy in America* (New York: Vintage, 1954), vol. 1, 9.

front more fully what he saw as the difficulties in achieving and maintaining public freedom in a large nationalized state where there were, he believed, tendencies toward centralization and elective despotism. His recommendation was for a decentralized political order, which, through the creation of associations and local communities, would "multiply to an infinite extent opportunities of acting in concert." This was his vision of America as manifest in the New England township and other municipal institutions. It was here, he believed, that "the people reign in the American political world as the Deity does in the universe." Even in America, however, there were threats to the kind of public liberty that Tocqueville had in mind, even though his warnings were probably directed more toward his homeland. His overriding and dramatically expressed fear was of what he perceived as the tendency in democratic society toward a kind of self-negating individualism and equality that left individuals isolated and weak. Tradition no longer tied generations together and served as an authority. Standards of judgment were relativized, and "men are no longer bound together by ideas, but by interests." Much of what Tocqueville emphasized was the new spirit of commerce, the pursuit of economic self-interest, and the desire for material gain. It was this that tended to depoliticize society and draw people away from public affairs and communal activity. He noted that "the desire of acquiring the comforts of the world haunts the imagination of the poor and the dread of losing them that of the rich," and in America "most of their passions either end in the love of riches or proceed from it."[47]

Tocqueville argued that with the demise of traditional social hierarchy and the rise of individualism, the only authority that remained was that of the "multitude" or majority. The majority that Tocqueville feared was not a definable majority interest, or even necessarily a numerical majority, but, as in Mill's essay *On Liberty,* a mass public opinion that was not really attached to any definable public, and that demanded conformity and threatened to cancel out the very value of individualism and reign as absolute and unchallenged. This was hardly the sovereign people that many wished to equate with democracy. What Tocqueville saw as the essence of democratic society was equality of condition and the propagation of interest. Equality, he stressed, was not the same as liberty. The extreme passion for equality in democratic society could lead people to believe that if they were equal, they were free. In these circumstances, despotisms of various kinds, whether of public opinion, centralized government, or a new economic

47. Ibid., vol. 1, 65; vol. 2, 103, 137, 239.

aristocracy, could threaten and arise almost by default. The principal answer, he claimed, to the extremes of individualism and equality in America and the anomic condition that they threatened to create, was to continue to propagate public rather than social and economic liberty. "When the members of a community are forced to attend to public affairs, they are necessarily drawn from the circles of their own interests," and consequently understand their interdependence and need for cooperation. But, as in the first volume, Tocqueville also saw benefit in the fact that there was a "habit of participation" whereby "Americans of all ages, in all conditions, and all dispositions constantly form associations" that did not have a "political object." Such civil associations not only combated the effects of individualism but also reinforced, and were reinforced by, political associations. Hopefully, in democratic society, enlightened self-interest or "self-interest rightly understood," that is, the knowledge that it is sometimes necessary to defer gratification and sacrifice some interests in order to save others and to see that there was interdependence, would combat the dangers of individualism and equality. Religion could also, he suggested, provide a cohesive force and turn people away from divisive material pursuits.[48]

It may seem strange that someone such as Ralph Waldo Emerson did not seem to recognize the manner in which the very conformity that he challenged could arise, as Tocqueville had suggested, from the spirit and practice of individualism, but whatever the merits of Tocqueville's insights, and no matter how some may interpret his work as prefiguring later hopes and fears about American democracy, it did not provide any clear answer to the question of what constituted the American political system as a democracy. Tocqueville did not really find an American people, and although he perceived individuals and associations, he did not have a clear image of how they added up to a democratic political form. Those in the United States who were actually attuned to Tocqueville were individuals such as Francis Lieber, who Tocqueville first met through a mutual interest in prison reform and from whose *Encyclopaedia Americana* he derived considerable information. Herbert Baxter Adams, and those in his school of historical and political studies at The Johns Hopkins University, already saw towns as the core of democratic society, and Lieber was a great advocate of decentralization and associational diversity. He did not believe that liberty and equality added up to popular government. There is general agreement that Tocqueville depended heavily on the *Federalist,* and Joseph Story, in a letter to Lieber, claimed that Tocqueville had "borrowed the

48. Ibid., vol. 1, 99–106; vol. 2, 4–7, 23–32, 108–14, 152–56, 334–48.

greater part of his reflections from American works," including Story's *Commentaries on the Constitution,* and that "you know ten times as much as he does of the actual workings of our system and of its true theory."[49] No matter how prophetic and profound we may now find Tocqueville's work, there was considerable skepticism on the part of his contemporaries. Jared Sparks, a historian who Tocqueville consulted at some length about the nature of New England town government, praised his work but at the same time said that he was "persuaded that his theories, particularly when applied to the United States, sometimes led him astray." This was particularly the case, he believed, with respect to the image of the tyranny of the majority, which Sparks believed was "entirely mistaken."[50] Tocqueville's work was used in college classes, but while he wondered if the United States really was a state, it was the adaptation of the Germanic theory of the state that dominated the emerging field of political science and the conversation about democracy.[51] And it was in the United States, beginning with the work of Lieber, another self-proclaimed "stranger" in America, that the theory of the state became a theory of democracy.

A case can certainly be made for the claims that there was conceptual continuity between the language of political science and its historical context and that the "state" was very much part of the vocabulary of both politics and political commentary from the point of the founding onward.[52] There is, however, reason to qualify this assessment. When the term "State" was used in the *Federalist* to refer to something other than the American states, it was to speak of states as members of earlier leagues or federations. As both a word and concept, it was absent, for example, from both Chipman's and Monroe's commentaries. When George Cornewall Lewis, at about the point that both Lieber and Tocqueville arrived in America, set out to illustrate "the various uses of the principal terms belonging to political science," his extensive survey of concepts did not include the "state."[53] Although not totally foreign to either American and English political discourse or discourse about politics, this word simply had little meaning apart from a generic synonym for a government or country. The

49. William W. Story, ed., *Life and Letters of Joseph Story,* vol. 2 (Boston: 1951), 330.

50. Herbert B. Adams, *Jared Sparks and Tocqueville* (Baltimore: Johns Hopkins University Studies in Historical and Political Science, No. 12, 1898), 43–44.

51. For an analysis of use of texts in American colleges, see Haddow, *Political Science in American Colleges and Universities.*

52. James Farr, "Political Science and the State," in *The Estate of Social Knowledge,* ed. JoAnne Brown and David van Kueren (Baltimore: Johns Hopkins University Press, 1991).

53. George Cornewall Lewis, *Remarks on the Use and Abuse of Some Political Terms* (1832; reprint, Columbia: University of Missouri Press, 1970).

state as a concept with a distinct theoretical meaning in the United States was the invention of academic discourse during the course of the nineteenth century, and while it had various uses and functions, it was the axis around which the second-order discussion of America as a democratic society would revolve.

Daniel Rogers has emphasized the antidemocratic implications of the concept of the state in nineteenth-century professional political science, but it is necessary to be cautious about this claim. There is some truth to his argument that those who created the vocabulary of state-talk were an emerging group of professional academicians who wished "to seize politics itself (if they could) from the grubby hands of the amateurs." And, even far more than Rogers indicates, the theory of the state was deeply involved in political science's search for both professional identity and epistemic authority, which, in turn, it hoped would lead to practical purchase. The very idea of a science of politics was predicated upon a political ontology that lay behind everyday political discourse and that revealed something more sublime than the images that composed the common-sense vision of political processes and institutions as well as the often distasteful facts of actual political life. The concept of the state, as Rogers also argues, sometimes played a significant "conservative" role as a "barrier to popular claims of rights" as well as a basis for arguing against government intrusion into economic and social affairs. But what Rogers fails to discern is the extent to which the commitment to the idea of the state transcended ideology and professional divisions. Its constituency was much wider than he indicates, and within the university, it was so pervasive that there literally were no dissenters. And Rogers is simply, literally, incorrect when he claims that "the State was the antonym of the People." On the contrary, it was, above all else, a synonym for the people. Rogers notes, but dismisses as insignificant, the distinction between state and government in this literature and characterizes it as the product of individuals who were attached to the ghostly thing because they found the "real thing," that is, government, "deeply unnerving."[54] But the displacement of "government" in the language of nascent political science, as a name for both the object and activity of political studies, was much more complicated. It represented in large part a continuation of the attempt to solve the problem of the relationship between the people and government that had haunted the founding period, which would again appear so starkly in the context of the Civil War when individuals such as John C. Calhoun would seek to identify the concept of the people with the peoples of the various states.

54. Daniel T. Rogers, *Contested Truths* (New York: Basic Books, 1987), 146, 165.

The American science of politics sought to assume the mission of political education that had been the goal of "practical ethics," as an aspect of moral philosophy, in the traditional university curriculum. The principal task was to teach citizens and leaders about the nature of the polity to which they belonged and about their rights and duties. Its self-consciously defined vocation was to provide an image of the polity and to justify that image, not only to mold citizens' behavior to conform to and reinforce the political system but to create a greater congruence between the ideal and the real. Although the discourse of the state that defined the evolving field of political science was at first as chary as the *Federalist* about using the term "democracy" to characterize the American system, one of its central goals remained that of explicating the manner in which the United States was a paradigm of popular government. The principal answer was found in the concept of the state itself. This concept represented a search for political coherence in a century when events, on the surface, often seemed to suggest fragmentation and differentiation, and it was closely tied to nationalism and, eventually, the defense of the Union. It also sought to engender a sense of social unity that traditional religion had failed to sustain. But whatever its uses and whoever its advocates, the theory of the state was most essentially a theory of popular sovereignty that spoke both to the general belief that the United States was a democracy and to the paradox that the *Federalist* and earlier commentators had confronted.

There is a cluster of confusion attached to many contemporary discussions of nineteenth-century academic discourse about the state. Some scholars suggest that it can be explained as a reflection of the rise of, and aspiration for, an American state—by which is meant the institutions of a strong central government. One difficulty with this idea is that many of the principal state theorists were very worried about such a government, but the contemporary use of the word "state" and phrases such as "state-building" represent a concept that is almost the very opposite of what this word meant in the context of the nineteenth-century literature. Although the word "state" as it is characteristically employed today cannot be fully understood as other than in part a consequence of the nineteenth-century legacy, this discursive past includes a decisive conceptual transformation that took place a century ago in the language of social and political science. The contemporary concept is now retrospectively utilized not only to designate phenomena that the nineteenth-century concept of the state was expressly not intended to denote, but to explain the emergence of that concept as well. Stephen Skowronek, for example, has argued that many nineteenth-century intellectuals and social scientists were part of "an emergent intelligentsia" who acted as a "vanguard" in "taking up the challenge of building a new kind of state in America."[55] While this characterization might fit the situation in late nineteenth-century Germany,[56] it obscures the position and vision of these individuals.

The introduction of the concept of the state was a much more accidental and novel event closely tied to the life and work of Lieber. One might argue that if the concept of the state had not been introduced, a functional substitute would have been found, but there is reason to be skeptical of such notions of historical determinism. And even if this were the case, the particular attributes of this concept shaped and propelled the discourse of political science in a unique manner. The suddenness with which the word "state" came, by the mid-nineteenth century, to represent a new concept in discourses about politics in the United States is both remarkable and palpable.

55. Stephen Skrowronek, *Building a New American State: The Expansion of National Administrative Capacities, 1877–1920* (New York: Cambridge University Press, 1982), 3.

56. See Daniel F. Lindenfeld, *The Practical Imagination: The German Sciences of State in the Nineteenth Century* (Chicago: University of Chicago Press, 1997).

THE STATE OF DEMOCRACY

The institutions of the United States
are the work of man, and can be
understood by men.

—*Francis Lieber*

Lieber was, in fact, not simply using the word "man" generically, since he viewed political science and politics as "manly" affairs, but he was both enunciating a hermeneutical principle and joining Tocqueville in the claim that "a new political science" was needed for the new world of American politics and democracy. It was not, however, the republican "science of politics" referred to in the *Federalist,* and it is somewhat ironic that the conceptual roots of this science sprung from the old world and that it was Lieber who initiated such a science. There can be no doubt that the *Federalist* imagination was in the background of the emerging conversation in political science, but it is also clear that this conversation was not primarily rooted in, or a continuation of, the political discourse of the founding period, but rather was a distinct second-order form of commentary. There may be some ambiguity about what Tocqueville meant by a "new political science," and whether its task was to understand or educate, since he was ambivalent about whether "publicists" were capable of exercising political influence, but despite its academic location, there need be little ambiguity about the ultimate practical purpose of this American science of politics. Lieber was quite consciously entering what had been, and would continue to be, the province of moral philosophy in America and engaging the task of political education. Political science was, from its beginning, a kind of *dislocated rhetoric* in that it assumed the task of explaining and justifying popular government such that in some respects it was an extension of political discourse but was also institutionally separate and in other respects sought to supercede it.

Lieber's contemporaries as well as later historians have all concurred regarding his singular role in adopting, importing, and adapting the German concept of the state to a description, explanation, and validation of American politics, and in laying the foundations of what would become the discipline of political science. Adams, for example, the founder of historical and political studies at The Johns Hopkins University, noted in 1887 that Lieber's "works represent the first real transmission of German political philosophy to the New World" and constituted "the first great original production of political science in America."[1] But by that point, however, even Daniel Coit Gilman, president of The Johns Hopkins, an impresario of emerging political studies, and champion of Lieber and his European counterparts such as Johann K. Bluntschli and Edouard Laboulaye, had lost sight of the exact character of the theory that Lieber had sought to promulgate. He claimed that Lieber knew where the "sovereignty of the State properly terminated and the sovereignty of the people began" and that he deplored "the inability of his countrymen to recognize the limitation of the power of the State as taught by the fathers of the republic."[2] Gilman's statement indicates the extent to which both the concepts of state and government, by that point, had begun to be used interchangeably and the theory of democracy attaching to the concept of the state was becoming obscured. Lieber's thesis, on the contrary, was that there was no difference between the sovereignty of the state and the sovereignty of the people and that government was something quite different. To understand how difficult it is to reconstruct Lieber's theory from a post-nineteenth-century perspective, one need only note that two of his principal biographers refer to him, respectively, as a "liberal" and "conservative."[3] In the

1. Herbert Baxter Adams, *The Study of History in American Colleges and Universities* (Washington, D.C.: Government Printing Office, 1887), 299.

2. Daniel C. Gilman, *Bluntschli, Lieber, and Laboulaye* (Baltimore: privately printed, 1884), 32.

3. Frank Freidel, *Francis Lieber: Nineteenth Century Liberal* (Baton Rouge: Louisiana State University Press, 1947); Bernard Edward Brown, *American Conservatives: The Political Thought of Francis Lieber and John W. Burgess* (New York: Columbia University Press, 1951). For other work on Lieber,

context of early nineteenth-century German, and generally European, politics, he is appropriately designated as a "liberal," despite the facts that the term would have had little meaning in America during the period in which he was active and that he did not label himself as such. Although his position corresponded in some ways to the manner in which the term "conservative" is employed today in political discourse, the concept to which the word now applies was not available to either him or his contemporaries. By adapting the discourse of the state derived from German scholarship to the indigenous concerns of American moral philosophy as civic training, Lieber joined two academic traditions devoted to practical purposes.

Lieber emigrated to the United States in 1827, and in his first major publication, the *Encyclopaedia Americana,* he enunciated the basic concept of the state that, he claimed, "would mark out the province of the political sciences" and give them their "distinct character." One of the functions of the concept was indeed to demarcate the emerging discipline of political science, but it was also the nucleus of a theory of popular government. Lieber was immediately emphatic that the "State" was something distinct from "government" and that the term had a substantive reference. Government, he argued, was an artificial and created entity and "merely a means of obtaining the great objects of the state." What, then, according to Lieber, was the state? In an Aristotelian sense, it was the "natural condition of mankind, because essential to the full development of his faculties" as well as because it emerged as part of human social evolution.[4] But whatever else was represented in Lieber's image of the state, it involved an attempt to identify a sovereign people and validate the United States as the paradigm case of popular sovereignty. Exactly what it would mean to say that the people were sovereign, even if the existence of such an entity as the people were accepted, was less than entirely clear, but Lieber's basic point was that they were the font of authority. Although in his first major work, *Manual of Political Ethics,* Lieber pointedly rejected contract theories as logically and historically "absurd," he claimed that there were natural universal rights and duties that attached to human beings qua social animals, and thus it was essential that beyond the family and other

see Lewis Harley, *Francis Lieber: His Life and Political Philosophy* (1899; reprint, New York: AMS Press, 1970). James Farr has written extensively on Lieber as well as the nineteenth-century image of the state: see "Francis Lieber and the Interpretation of American Political Science," *Journal of Politics* 52 (1990); "Hermeneutic Political Science: the Forgotten Lesson of Francis Lieber," *History of Sociology* 7 (1987); See also Steven Alan Samson, "Francis Lieber on the Sources of Civil Liberty," *Humanitas* 9 (1996).

4. Lieber, *Encyclopaedia Americana* (Philadelphia: Thomas Desilver, 1835), vol. 10.

rudimentary associations "a union of a different character is required—it is called the State." Lieber labeled this a "jural" society, which was different from, for example, a religious society. It was not only qualitatively different but also quantitatively greater. It was the "society of societies," a particular form of the social whole that constituted a "res publica," "res communis," or "res populi" and that was the seat of sovereignty expressed in both public opinion and law. The jural society was, he claimed, "aboriginal" in that it existed before government and law and continued to exist as a distinct entity after they came into existence. He conceived of government as the institutional vehicle or "contrivance through which the state . . . acts in all cases in which it does not act by direct operation of its sovereignty."[5] Government was an artificial creation of the state.

For Lieber, it was essential that the concepts of state and government not be "confounded"—both that sovereignty not be attributed to government and that, in most instances, sovereign power not be exercised directly but rather through the institutions of government. This notion of separate government echoed the *Federalist,* but while the authors of the latter were ambivalent or even paradoxical in their claims about one sovereign people, Lieber was totally committed to the existence of such a people and adamant in his claim that the state *was* the people. Although he postulated ultimate ethical principles for judging the worth of various forms of government, such as impartiality in the dispensing of justice, he insisted that governments were necessarily relative to time and place. He criticized "philosophical politicians" who would suggest that the "people have absolute power," since "democratic absolutism" was even more dangerous than monarchial absolutism. When power was delegated to government by the state, it took on a secondary form and could be restrained by various constitutional arrangements and was always to some extent a function of "reputation." Democratic government, however, such as that which came to characterize ancient Athens, manifested direct and "real power, a torrent which nothing can stem." At least in the case of monarchy, he suggested, power was "visible" and locatable, since it was "lent" and required support in one way or another in order to be sustained. Thus the real justification for representative government was, as in the case of the *Federalist,* less that it was a vehicle for conveying the will of the people than a way of insuring "that the people, if they hold the supreme power, must not act themselves but through agents."[6] But in the process of explicating his

5. Lieber, *Manual of Political Ethics* (1838; reprint, Philadelphia: J. B. Lippincott & Co., 1875), 145, 152–53, 159, 162, 238.
6. Ibid., 316, 322, 328, 329–30.

vision of social reality, the people remained an organic entity and did not dissolve into individuals and factions.

Lieber rejected analyzing governmental forms in terms of the traditional categories of monarchy, aristocracy, and democracy. Instead, he focused on determining the functional and systemic form of the "polity," that is, the "character the power is, and in what mode the government operates." These, in turn, he divided into two basic types—"autarchies" in which power "rests somewhere" and is absolute, such as with a monarch or particular social class, and "hamarchies" or systems of cooperative or joint rule in which unity is joined with diversity. A hamarchy, however, was nevertheless "an organism . . . in which a thousand distinct parts have their independent action, yet are by the general organism united into one whole, into one living system." Such a system was "materially republican" whatever particular institutional character the government might take. The hamarchy was, he suggested, like "the living animal body," a "republic of action" that reflected and represented the natural character of society.[7] This kind of government was historically, in Lieber's view, a relatively recent achievement that was grounded in a kind of national unity, which had not actually existed in either ancient or medieval times. Although the decentralized social universe of the Middle Ages may have provided a check on concentrated power, it had not achieved the overall integral unity and homogeneity that was the basis of modern liberty and the kind of popular sovereignty that characterized a nation. It has been noted that "as late as 1841, the publishing firm of Harper & Brothers claimed that no American book on democracy existed,"[8] but although Lieber may not have been fond of the term "democracy," he was addressing the concept and formulating a theory that would endure well into the next century.

Fifteen years after his work on political ethics, Lieber elaborated his vision of "liberty" and "self-government" more fully in a book that in part reflected his concern about the trends in Napoleonic France and his wish to distinguish between what he called "Anglican" and "Gallican" liberty, which amounted to the difference between centralized and decentralized power. It also represented his dimming hopes, after the events of 1848, that Germany would achieve national unity and, at the same time, realize institutions that would foster and sustain individual liberty. As in the case of the earlier work, however, this book was primarily an attempt to render a theoretical image of the American polity for students in American colleges and universities who were "preparing themselves for the citizenry

7. Ibid., 353, 357.
8. Wiebe, *Self-Rule*, 55.

of a great republic."[9] It also included a theme that had been adumbrated in his earlier work but that might have seemed difficult to reconcile with certain of his claims about the state. He insisted that despite the fact that the state is "natural" and "indispensable" and serves the "highest end" of human being, membership in a state or life as a political being is not, in contrast with the claim of the ancients, an end itself, but rather it "always remains a means" for maintaining "individual and primordial rights" and achieving "certain objects both for the individual and for the social collectivity."[10] Lieber's principal concern at this point was with what he considered to be the danger inherent in the "encroaching power" of government. What he recommended, and presented as characterizing the United States, was what he called "institutional liberty," which, he argued, protected against threats from government as well as from the "masses." In this analysis, hamarchy gave way to the concept of "self-government," but he still did not want to equate this with what was often taken to be democracy. Lieber, like Tocqueville, saw dangers in democratic movements and in the search for equality, and he maintained that equality, and democracy either as a form of government or a social condition, did not ensure liberty. He conceived of a variety of institutions and associations as a bulwark against both government centralization and majorities. But, also like Tocqueville, he was not a medievalist. His vision of institutions was not of exclusive entities but of something more fluid, encompassing a variety of individuals who in turn participated in various associations—an image that would again appear in the discourse of political science after the underlying sense of unity embraced by Lieber had largely disappeared. Lieber did not conceive of civil society as a communal unity, but individuals as members of the institution of the jural society of the state did, in his view, become a homogeneous organic body. Thus German philosophy recaptured and reconstituted republican imagery.

In this second work, the state was again presented as a "union" and a "sovereign society" with an "indelible character and individuality," but the focus was on the state as an "institution which acts through government." Government was also again conceived as "a contrivance which holds the power of the whole, opposite to the individual." Although in some respects the state was, in his view, universal in both space and time, its contemporary form, which offered "Anglican" and then "American" and "modern

9. Lieber, *On Civil Liberty and Self-Government* (1853; reprint, Philadelphia: J. B. Lippincott & Co., 1877), v.

10. Lieber, *Manual of Political Ethics,* 159; *Civil Liberty and Self-Government,* 44, 46.

liberty," was, as he had suggested earlier, quite recent. England was, for Lieber, a paradigm of a nation and of republican liberty, but he argued that prior to the Revolution, Americans had developed a sense of themselves as a distinct nation that was finally given organized expression in the Constitution. What distinguished American self-government, he argued, as would American historians a century later, was that the republican elements of the British system "found a peculiarly favorable soul in America," which resulted in a more "popular or democratic cast of the whole polity" with attributes such as greater social equality, separation of church and state, and federalism. But what was more important than particular constitutional arrangements was the basic character of "institutional liberty." This involved assuring "publicity" through the device of representative government whereby "public opinion organically passes over into public will, that is, law," which was supreme, and this in turn entailed a strict separation between the electorate and the governmental "trustees."[11] In other words, there was no mixed sovereignty here, and government did not virtually represent the people but rather was the creation and agent of the people. Again, while this might seem to echo the *Federalist,* the fundamental difference was the substantive vision of the people that marked Lieber's formulation.

Although Lieber, like Tocqueville, claimed that liberty and self-government were ultimately rooted in "love and habit," they were "obtained and perpetuated" through a "vast system of institutions." The kind of diversity represented in this vision was, however, quite different from that articulated in the *Federalist.* What Lieber meant by "institution" was less an association of interest than "a system or body of usages, laws, or regulations of extensive and recurring operation, containing within itself an organism by which it effects its own independent action, continuance, and generally its own further development." Institutions created spheres of liberty, and, he claimed, "the idea of an institution implies a degree of self-government." What Lieber envisioned, concretely, was a variety of associations such as the family and the church, and although some institutions might be more temporary or "deciduous" than others and although they could be "instituted" or "established," most were "crescive" or had "grown" rather than having been expressly "enacted or contrived." And they transcended the individuals who participated in them both in terms of their "perpetuity" and the manner in which they went beyond "subjective

---

11. Lieber, *Miscellaneous Writings,* vol. 2, 232–37; *Civil Liberty and Self-Government,* 44, 50, 55, 165–68, 256–57, 298–300.

conception, individual disposition, and mere personal bias," and were governed by an "elemental law of moral reduplication." Some institutions were, he claimed, more "favorable" to the creation and maintenance of liberty than others, since, in his view, organizations such as trade unions and the Society of Jesus were distinctly "unfavorable" in that they tended to be destructive of the larger organic community of which lesser institutions were a part.[12]

In many respects, what Lieber claimed to perceive in America was exactly the kind of unity that his friend Tocqueville had found lacking. What Lieber termed "institutional self-government" was, again, a "popular government which consists in a great organism of institutions or a union of harmonizing systems of laws," that had a "cooperative character, and thus the opposite of centralism." This concept was different both from "an unarticulated government of the majority" and from a government based on "extra-popular principles, such as divine right." It possessed what he termed an "inter-guaranteeing, and, consequently, inter-limiting character" and manifested "a self-evolving and genetic nature" based on "realities" rather than "abstraction." This, he claimed, produced a system of political education that bound individuals together in common traditions and forms of activity. For Lieber, the only way to avoid the "appalling dilemma" of power being located either in the government or the people was "to unite the people and government into one living organism," and essential to his vision was the manner in which the diversity of local forms of self-government was amalgamated into a national system of self-government.[13]

It may be interesting to sort out the putative influences on Lieber's formulation. In various, and sometimes contradictory, ways he sounded like Locke, Kant, Burke, the *Federalist,* Mill, Tocqueville, and Hegel. But while we may assume his familiarity with the work of these individuals, it is more important to be clear about what he was saying and some of the more concrete conversations in which he was engaged. Lieber's theory of the state was in part informed and reinforced by the work of Bluntschli, whose own textbook, when translated in 1885, was widely used in American higher education.[14] Like other European intellectuals such as Laboulaye and Tocqueville, with whom Lieber was closely associated, Bluntschli saw American representative government, despite certain problems attaching

12. Lieber, *Civil Liberty and Self-Government,* 303, 305, 311, 313–14, 319.
13. Ibid., 366.
14. Johann Kaspar Bluntschli, *The Theory of the State* (Oxford: Clarendon Press, 1885).

to it such as slavery, as the leading edge of the evolution of the state in human history. Although Laboulaye, who initiated the efforts to produce the Statue of Liberty, never visited the United States, he was the most consistent and thorough, but now forgotten, European advocate of and commentator on American history and the American political system. He held up the United States as a model of liberty that produced both order and progress, and he became one of the principal voices in opposition to the Empire of Louis Napoleon.[15]

While Tocqueville and Laboulaye characterized America as a "democracy," which, politically, meant basically self-government and individual freedom, and while Lieber usually took pains to avoid the term, both Lieber and Tocqueville were more concerned with the breakdown of national community than Laboulaye, the more classic French liberal. Lieber's fears about democratic absolutism were, however, ultimately quite different from those of Tocqueville, despite their common concerns about such things as centralized government and the dangers of democratic extremism and their belief in the efficacy and benefits of associations. Tocqueville hearkened more to an image of public liberty that he feared would be lost in an atmosphere in which individual rights were valorized above all else. There is little in Lieber's work that would suggest the image of a tyranny of the majority such as that depicted by Tocqueville and Mill. And despite Tocqueville's concerns about social atomism and anomie and the loss of tradition, social structure, and community, there is little to suggest that he conceived of the possibility in democratic society of an organic people such as that postulated by Lieber or that he saw the state as other than government. Lieber's concept of the state was a distinctly German construction injected into, or grafted onto, an indigenous American tradition. As was the case for many of the nineteenth-century theorists, part of Lieber's agenda was not only to make sense of the American system in some abstract sense and to offer an image to be utilized in political education, but to give a theoretical ground to the claim that, despite the approaching break in the Union, there was in fact one American people that was sovereign, and constitutive of and represented by all the forms and levels of government.

---

15. See Walter D. Gray, *Interpreting American Democracy in France: The Career of Edouard Laboulaye, 1811–1883* (Newark: University of Delaware Press). Among Laboulaye's works were studies of the American Constitution and founding as well as political history of the United States during the mid-nineteenth century. There was also a satire (written under the pseudonym Dr. Rene Lefbvre and translated into English) recounting the adventures of a Parisian suddenly transported to America.

There were, however, some ideas in the intellectual milieu of the nineteenth century that reinforced the image of democracy that dominated the early discourse of academic political science but which had little to do with German philosophy. Although Orestes Brownson dedicated *The American Republic* (1866) to the historian and statesman George Bancroft (after earlier disagreements), his inspiration was not, as in the case of Bancroft, Hegelian. Probably no one so consistently attempted to hold on to a bond between the practice of Democratic politics and a theory of democracy as Bancroft,[16] but his ten volume *History of the United States,* finally completed in 1874, was a romantic attempt to discern laws of divine providence guiding an American people and transcending the venality characteristic of everyday government and politics. Brownson had begun, like many American reformers, as a kind of Christian socialist dedicated to bettering the lot of the working man. Although a proponent of democracy, he repudiated (in an essay titled "Democracy") egalitarian and majoritarian theories in favor of an image of law as sovereign. He had originally conceived of democratic principles in terms of such things as social amelioration and states' rights and had even supported Calhoun as the Democratic candidate for the presidency in 1844. His attachment to various Protestant persuasions was finally severed when he converted from Unitarianism to Catholicism, but he also became politically "conservative" in the course of his religious transformation and his more pointed defense of the Union. He never allied himself with the Whigs, but he turned away from Jacksonian views.

In his most mature work, Brownson addressed the nature of the American founding as well as the general question of political legitimacy, without which "politics cannot be a science and there can be no scientific statesmanship."[17] Like Lieber, he vigorously rejected all forms of social contract theory in favor of an idea of society as an organism that was natural and primordial and carried with it individual rights and duties. His account of American democracy began with the claim that there was an "unwritten constitution" that existed before 1787 and that was an expression of the American people, ordained with God's authority. This people had, he claimed, emerged from British rule as one organic sovereign community which, in turn, had created the written Federal constitution and subordinate state constitutions, which then gave rise to governments. Brownson argued that even though the integrity of the nation was not, in a practical sense, finally validated until the Civil War, the federal and state

16. See Lilian Handlin, *George Bancroft: The Intellectual as Democrat* (New York: Harper and Row, 1984).

17. Orestes Brownson, *The Works of Orestes A. Brownson,* vol. 18 (Detroit: T. Nourse, 1882–87), 18.

governments represented and expressed the organized form of the American people, which, in world-historical terms, signified the fulfillment of the Greco-Roman republican tradition.

Within the university, however, it was Lieber's work that gained the most attention, and it was enthusiastically promulgated, among others, by Theodore Woolsey at Yale, who edited a revision of *Civil Liberty and Self-Government* in 1874 and the fourth edition of *Political Ethics* in 1875. Woolsey published his own widely used text in 1877 and was the teacher of Gilman as well as other founders of American social science such as Andrew Dickinson White at Cornell.[18] Within a generation of the publication of Lieber's principal work, however, some of the inherent tensions in the theory of the state had begun to emerge as well as pessimism about the efficacy of moral philosophy and religion as guarantors of democratic unity. Henry Adams's anonymously published novel, *Democracy,* and his nostalgia for medieval society, was one example of the doubts about democratic solidarity that confronted theorists of the state. In this story, Mrs. Lightfoot Lee had gone to Washington in search of both power and "the heart of the great American mystery of democracy and government," but barely "saved herself" from both the person of the politician Silas Ratcliff and the general "atrophy of the moral senses" that the politics of interest induced. "She had got to the bottom of the business of democratic government, and found out that it was nothing more than government of any other kind."[19] There is reason to suggest that even Lieber had not always been fully successful in holding to the conceptual distinction between state and government, and by the beginning of the post–Civil War era, political studies in the university had begun to move away from the idea of joining moral philosophy and civic education and toward a greater emphasis on the authority of science as a way of affecting public life. In many respects, the emerging social sciences were spawned by, one might even argue, a displacement of, religious passion, but science was also viewed as a means of achieving values that were rooted in religious faith—something that was still quite evident in the origins of pragmatism.

When Charles Eliot became president of Harvard in 1869, his concern, and in part his mandate, was to move the educational core further away from theology to science. The professionalization of science had begun with

18. Theodore Woolsey, *Political Science or the State Theoretically and Practically Considered* (New York: Scribner, Armstrong, 1877). For a biography of Woolsey, see George A. King, *Theodore Dwight Woolsey: His Political and Social Ideas* (Chicago: Loyola University Press, 1956).

19. Henry Adams, *Democracy* (1880; reprint, New York: Farrar, Strauss and Young, 1952), 9, 233, 255.

the appointment of Louis Agassiz, and it would have some anomalous consequences. Despite Agassiz's insistence on separating religion and science, much of his career was devoted to pursuing certain values such as the inferiority of blacks. The use of science to validate social judgment would be even more apparent in the case of the social sciences. In 1872, Noah Porter, former professor of moral philosophy but then president of Yale, concluded that it was necessary to make a bow toward the emerging secular sciences without endangering the religious basis of the traditional university curriculum. He concluded that a young alumnus who had been trained as a classicist in America and Europe but who was also familiar with the new science of political economy, and then serving as a minister in a small parish, would be the perfect answer to the needs of the Yale Corporation. But Porter got more than he bargained for when he found that the work of Herbert Spencer had suddenly been introduced into the classroom. Despite his personal religious convictions, William Graham Sumner, like so many others of a quite different ideological persuasion, was convinced that science rather than the church was the answer to social improvement and change as well as the key to enhancing the role of university intellectuals in public affairs.[20] Another, less well-known but ingenious cleric who embraced philosophy and social science was Elisha Mulford, but Mulford, as in the case of Lieber, found his inspiration in German philosophy and attempted to integrate moral philosophy and political science.

Although initially a Calvinist, with an LL.D. from Yale, Mulford, like Brownson, on whose work he explicitly drew, found greater intellectual comfort in more doctrinal religion. After a short career as a pastor, he became a private scholar, identified with theologians who wished to meld Christianity and philosophy, converted to Episcopalianism, and ended his career as a lecturer in the Episcopal School in Cambridge, Massachusetts. He had first confronted politics when he had taken up the cause of the Union in an unsympathetic town in New Jersey, and this led him to the view that the American political system, as well as the Civil War, required an explanation and that such knowledge should be part of American political education. In the *Nation,* published in 1887, he acknowledged his debt, both substantively and methodologically, to Hegel and Bluntschli. In his account of the state, which he viewed as synonymous with the nation, he presented it as "moving toward realization" in institutions that allowed it to be "an object of political knowledge" and the "condition of political sci-

20. See Julie Reuben, *The Making of the Modern University: Intellectual Transformation and the Marginalization of Morality* (Chicago: University of Chicago Press, 1996).

ence," which, in turn, was "the ground of political education." The book was presented as a general treatise on the history and theory of the state, but in addition to particular examples drawn from the American experience, it was, as a whole, like many subsequent general theories of politics produced by political scientists, an abstracted version and universalization of the history and structure of the government and politics of the United States. The state, Mulford claimed, was both an "organism" and "moral being" manifesting "unity and continuity," and thus ethics and politics must be studied together. Mulford rejected contract theories and all other general theories of the beginning of the state. Individuals were, he maintained, always part of an organic social unity. This condition was, he argued, natural, as Aristotle had long ago noted, but, like all natural things, it had a "divine" origin, and its "sovereignty," although vested in the "people," ultimately came "from God." Since the state was a "conscious organism" and "personality," it reflected upon and determined its own path, but the general purpose was the realization of freedom manifest in rights embodied in law. The evolution of the state constituted the core of human history.[21]

Mulford maintained that just as the family preceded a more complex society, the "civil order of society," which he called a "commonwealth," was historically and logically prior to the nation and, among other things, represented its economic organization. The commonwealth, however, was incomplete, and the state or nation was "immanent" in it. Like Brownson, he claimed that there were two "constitutions," one that represented the development of the nation or state as a people and organism and the other a "formula" or "enacted constitution," which was the form of organization that the nation prescribed for its order. The sovereignty of the state, which existed before the formal constitution, found initial expression in a "convention" through which the people ordained the constitution, and thus they could also subsequently alter it through an act of "revolution," as in the case of the American Revolution that manifested the "realization" of the nation. Mulford claimed that the individual American states could be best understood as "commonwealths," as in the case of Massachusetts. These commonwealths, although incomplete in themselves and presuming the nation, did have an organized dimension and a kind of sovereignty like the state itself, but this was only a "formal" or instrumental sovereignty. The "real" or organic sovereignty, which performed functions such as international agreements and basic law, resided in the nation, which was "external" to and encompassed the commonwealths. Mulford argued that there

---

21. Elisha Mulford, *The Nation* (Boston: Houghton Mifflin, 1887), v, vi.

was a fundamental conflict between the idea of a nation and the idea of a confederacy and that, in the end, this was what the Civil War had been about. A confederacy was, first of all, an artificial and contractual entity, although it might be an intermediate stage on the way to a national constitution, and the war was a historical example of the fundamental "antithesis" that required resolution in the unity of the state. But he also claimed that there was a fundamental antithesis between nation, on the one hand, and "empire" and imperialism, on the other, since an empire was also an artificial and inorganic entity.[22]

Lest one assume that these sentiments would soon become atavistic, one need only look at how close Mulford's position was to that of a young philosopher who would dominate the intellectual life of the next generation. In the same year that Mulford published his book, John Dewey took it upon himself to respond to Henry Sumner Maine's critique of democracy as rule by the masses (*Popular Government,* 1885). His defense, however, was very different from something such as Walt Whitman's *Democratic Vistas* (1871). Dewey argued that Maine made the mistake of treating democracy as a form of government when it was in fact an "ethical conception" based on values such as freedom and equality that, even if not always perfectly realized, presupposed a community or society with a "common will" of which the majority voice was the manifestation. Dewey argued that "the whole drift of political theory since the abstract natural right philosophy of the French Revolution has been toward the conception that society is an organism, and government an expression of its organic nature." Although Maine, to his credit, rejected contract theory, he made the mistake, Dewey claimed, of accepting the premise that society was a collection of individuals when, in fact, humans were by nature social beings who found their identity in the "social organism." Dewey argued that we should not be fooled by looking at institutions such as voting, since the notion that society is an aggregate of individuals is a fiction. Although he did not claim that it was necessary to go as far as Bluntschli and view society as if it were actually a biological entity, it was only because individuals were bound together in a political community that "the whole lives truly in every member" and "every citizen is a sovereign." For Dewey, the government was merely the institutional agent of the state—"government is to the state what language is to thought."[23]

22. Ibid., 13, 16, 53, 144, 152, 283–84, 302, 321, 342.

23. John Dewey, "The Ethics of Democracy" (1888), in *The Early Work of John Dewey, 1882–1898,* vol. 1 (Carbondale: Southern Illinois University Press, 1969), 230, 232, 237–38, 246.

The image of the government as an agent of the people was part of the folklore of democracy as well as a doctrine of political science, but it had also worked its way into the more formal dimension of the language of politics. In a series of Supreme Courts cases, it was affirmed that a state was a "political community" of citizens organized under a government limited by a constitution and that "the distinction between the government of a State and the State itself is important, and should be observed." Even though in everyday speech the two might often be "confounded," the distinction was, in the end, what differentiated "free government" based on the "sovereignty of the people" from despotism. The Court concluded that the Civil War was not a war between states at all but rather a war between the United States and unlawful usurping governments.[24] By the last quarter of the century, however, the conceptual tension inherent in the distinction between the state and government had begun to surface in the discourse of political science.

In their influential textbook, William Crane and Bernard Moses (the founder of political science at Berkeley) distinguished, as had previous theorists such as Lieber and Bluntschli, between "analytical politics," or "politics as a science," and "practical politics" or "politics as an art," which had to do with what the state "should" do. This distinction was not the consequence of an attempt to insulate these spheres from one another but rather one of the first instances of a growing belief, which would find its paradigmatic expression in Max Weber's essays on science and politics (1919) but was very early on manifest in the American literature, that making political science apolitical and scientific would provide it with greater practical purchase. The "science of government," they claimed, was concerned with "the structure and development of the state as an organism," but in their analysis, the concept of the state as formulated by individuals such as Lieber increasingly slipped away as they attempted to present an image of "democratic self-government."[25] They maintained, as usual, that a "nation" was a natural and organic entity and that a "people" was a "politically united body" and that in America, by the time of the Revolution, "the whole people constituted a nation" even if individuals were not fully conscious of it. The revolutionaries, however, had fatefully allowed a division of the people into states, and the idea that there existed two political wills had forever after plagued American politics. Crane and Moses, like so many commentators reflecting the concerns stemming from the Civil

24. *Texas v. White* 74 US 1869; *Poindexter v. Greenlaw* 114 US 270 1887.

25. William Crane and Bernard Moses, *Politics—An Introduction to the Study of Comparative Constitutional Law* (1884; reprint, New York: G. P. Putnam's Sons, 1898), 1.

War and other instances of federal and state conflict, took the position that the problem could be solved by a clearer account of sovereignty as the entity that "expresses and enforces its supreme will" and makes the laws. They concluded that the American states were not sovereign, but although they held to the now traditional claim that governments were "merely the instrumentalities through which the whole given community expresses its will, and uses its force," they maintained, influenced in part by parliamentary images of government and virtual representation, that sovereignty was, in effect, for all practical and legal purposes, located in the government. This, however, was an anomalous and subversive idea for the future of democratic theory based on the concept of the state. To dislocate sovereignty from the concept of the people created a theoretical perplexity.

Crane and Moses admitted that in a country such as the United States, where there was a federal structure and "shifting power," sovereignty might be difficult to locate, but, like the influential John Austin, they maintained that there must be an "ultimate body of persons who in the last analysis can declare the will of the nation." Since "it is inaccurate to say of a representative republic that the people are sovereign," the sovereign in the United States "is not the whole body of the people nor the whole body of the voters of the several states." In the United States, they concluded, much like Austin, "the ultimate or primary sovereign, is a collegiate sovereign" composed of federal and state legislatures. They claimed, on the one hand, that the "people" were the "sovereign-makers," since the "motive power . . . behind the carriers of sovereignty, in a popular government, is public opinion" and "the consent of the governed." But, on the other hand, they concluded that "politically speaking, there is no such community as the people of the United States regarded as constituting one nation" and that what is really involved is not a government presiding over "the masses of citizens as masses" but officials in their various capacities relating to individuals.[26] The contradictions or tensions in Crane and Moses's analysis, and their return in some respects to imagery more characteristic of the *Federalist,* adumbrated the theoretical dilemma that would occupy the minds of political scientists for many years and ultimately undermine the identity of the concepts of state and democracy. By the end of their treatise, the people as an entity seemed to have evaporated, but Moses continued, in his own work, to maintain the "universal prevalence of democracy in America."[27]

26. Ibid., 39–41, 50, 147, 151, 233, 253.
27. Moses, *Democracy and Social Growth in America* (New York: G. P. Putnam's Sons, 1898), 12.

Woolsey, like many of those who succeeded Lieber such as Moses, had gone to Germany to imbibe the theory of the state directly, and John W. Burgess was also among this group. It was Burgess who succeeded Lieber at Columbia and who most forcefully and systematically attempted to eliminate the ambivalence expressed in work such as that of Crane and Moses. He directly confronted the basic dilemma in American democratic theory and elaborated most fully the theses that the state and government were two distinct entities and that the state was identical with the sovereign people. More than anyone else, Burgess established the disciplinary, professional, and intellectual foundations of modern political science; grounded political science on the concept of the state; and established the idea of political science as a science devoted to an account of democracy and to the study of the United States as a democracy. Even many of the next generation of political scientists who diverged ideologically from Burgess were subject to his theoretical tutelage. His most influential book, *Political Science and Comparative Constitutional Law,* was published in 1890, but in 1917, with the aid of his longtime student and admirer Nicolas Murray Butler, president of Columbia University, he drafted a condensed version, which, although not actually published until 1933, placed greater emphasis on the theory and practice of democracy. Butler, like Burgess, believed that since government and liberty were two different spheres, the university should be a private institution. Shortly before the fiftieth anniversary of the School of Political Science that he founded, Burgess, in Butler's words, "stepped off into the clouds to continue the Great Adventure."[28] By this point, Burgess's analysis had become hardly intelligible, let alone credible, to most political scientists, but in subtle ways, his legacy was perpetuated not only during the Progressive era but beyond.

Burgess argued that the state and the government were definitely not the same thing, and he claimed that the nation, although the foundation of the state, was also something different. A nation was a geographical and ethnic entity, which became political when it took the form of a state. Modern constitutional states, and particularly the United States, were the prime examples of those founded on a national unity, and they represented "the self-conscious democracy, the *ultima Thule* of political history."[29] Nations, he claimed, tended, in the natural course of history, to become states, and the highest examples of the latter were those that had achieved

28. John W. Burgess, *Reminiscences of An American Scholar* (New York: Columbia University Press, 1934), 345–46.
29. Ibid., 254–55.

the "popular or democratic form." However, he argued that not every nation, such as those of Asia and Africa, would become a state, and thus Burgess, unlike Mulford, or Sumner for that matter, viewed "the political subjection or attachment of the unpolitical nations to those possessing political endowment" as right and inevitable. It seemed reasonable to Burgess that unless a nation achieved democracy, it could not claim the privilege or ability of self-government. As much as Burgess shared with Lieber, Woolsey, Bluntschli, and most European "publicists," they had, in his view, still somewhat "confounded" or failed to hold fully to the difference between the concepts of state and government and thus remained hostage to the problems that this created. Burgess saw his task as not only defending this distinction but articulating it, both logically and historically, in a manner that had not heretofore been achieved.

Despite his German education and his deep involvement in German philosophy, which commentators have so often, and properly, stressed, his concerns were, maybe even more than in the case of previous writers, distinctly directed toward American government, and he viewed many American authors as too beholden to European ideas. He argued that just as the objective institutionalized form of the state found its fullest expression in the United States, notwithstanding the fact that it was "the creation of Teutonic political genius," European thought was but "a stepping stone to a higher and more independent point of view," which at its core involved a definite distinction between state and government. In the past, he suggested, both in theory and practice, the line often tended to blur. Thus he insisted that it was important to stress the distinction in principle even if it was sometimes difficult in particular cases to discern a strict division between the subjective or ideal, that is, the "pioneer" idea of the state as "perfect and complete," on the one hand, and the objective and actual "concept of the state," on the other hand, which represented the state "developing and approaching perfection"[30] in the course of history. Without vigilance regarding this crucial distinction, he argued, the theory of democracy could not be sustained. This German phrasing, so typical of Bluntschli and other German theorists, may today appear very obscure, but what it amounted to was the basis and beginning of what in later political science would become the conceptual distinctions between democracy as a form of government and democracy as a set of institutional practices, between theory and practice, between value and fact, and between normative and empirical theory.

30. Burgess, *The Foundations of Political Science* (New York: Columbia University Press, 1933), 6, 40, 74.

In Burgess's view, however, the United States marked an instance where theory and practice tended to merge. He maintained, in effect, like so many after him, that the theory of democracy was to be found in the practice of American politics. A description of American politics equaled a theory of democracy. Here, at the highest point in the evolution of the state, the matter could be studied as "objective fact" and with the same method that was utilized in natural science. The national popular state as realized in America furnished "the objective reality upon which political science can rest in the construction of a truly scientific political system. All other forms contain in them mysteries which the scientific mind must not approach too closely." In the United States, he claimed, there were "objective aids and supports upon which to steady our reflection and by which to guide our science."[31] More than a half a century later Robert Dahl and other political scientists who viewed themselves as ideologically and scientifically far removed from Burgess enunciated a very similar idea of political science and their own version of the American "hybrid" that supported both an empirical and normative concept of democracy.

Burgess emphasized that in the case of the United States, "the government is not the sovereign organization of the state. Back of the government lies the constitution; and back of the constitution the original sovereign state." He attempted to validate this picture both with a singular and imaginative account of American history and in terms of a contrast with England and past regimes. He argued that in England prior to 1066, the king had been both state and government, but subsequently the nobility became the state, and thus the sovereign, and the king became the government, even though neither king nor nobility quite admitted nor comprehended this fact. In the United States, however, things were historically and scientifically much clearer. The American "system," he argued, rested entirely on a "revolutionary" basis, since any organization of the state prior to 1774 had been completely destroyed. The old state did not reappear, as it had in England after the restoration of the monarchy in the late 1600s, as an element of government that claimed a portion of the sovereignty. In ancient Greece, state and government were also in practice the same, but in the contemporary world, in both theory and practice, forms of government and states were becoming two different things as were forms of government and types of governmental institutions. In the case of the form of "immediate government," or direct democracy, the state exercised the function of the institution of government, while the "real principle"

---

31. Burgess, *Sovereignty and Liberty,* vol. 1 of *Political Science and Comparative Constitutional Law* (Boston: Ginn and Company, 1890), 58, 70.

of a "republican" form of government, toward which history was moving and which should be embraced as a value, was a "democratic state with an aristocratic government." This evolution, he suggested, was accompanied by the decline of past forms such as monarchy and aristocracy.

Burgess claimed that there was, in the modern world, a movement away from "immediate" and "unlimited" government or a situation in which the state exercised the function of government (which could be monarchial, aristocratic, or democratic), toward representative government where the state vested power in an institutional entity that was distinct from its own organization. "Modern states," of which the United States was the archetype, were "those based on the principle of popular sovereignty; i.e., they are democracies." Such states, Burgess claimed, were grounded in a "natural harmony" and "consensus of opinion" and cemented by a common language, psychology, and set of basic interests. Thus there was a tendency to use the terms "nation" and "state" interchangeably even if they were not actually, and strictly speaking, identical. The purpose of government was to further the ends of the state by exercising the highest degree of power consistent with the highest freedom of the individual.[32] What had happened in the case of America, Burgess claimed, very much as Lieber and others had before him, was that during the colonial period there arose not merely a national consciousness but a new state, a distinct people, which was different from England. Eventually there was an "irresistible impulse" to give this subjective fact an objective institutional expression, and this was manifest in the Continental Congress—"the first organization of the American state." The actual revolution, giving rise to the American state, was achieved prior to 1776, and even the Declaration of Independence was but a recognition and "notification" of this fact. The Articles of Confederation, however, were defective, and consequently, at that point, "the American state ceased to exist in objective organization" and, lacking a real central government, it "returned to its subjective condition." Since, in this disembodied situation, there was no way for the sovereignty of the state to be adequately expressed, it "was a perfectly unbearable condition of things in theory, and was bound to become so in fact." Certain "astute" individuals, however, such as Alexander Hamilton and James Bowdoin, sensed the problem. Bowdoin had urged the Massachusetts legislature to instruct delegates to call for a national convention to undertake a revision of the Articles, which, in the language of "political science," would have involved "a reorganization of the state by

32. Ibid., 57, 72, 81.

representatives of the people," but they failed to do so. According to Burgess, however, the clever Hamilton managed to finesse the situation and transform a meeting that had been called to deal with commercial matters into a constitutional convention. The actions of the convention amounted to a new "revolution" by assuming the "constituent powers" of the state, drafting the Constitution, and calling for a plebiscite. Burgess argued that "the all-important hermeneutical conclusion" must be that "the original construction of the American state cannot be interpreted by juristic methods," but only by "history" and "political science."[33]

Burgess's formulation can hardly be construed as an example of the sterile legalism and formalism that is often attributed to him and his contemporaries, a formulation he pursued a few years later in the *Political Science Quarterly*. The initiation of the journal in 1886 had been predicated upon the autonomy of the subject matter of the state and upon the increasingly "dominant position" of political science as "the science of the state," yet even this organ of the Columbia school did not evince an entirely clear position on the issue of the relationship between state and government. Although the state was the deemed the "domain" of political science, Munroe Smith, in the journal's first issue, claimed that this was basically a "point of view" for looking at the social "whole" and was dictated by the fact that the state was assuming greater functions and becoming the "central factor of social evolution."[34] This was not exactly the perspective that Burgess wished to emphasize, but it indicated the difficulty in hanging on to the distinction that underlay the theory of democracy to which he subscribed. Already Smith and others at Columbia were tending to identify the state with government, and subtly moving away from Burgess's ideology while in many ways remaining within his theoretical orbit.

Although the Civil War and the arguments of individuals such as Calhoun were long past, Burgess maintained that the propensity of state governments to encroach on liberty made it necessary to once again "excite skepticism" about the "dogma that our political system is an indestructible union of immutable states." Despite the fact that some might read the Constitution as providing the individual states with some residual sovereignty, he maintained that this document was not itself the "creator" of anything, but only a necessarily imperfect attempt to "express" verbally the sentiment of the underlying state or sovereign people. All legal right flowed from the state, which was the emanation of "nationality," a homogenous

33. Ibid., 100–108.
34. Munroe Smith, "The Domain of Political Science," *Political Science Quarterly* 1 (1886): 4, 8.

people, and based on "geography and ethnography."[35] The individual American "states," according to Burgess, were not literally states at all, but rather "a meddlesome intruder" that was "the tool of the stronger interest, the oppressor of the individual." This was surely a resurrection of Federalist imagery, but now coupled with an unrelenting attempt to claim that there really was a people behind the apparent diversity in society. Although the states, he argued, were in part the institutional residue of the original colonies based on grants from the English crown, their real significance, as Mulford had claimed, was that they had developed into "commonwealths" or "natural communities" from which, over time, had arisen the general national sentiment that issued in the Continental Congress and constituted a sovereign claim to independence. The Articles, however, which recognized separate and independent states, amounted to an act that "usurped the sovereignty of the people of the nation." The ratification of the Constitution was in essence a "revolution against usurpation," which finally culminated in a national government as the representative of the people or the state.[36]

From the perspective of the twenty-first century, it may be quite correct to categorize Burgess as an ultra-nationalist, an imperialist, a racist, an apologist for resistance to government interference in the economic enterprise, and an opponent of what many might consider democratic politics. And it is difficult to read his work or that of many of his predecessors as other than a defense or rationalization of the Union. Even more than Lieber, he was attached to a veneration of Germany as the source of Anglo-Saxon liberty and immersed in a Hegelian metaphysic and philosophy of history. It may not be untoward to suggest that "the whole of Burgess' political science is built upon a tension between the German doctrine of the state which, like his colleagues, he considered the cornerstone of modern political science, and an ideological commitment to the individualism of traditional Anglo-American liberalism." And one might conclude that for all the state theorists of the period, "the difficulties they encountered arose ultimately from their inability to apply the German idea of the state to the American political tradition."[37] But all of this neither elucidates nor explains away the manner in which the concept of the state was the paradigm at the core of a theory of democracy.

35. Burgess, "The American Commonwealth: Changes in Its Relation to the Nation," *Political Science Quarterly* 1 (1886): 12–13.

36. Ibid., 34.

37. Sylvia D. Fries, "*Staatstheorie* and the New American Science of Politics," *The Journal of the History of Ideas* 34 (1973): 401. See also Bert James Loewenberg, "John William Burgess, the Scientific Method, and the Hegelian Philosophy of History," *Mississippi Valley Historical Review* 42 (1955).

We might want to say that these nineteenth-century theorists were limited by the vocabulary of state theory and their belief that it was the basis of a science of politics, but this would be something like saying that Aristotle's theory of motion was inhibited by not having access to the vocabulary of Newton. The problem was less one of the limitations of the concept of the state in accommodating to the American political tradition than one of solving the anomalies inherent in that tradition. The concept of the state was part of a continuing attempt to validate the idea of the American polity as a manifestation of popular sovereignty. Today, for various reasons, we may find Burgess's ideas less than philosophically, morally, and empirically credible, but there is no easy standard to which we can repair to diminish his conception in comparison with the formulations that would be advanced in the course of the following century. The commitment to the idea of the state during the nineteenth century transcended any narrow ideological persuasion, and it was not limited to the discipline of political science. It was, however, within the discourse of political science that this idea was most distinctly elaborated, and it was around the idea of the state that the American polity was most consistently imagined as a democracy. And this inevitably entailed that a crisis in the theory of the state, whatever factors may have contributed to that crisis, would constitute a crisis in democratic theory.

Both Burgess and Herbert Baxter Adams had been educated at Amherst College under Julius Seelye, who was deeply committed to German philosophical perspectives. While Burgess went on to study in Germany, Adams drew continual inspiration from Bluntschli's work. What emerged from Adams's school at The Johns Hopkins University, however, was a less coherent account of the state, and, as in the case of the next generation at Columbia, the line between the concepts of government and state began to blur. Democracy, by this point, was not an uncontentious value. Austin's influential account of sovereignty seemed, for many, to place sovereignty within the institutions of government, and Maine, for example, had attacked democracy even though he argued that the United States, although a popular government, was not actually a democracy. Woodrow Wilson may not have felt it necessary to travel from Baltimore to Washington in order to study the institution of Congress, but he injected a new kind of realism into the conversation when he set out to demonstrate the difference between the "literary" Constitution and the "actual practices" or "real government of the Union." According to Wilson, the so-called balances in the constitution were "only ideal," and, in his view, the fact of the matter was that the federal government was dominant over the states and the Congress was "predominant" over the other branches.[38] But although the legislature had become supreme because of its organization and efficiency, its time was taken up with legislation, which diverted it from oversight. And, Wilson claimed, the American Congress lacked the center of authority and responsibility of a parliamentary system and the capacity adequately to inform and guide public opinion.

Wilson soon began to question those dimensions of popular government that had "enthroned public opinion" and inhibited administration and efficiency in government; but, more significantly, he argued that "the sovereign's mind has no definite locality" and that this "unphilosophical bulk of mankind" is influenced by "favorites" that distort good judgment and make us "crude democrats." It was on this basis that Wilson advocated his famous distinction between politics and administration and argued that "administration lies outside the proper sphere of *politics*. Administrative questions are not political questions." Although there was an "admirable movement" to enhance "political education" and make sure that political science was part of every college curriculum, this could not be a substitute for agencies that would do the "business" of government. The role of public opinion, he argued, should be that of an "authoritative critic" that avoided being "meddlesome," and while we might not want to adopt the political principles of European countries, we could safely appropriate some of their techniques of governance.[39] The climate of opinion at Hopkins, earlier than for the younger generation at Columbia, was, with individuals such as left-wing economist Richard Ely, considerably more inclined toward activist government and less committed to the image of the state as a sovereign people, and Wilson was representative of this cast of mind.

What is most important about Wilson's influential treatise on the state is that he was not actually, in the end, talking about what had been called the state by Lieber, Burgess, and others, including many of those at Hopkins such as Adams who had been so attached to Bluntschli's work. Although a large section of his book was published as a separate text on American government,[40] it was also not primarily a study of American democracy. Although he capitalized the word "State," paid lip service to the idea of its Teutonic origins, spoke of it as the organization of society, and went through the motions of summarizing some of the basic tenets of the traditional theory, he actually seldom used the term, and the concept

38. Woodrow Wilson, *Congressional Government* (New York: Houghton Mifflin, 1885), 52.

39. Wilson, "The State of Administration," *Political Science Quarterly* 2 (1887): 208–10, 215–17, 219.

40. Wilson, *The State and Federal Governments of the United States* (Boston: D. C. Heath & Co., 1891).

seemed to dissolve in the course of his discussion. The book was really about government institutions and, as the subtitle indicated, "*historical and practical politics*" from the ancient world to the present. It was probably fair for him to claim that his "textbook" had "no model," since it was the first systematic study of comparative government in American political science. Although he claimed that "government is merely the executive organ of society" and that society is "natural," that is, "Society an Organism, Government an Organ," and although the state was presented as the "organic body of society" without which society is only an abstraction, the state faded discursively into government in the course of his analysis, as in the case of Crane and Moses. And no subsequent theorist came along with any decisive attempt to rescue it from theoretical atrophy.

For Wilson, "the essential character of all government, whatever its form, is authority," and this ultimately rested on "force." What characterized modern times was, he claimed, that "democracy seems about universally to prevail," but what Wilson meant by democracy was representative or "mediate" government, which involved a separation between government and the governed. He held on to the idea of separate government, but what it was separate from, if something other than a mass of individuals, was less coherent. In ancient democracies, government, he argued, was both the "embodiment" of society and "immediate," just as a human being is at once spirit and body. In this case, "government was as old as society." During the Middle Ages, however, government "suffered eclipse," and society dominated until the Teutonic period when the individual rights that were first discovered by Christianity found political expression. The "modern State has been largely *de-socialized*" and now serves the individual. He claimed that "the state, as it appears in its organ, the government, is the representative of the individual."[41] The question that was emerging was that of in whose name government should or should not act. What was missing in Wilson's analysis was a clear notion of a sovereign people that stood behind government, and what was becoming apparent was that the search for democracy would soon require seeking it within, rather than behind, government and politics.

In addition to Lieber and Tocqueville, another self-identified "stranger" sought to describe American democracy and in doing so had a significant impact on the conversation in American political science, including its increased "Americanization" after the turn of the century. James Bryce,

---

41. Wilson, *The State: Elements of Historical and Practical Politics* (1889; reprint, London: D. C. Heath & Co., 1899), 572, 576, 581, 618–19, 631.

who visited the United States on three occasions between 1870 and 1885, did not, any more than Tocqueville, doubt that he was investigating a democratic regime, maybe *the* democratic regime. America was democracy, and to understand one was to understand the other. After successively winnowing "a swarm of bold generalizations," he presented the most thorough, concrete, and systematic account of American political institutions and culture that had heretofore been offered.[42] He believed, at this point, that so many individuals had attempted to describe and explain the American polity that some justification beyond the fact of rapid change in the society was needed. He argued, probably quite correctly, that "no one author has proposed to himself the aim of portraying the whole political system of the country in its practices as well as its theory," "both as a Government and as a Nation."

Realizing that his work would be compared with that of Tocqueville, Bryce stressed that he was undertaking something "quite different." Although he claimed to benefit from a certain "detachment" and a capacity to see what a "native" might miss, he also indicated that it helped to be "English" and more culturally attuned than some other external, and by imputation French and German, observers. And while Tocqueville's ostensible concern was in part to "estimate the strengths and weaknesses of democratic government as it exists in the United States" as well as to compare it with European speculation about democracy, the real concern, Bryce suggested, as most subsequent commentators on Tocqueville would also note, was less with a description of the United States than with writing a general treatise on democracy that was based on illustrations from America and that could provide lessons for France and Europe in general. According to Bryce, "Democratic government seems to me, with all deference to his high authority, a cause not so potent in the moral and social sphere as he deemed it; and my object has been less to discuss its merits than to paint the institutions and people of America as they are, tracing what is peculiar in them not merely to the sovereignty of the masses, but also to the history and traditions of the race, to its fundamental ideas, to its material environment." One need not give full credence to Bryce's claim, anymore than that of Darwin, that he avoided "theories" and the "deductive method" in order "to present simply the facts of the case, arranging and connecting them as best I can, but letting them speak for themselves rather than pressing upon the reader my conclusions." But his work did provide a model for important dimensions of political science as it moved

42. James Bryce, *The American Commonwealth* (New York: Macmillan, 1890), 4, 7.

away from the framework of analysis associated with the concept of the state and focused more on the description of particular political institutions and processes and on the manner in which they added up to democracy.[43] But what it meant to speak of the "sovereignty of the masses" was something that required considerable clarification.

Since Bryce assumed from the outset that the United States was a democracy, he was less concerned with locating the ground of popular sovereignty in an entity such as the state than in describing the "constitutional machinery" and the "methods" and "forces" that were involved in democratic practices. Much like Lieber and Tocqueville, however, he still believed that the core of American democracy was to be found in the power of "public opinion" and the existence of a general "mind or consciousness" that "stood above parties, being cooler and larger minded than they are; it awes party leaders and holds in check party organizations. No one openly ventures to resist it. It determines the direction and character of national policy. It is the product of a greater number of minds than in any other country, and it is more indisputably sovereign. It is the central point of the whole American polity."[44] But this was a public opinion that was not, anymore than in the case of Tocqueville and his worry about the tyranny of the majority, the opinion of any identifiable public or people. It was largely a functional entity, and the question of the location of democratic will would loom large.

For most American political scientists, however, the assumption that America was a democracy required theoretical validation, and the concept of the state remained the key for most. Many held on to the belief, which they attributed, among others, to Lieber, that there was a "national sovereignty" and a people "with a capital 'P'" no matter what Austin and Maine might claim.[45] Contemporary scholars who cling to the notion that the theory of the state was the special property of conservative nationalists need only consult the career of individuals such Ely.[46] Whatever theoretical and ideological variations may have appeared, the theme was not lost. For indigenous students of politics as well as for the German publicists from whom they adapted their theoretical paradigm, to conceive of democratic institutions was, as Frederick Grimke had averred in his popular mid-century text, to think of the United States;[47] to think of democracy was to

43. Ibid., 4, 6.

44. Ibid., 6.

45. See, for example, John A. Jameson, "National Sovereignty," *Political Science Quarterly* 5 (1890).

46. For a discussion of Ely, see Gunnell, *Descent of Political Theory*, chapter 2.

47. Frederick Grimke, *Considerations upon the Nature and Tendency of Free Institutions* (New York:

postulate the state; and, well into the twentieth century, to give identity to political science was to see it as the theory of the state.

Although by the last decade of the nineteenth century the basic tenets of state theory as advanced by Burgess were, one might say, in the process of decay, they had nevertheless become paradigmatic in the emerging discipline of political science. In a text for advanced students, Frank Sargent Hoffman of Union College, who had studied with both Seelye and Burgess, summed it up well, and his formulation indicated how the concept of the state was not ideologically specific, whatever the political disposition of someone such as Burgess. It was the "State," Hoffman claimed, that provided a resolution to the tension between the "two great truths" of "individuality and brotherhood." Since the state was the source of all rights and duties, individuals could possess no rights that conflicted "with the good of the whole," and the state was not "a mere collection of individuals." The state represented a natural organism with a perfect integration of part and whole. It was "the organic brotherhood of man." Sovereignty was the essential attribute of the state, and this entailed that the people were sovereign, because "the people in their organic capacity are the state."[48] Thus, he argued, like Burgess, it was technically inappropriate to refer to the several American "commonwealths" as "states," and it was necessary to recognize that a state can change or "revolutionize" its government without losing its basic identity. Although Hoffman subscribed to Burgess's notions regarding the Teutonic origins of the modern state and the propriety of more advanced states assuming sovereignty over "barbarians," he suggested a much more active role for the state and the people. "The people of the State can change their government and ought to change it as often as the public good requires." He noted that "no term in political science is so commonly misapprehended or so frequently misapplied" as government, and the basic source of error was to confuse it with the state. The government was no more the state than "a man's words are the man himself." Although contract theories of the origin of the state were, he claimed, surely incorrect, they conceivably represented a "true doctrine" with respect to the origin of government. It was, however, the role of the government, as an "organ of the State," to "enlighten the people as to what the good of the State requires," and the best government was not necessarily one that

H. W. Derby, 1848), 4. See Stephen Leacock, *Elements of Political Science* (Boston: Houghton Mifflin, 1906) for a characteristic statement of these propositions as well as the notion that the "separate 'states' of the American Union are not states in the technical sense of the term" (14).

48. Frank Sargent Hoffman, *The Sphere of the State or the People as a Body-Politic* (New York: G. P. Putnam's Sons, 1894), 1–6.

governed the least but one that served the real needs and interests of the subjects.[49] What this indicates is just how easy it was to accommodate the theory of the state to a set of policies that were quite out of tune with its composers, that is, to Progressivism and to Progressive political science. What Hoffman's work indicated was just how much the idea of the state transcended ideological differences and how after it had been emptied of its original theoretical content and equated with government, it persisted in the minds of many as an answer to the problem of the public interest.

Dewey's next major intervention in the conversation of political science was a critique of Austin's theory of law and a defense of popular sovereignty and the idea of government as an organ of popular will. He referenced with approval Burgess's distinction between state and government as a way of attacking what he believed to be Austin's confusion between sovereignty and the organs of its exercise. Dewey noted that Austin admitted that the sentiments of the mass of the people were often stronger than the sovereign, but this only pointed to the fact that his attempt to locate sovereignty in some "determinate" entity was a mistake and, if accepted, would lead to the conclusion that "popular sovereignty is obviously wrong." Dewey argued that Austin's theory was ultimately contradictory, since Austin claimed that in the case of the United States, sovereignty was located in the aggregate electorate of the several states. This, Dewey argued, only indicated that, in fact, the sovereign was not "determinate" or located in "some one part of the social organization," but was to be found in the "forces" behind government and "in the whole complex of social activities."[50] Probably few scholars have so often been misinterpreted and misrepresented as Austin, but whatever Austin truly may have meant by sovereignty, it was clear what Dewey had in mind, which, at its core, was not really far removed from Burgess's theory.

In 1895, Burgess was asked to address the "ideal" of the American commonwealth, and he not only accentuated his racist position that the polity was the culmination of Aryan institutions and that "American Indians, Asiatics, and Africans cannot properly form any active, directive part of the political population," but argued that the commonwealth was "ever moving toward the realization of genuine democracy" and presenting a model for the world. The danger of claims to individual state sovereignty had been overcome and now the most immediate threat to the ideal of national sovereignty came from the intrusion of "socialistic" ideas from

49. Ibid., 18–24.
50. Dewey, "Austin's Theory of Sovereignty," *Political Science Quarterly* 9 (1894): 34, 37, 43, 51.

Europe and from "young professors" who looked too much to government in seeking reform and who talked about the need for "state interference" when they actually meant government interference.[51]

Many of these "young professors" were, in fact, his own students, and the growing ambivalence on the part of some about the relationship between the concepts of state, sovereignty, and government prompted a solution in terms of a distinction between political and legal sovereignty and the suggestion that the former amounted to little more than "opinion," which was the real meaning of the "sovereignty of the people."[52] One political scientist undertook an exhaustive analysis of the literature in terms of this distinction and attributed to individuals such as Austin a concern with legal sovereignty, which was very different from political sovereignty and which, he argued, resided in the state or the organic aggregate of the elements of society and was expressed in voting and carried out by government.[53] During the next quarter century, this position would gain currency as a way of retaining the juristic significance of sovereignty in the face of a waning substantive theoretical image, but it also cut deeply into the concept of popular sovereignty.

Even more than in the case of Burgess, it was a concern with the identity of political science as a discipline and profession that informed Westel Woodbury Willoughby's account of the state. As much as Willoughby, like other graduates of Hopkins such as Wilson and Ely, distanced himself from Burgess's Hegelian assumptions, the terminology was nearly identical, and this has made it difficult for commentators to untangle exactly what he was saying. It is also fair to assume that his arguments did not remain as consistent as those of Burgess. The kind of conceptual tensions that were manifest in the work of Crane and Moses also emerged in Willoughby's work. He received his Ph.D. from Hopkins in 1891, and although there was no political science department, he took courses on comparative politics and administration from Wilson. He initially practiced law for a short period but returned to teach political science at Hopkins and, except for a few years at Stanford, remained there until 1933. Willoughby considered much of his own work as falling within the realm of political theory or political philosophy, which he designated as a "philo-

---

51. Burgess, "The Ideal of the American Commonwealth," *Political Science Quarterly* 10 (1895): 406–7, 411.

52. David Ritchie, "On the Conception of Sovereignty," *Annals of the American Academy of Political and Social Science* 1 (1890): 401–2.

53. Charles Malcolm Platt, "A Triad of Political Conceptions: State, Sovereignty, and Government," *Political Science Quarterly* 10 (1895).

sophical examination of the various concepts upon which the whole science of politics rests." The primary concept was that of the state, but few
did more than Willoughby in the course of his analysis to bring the cur-
tain down on the "state of democracy." He argued that the domain of political science was defined by its object of inquiry, and this was the state,
which could be studied both from the perspective of political theory and,
descriptively and historically, as administration and government. A major
difference between Burgess and Willoughby was that for the latter, the
"state" referred less to some preconstituted entity than to an analytical concept of the political scientist, and this difference would emerge ever more
clearly in his later scholarship. The idea that the subject matter of political science was something that was analytically distinguished by political
scientists rather than something intrinsically or substantively political
would eventually come to dominate the discipline—and exercise the minds
of its critics. By mid-twentieth century, the constructed character of the
object of political science would be apparent. The demise of the theory of
the state entailed a transformation in the manner in which political science would ever after conceive of its object of inquiry. The political realm
would never again be understood as an independent and intelligible entity,
but as process and an arena of interactions requiring the imposition of conceptual—and often practical—order.

As in the case of Burgess and others, Willoughby noted the difference
between the idea of the state abstractly conceived and the state as an
"empiric conception" referring to various historical manifestations, but he
rejected Burgess's normative Hegelian image of degrees of completeness
and perfection. Although Willoughby claimed that it was possible to assess
governmental machinery in terms of various criteria, states as such "do not
admit of comparative degrees of excellence." He claimed that practical
issues relating to the scope of the state's actions and the establishment of
rights was a matter belonging to "politics or the Art of Government, and
not within the domain of political theory" and political science. What is
apparent in Willoughby's work is, again, a set of discriminations that
would become central to mainstream political science during the succeeding century.[54]

For Willoughby even more than for Burgess, a principal focus of concern was to establish the autonomy of political science among the emerging social sciences and to provide it with a professional identity. It was

---

54. W. W. Willoughby, *An Examination of the Nature of the State—A Study in Political Philosophy*
(New York: Macmillan, 1896), 5, 17, 338.

particularly important that the subject matter of political science be distinguished from the larger field of sociology, because the former "deals with society solely from its organized standpoint." The "body politic," he argued, was something different from the various interests composing society at large. It is the "social body plus the political organs" that established a "controlling authority." This is a "State"—"a community of people socially united" with a "political machinery" or government. Although Willoughby was reiterating the characteristic litany about the difference between the state and government, he had increasing difficulty holding on to the distinction as well as specifying clear differences between people, state, and nation. And while he continued to claim that there was a "fundamental distinction" between the state and government, since the latter is the "organization of the state" or the device that has been developed for formulating and executing its purposes, the difference was little more than definitional. State and government, he claimed, should no more be confused than a "person" and their "bodily frame," but this very analogy suggested identity rather than difference and was difficult to reconcile with his often pointed rejection of organic images of the state. A state, Willoughby claimed, was not simply either a people or nation, even though most nations, which consist of a people or "aggregate being" held together by ethnic and/or psychological bonds, tend to constitute themselves as states.[55]

Burgess viewed democracy primarily as a form of government rather than a particular set of institutions, and Willoughby also considered modern states as generically democratic because they represented a people. Willoughby was emphatic in his designation of democracy as a kind of government, a particular form of political organization. Despite its "defects and difficulties" and the high degree of education, morality, material and social equality, self-control, and leadership that was necessary for it to exist and prosper, it was the "best type that developing civilization has thus far disclosed, and in the continued existence of democratic control we see the highest types of human progress." Something on the order of popular sovereignty was, for Willoughby, the basis of all states and of political life, since the "essence of the state is the national feeling that unites the People"; but for Willoughby, as for Bryce, this tended to be a largely functional concept. Both a constitution and a government were, he claimed, "juristic" and "artificial" expressions of this prior, "natural," and "organic" condition. In a crucial theoretical turn, however, he defined sovereignty as a legal concept and located it in the person who has the "power, in the last

55. Ibid., 2–4, 6.

resort, to impose his will *in a legal manner* upon the whole body of persons that constitute the state." Sovereignty, strictly speaking, was, for Willoughby as for Wilson, in the government. He argued that there could not be a "federal state," since the "state is by nature a unity," yet even though he rejected contract theory, he also rejected the idea that the state is literally "an organism," since although it is more than the wills of the individuals composing it, it is, unlike a natural organism, "influenced and largely determined by such individual volitions."[56]

Willoughby concluded, first of all, that "the creation of a State and of a People are necessarily synchronous, . . . a State is created by a community of men, which, by reason of a sentiment of unity, is *potentially* a People, and that this community becomes *actually* such when the State is established." And while he maintained that the origin of the state was "an act of a People rather than individuals" and that it was predicated on a "general will" that was prior to government, he also believed that the body politic, that is, the state, only came into existence with "the erection of a common governing authority."[57] The distance between his formulation and that of earlier state theorists would become increasingly apparent in his later work, but already the distinction between state and government and the theory of democracy that it supported was losing coherence. Willoughby would reiterate his analysis of the state, almost verbatim, in numerous venues, but it would be become an increasingly "juristic" and theoretically nonsubstantive concept. Willoughby had, in effect, largely abandoned the core of the traditional concept of the state despite retention of the verbiage that had attached to it, and this transformation was apparent to some of his peers.

William Archibald Dunning, the leading scholar of the history of political theory at Columbia at the time, noted that despite Willoughby's attempt to distinguish between government and state, the boundary between the two concepts ultimately collapsed in his analysis, which "discards alike the doctrine of Burgess" and others. Dunning saw a distinct danger to democratic theory in this view that "government is sovereign" as well as in Willoughby's formulation of the activity of studying politics, which seemed to him to indicate that "the political philosopher commits scientific suicide."[58] What Dunning was getting at was the fact that Willoughby was denying that his subject matter had any "natural" existence,

56. Ibid., 35, 38, 131–32, 243, 280, 438–39.
57. Ibid., 119–20, 123, 129.
58. William A. Dunning, review of *The State,* by Willoughby, *Political Science Quarterly* 11 (1896): 547–48.

a type of criticism that, as already noted, would be leveled by various critics of mainstream political scientists a half century later. Franklin Giddings,
the founder of sociology at Columbia who had developed a social theory
based on "consciousness of kind," also stepped up to defend Burgess's idea
of the "state behind the constitution," and popular sovereignty, against the
charge of commentators such as William Lecky (*Democracy and Liberty,*
1896) that democracy was nothing more than government by ignorant
"masses." Giddings, too, saw the "people" as a "mass," but then claimed,
strangely for someone in this period, that there was no need to worry,
because they were *only* sovereign and did not actually rule. Giddings, like
later elite theorists, argued that despite all the famous works on democracy such as the favorable accounts of Tocqueville and Bryce and critical
assessments such as that of Maine, they all failed to grasp what democracy
was all about. He argued, much like Burgess, that while the masses participate through universal suffrage and representative government, it is the
"aristocracy that rules the state behind the constitution" and not the people themselves. It was important, however, not to allow "bosses" to gain
positions of leadership or to let the Catholic church displace "Protestant
liberalism." Giddings claimed that "the student of political science will
never understand democracy until he sees clearly that its origin is not due
to the formulation of any positive program by the masses themselves."[59]
This left the question of what, exactly, democracy was.

By the end of the century, political scientists were beginning to take up
the idea of reform that had been the province of the more amateur social
science practiced by the American Social Science Association and those
associated with Gilded Age reform, such as the Liberal Republicans and
Mugwumps who, like Mark Twain, had jumped ship and supported Grover
Cleveland over James Blaine in 1884. Individuals such as Carl Schurz and
E. L. Godkin were not egalitarian in their perspective. They were secular,
but held to the kind of classical republican principles regarding virtuous,
nonpartisan, and active citizens advanced in moral philosophy by individuals such as Francis Wayland (*The Elements of Moral Science,* 1835). Godkin,
the founder of the *Nation* was, like Shurz, an emigrant (in his case, from
Ireland) and in his analysis of the "unforeseen tendencies of democracy" he
decried the lack of dedicated and impartial leaders, the domination of
bosses, the vagaries of public opinion, the breakdown of common morality, the corrupting force of money, the loss of tradition, and the problems

59. Franklin H. Giddings, "The Destinies of Democracy," *Political Science Quarterly* 11 (1896):
728, 730.

of modern complexity.[60] Like many of the Progressives after them, however, these reformers held to the idea that there was an American people, and they believed that just as the educated middle class elite had led the battle against slavery, it was now their task to awaken the public and achieve reform in areas such as civil service. Godkin was among the most able of the Mugwump critics of late-nineteenth-century society and politics, but by this point, in a move not unlike that of Brownson and Mulford, he had shifted his intellectual allegiance from Mill to Burke. He suggested, for example, that the reason the United States could not support a continuing magazine devoted to humor was that the country was too homogeneous. But the underlying consensus needed to be awakened and galvanized.

Henry Jones Ford, along with Frank Goodnow, the first president of the American Political Science Association (APSA), was one of the principal founders of professional political science. He was a newspaper editor who, after the creation of the APSA, lectured at Hopkins and the University of Pennsylvania before Wilson appointed him to the Princeton faculty and later, after Wilson became president, to various government positions. Goodnow, who became president of Hopkins in 1914, taught administrative law at Columbia and specialized in municipal government. Following Wilson, Ford and Goodnow both emphasized the need for and role of administration, but while Goodnow advanced his famous dichotomy between politics and administration as part of a vision of democratic reform, whereby citizens at various levels would make their wishes known while the execution of policy was undertaken by impartial experts,[61] Ford focused on the need for greater national unity and coordination. He urged administrative centralization and party government as a way of keeping control out of the hands of local and less politically evolved authorities. It was, in his view, not so much "bosses" and corruption that, in the end, inhibited democracy as a lack of coordination between the president and Congress. He argued that while government received its strength from its popular base, what was required was a system that was functionally parliamentary and in which parties provided a union between the legislative and executive branches. In taking this position, he initiated an argument that would persist for a century as one answer to the problems of what would later be called pluralist politics. Ford called upon Spencer's evolutionary vision and biological analogies, such as designating advanced forms of national government as "vertebrate," in claiming that "the extension of

60. Edwin L. Godkin, *Unforseen Tendencies of Democracy* (Boston: Houghton Mifflin, 1898).
61. Frank Goodnow, *Politics and Administration: A Study in Government* (New York: Macmillan, 1900).

executive authority is still the only practical method of advancing popular rule" and checking "special interests." The development of the "social organism" required a natural aristocracy of administrators tied to an "elective kingship" that would increase efficiency and release individual citizens from the burden of making politics a vocation. For Ford, national politics rather than piecemeal political reform was the answer to political change, and he clamed that it was the role of a science of politics "to guide exercise of reason in affairs of state."[62]

Burgess also recognized the fact that it was actually government, rather than the sovereign people, that called the shots, but consequently, as opposed to what Ford postulated, this meant for him that government must be restrained. He claimed that corporations were not only good things in themselves and an integral part of the political system, but served as a bulwark against the encroachment of government on liberty. Even in Burgess's work, there was support for the emerging idea that special interests played a democratic role. And he was also sympathetic to the idea of electing senators by popular vote, which he saw as an affirmation that the polity was "a system of national popular sovereignty" and that one could attribute to "the people of the United States, as one people, the original and ultimate authority to constitute and empower government" as well as elect representatives.[63] Willoughby, however, by the end of the century, turned away entirely from a discussion of the state and focused on the issue of social justice that was becoming the concern of so many reformers. Although the most immediate impetus behind this work was to confront "socialistic, or communistic" theories and demonstrate that other more democratic solutions were possible, a broader purpose was to call into question the application of any abstract absolute idea of distributive justice including the "anarchistic" claims of individuals such as Spencer.[64]

Willoughby argued that every age develops its own conceptions of fairness and right, and the task was always to reconcile "popular thought and objective conditions." He argued that it was necessary to test ideals against some rational standard, and he drew on the tradition of "higher" utilitar-

62. Henry Jones Ford, *The Rise and Growth of American Politics: A Study of Constitutional Development* (New York: Macmillan, 1898), 356–57, 362, 365, 373; "Politics and Administration," *Annals of the American Academy of Political and Social Science* 17 (1901); "The Results of Reform," *Annals of the American Academy of Political and Social Science* 21 (1903), 235; "Principles of Municipal Organization," *Annals of the American Academy of Political and Social Science* 23 (1904).

63. Burgess, "Private Corporations from the Point of View of Political Science," *Political Science Quarterly* 13 (1898); "The Election of United States Senators by Popular Vote," *Political Science Quarterly* 17 (1902): 650.

64. Willoughby, *Social Justice* (New York: Macmillan, 1900), viii.

ianism represented by T. H. Green, which entailed ensuring each individual the opportunity to realize their ethical self and to recognize the same value for others. He rejected any theory of natural law and insisted on the "relativity of all rights." Looking back over the whole course of Western political thought, he found that "no laws of justice have been discovered which may be universally and rigidly applied." It was precisely the fact that justice was relative to "circumstances" that made social science part of the "science of right living" and contributed to undercutting "dangerous revolutionary and socialistic schemes and the ethical support that is claimed for them."[65] Like so many later political scientists, Willoughby eschewed any vision of moral absolutism. He argued that even notions like equality, as abstract principles, must be rejected and approached in terms of "some ascertainable conditions of time, place, or person." Various canons of distributive justice and state compulsion advanced by socialists were deficient, but there was also no general right to freedom from government constraint such as that advocated by crude evolutionists such as Spencer or theorists such as Burgess. All property ownership was, Willoughby claimed, a "trust," which carried with it an obligation to utilize it for "promoting the true welfare" of the individual and "humanity," but there were no simple rules of public policy that flowed from this. The proper sphere of social and political control could not be established a priori and "in every case conditions of fact should govern." Even though Americans might be attached to the competitive principle as contributing to the progress of society, this "would carry with it no necessary demand for a diminution in the functions of government," and in principle "it would permit a vast extension of the present regulative and educational functions of the governing powers."[66] Although many commentators have counted Willoughby among conservative institutionalists, in many respects he prepared the way for those who supported interventionist liberalism and shaped the perspective of contemporary social science.

Just as the theory of the state cut across ideological lines, so did its critics. When Sumner wrote his essay on *What the Social Classes Owe to Each Other* (1883) and concluded that the answer was, in fact, nothing, he derided any attempt, especially by German writers, to conceive of the state as an entity with will and power. Although he held on to the idea of society as an organism, the "state," he claimed, was either just an abstraction designating "All-of-us" or a term referring to some haphazardly chosen

65. Ibid., 10, 22–27.
66. Ibid., 77, 212, 263, 269, 306.

group, or even "obscure clerk," instructed to perform various services.[67] But while some who embraced socialist ideas, such as Ely, found support in the idea of state, others such as Edward Bellamy (*Looking Backward*, 1888) and Thorstein Veblen (*The Theory of the Leisure Class*, 1899) stressed a basic division between the rich and the poor that implied there was no organic people. When Willoughby made one of the major statements regarding the purpose of the APSA, which had been founded in 1903, he hardly mentioned the concept of the state and focused instead on the study of government and various specific political phenomena.[68]

At the Congress of Arts and Sciences at the Universal Exposition in St. Louis, Missouri, Willoughby once again attempted to confront these issues in a symposium on Political Theory and National Administration. The term "Political," he emphasized, simply referred to "the organization of men in corporate communities over which some paramount ruling authority is generally recognized as the legitimate source of all legally binding commands,"[69] and this was the meaning of "state." Political philosophy dealt with the "theoretical," that is, general, abstract, and fundamental characteristics of the state, and consisted of "methods and aims" that were both "teleological or ideal" and "scientific or analytical." It was concerned both with the universal "nature of political society and the legitimate sphere of its authority" and with creating generalizations about "the state as it is," which, by ordering and making sense of the "multitude of phenomena," would render possible a scientific study of politics. Willoughby emphasized that until "recent times" the analytical dimension of political philosophy had received little attention and had been dominated by a search for ethical absolutes, but now "in both ethical and political speculation, the absolute has given way to the relative." While this called into question such pursuits as natural law theory and a search for utopias, it did not mean abandoning ethical considerations. Willoughby's basic concern, however, was with the theoretical basis of a "true political science" based upon "exact observation" and "arranged in a rational system" of concepts and definitions that would not only provide "pure intellectual delight" and satisfy the "search for the essentially true," but would have value for practical reasoning in areas such constitutional law.[70] Willoughby was con-

67. William Graham Sumner, *What the Social Classes Owe to Each Other* (New Haven: Yale University Press, 1925), 9.

68. Willoughby, "The American Political Science Association," *Political Science Quarterly* 19 (1904).

69. Willoughby, "Political Philosophy," in *Congress of Arts and Science,* ed. Howard J. Rogers, vol. 7 (Boston: Houghton Mifflin, 1906), 309.

70. Ibid., 310–14, 325.

cerned with establishing and defending the domain of political science as both a discipline and profession. While certain aspects of the field were closely allied to metaphysics and ethics, the focus on the state gave it autonomy and even precedence with respect to fields such history, economics, law, and especially sociology, which sometimes treated the state as a development "from some lower social unit" or viewed it as simply part of the study of "social groups."[71] While he had largely emptied the concept of the state of its theoretical meaning, he was not willing to embrace the pluralist alternative that was already beginning to take shape.

A short time later, Willoughby pointedly turned to distinguishing his position from that of Burgess. While he suggested that, subsequent to Calhoun, Burgess had made the greatest contribution to advancing political theory, he argued that Burgess's work was still encumbered by a failure to separate political theory from politics. While Calhoun's analysis had, understandably, been motivated by certain concrete political concerns, Burgess had attempted, Willoughby argued, to deduce principles of "political expediency and morality" from political theory and philosophy. He had thus "overstepped the boundaries" of "pure political theory" and, more like a constitutional lawyer than a political theorist, entered the realm of "Politics or Statesmanship."[72] It was not simply that Willoughby disagreed philosophically and ideologically with Burgess. It was clear, for example, that he had a less vigorous view of American expansion and that he favored more energetic national social policies, but he was also worried, after witnessing the punishment meted out to a generation of social scientists such as Ely who had attempted to speak politically from within the academy, about the status of the scientific authority of political science if it were involved with the particulars of political judgment and if it attempted to give substantive and normative meaning to the concept of the state. Despite Burgess's extreme emphasis on the distinction between state and government, Willoughby argued that he had actually confused the two concepts in his account of such matters as English history and the American founding. If, for example, state and government referred to two different things, how, Willoughby asked, could Burgess claim that in England there was a time when the king was both state and government? What this question indicated was a very fundamental theoretical shift whereby the old paradigm no longer seemed to make sense.

---

71. Ibid., 315–23. See also Willoughby, "Political Science as a University Study," *Sewanee Review* 14 (1906).

72. Willoughby, "The Political Theory of John W. Burgess," *Yale Review* 17 (1908): 61, 64.

Willoughby argued that Burgess's distinction between the idea of the state, that is, the state as ideal and perfected, and the concept of the state, that is, the state as it existed historically, characteristic of Bluntschli and other German theorists, was untenable. Given the core meaning of sovereignty to which Burgess subscribed it made no sense to talk, as Burgess did, about a "world state" or to suggest that political regimes in Asia were not "real states." Burgess's historical theory of the Teutonic state and the mystical image of its manifest and divine mission was, according to Willoughby, no better than contract theories and theological theories. Although Willoughby still had no difficulty with the idea that more advanced political societies could ethically dominate others who were not morally and intellectually prepared for self-government, he worried that Burgess's position underwrote an imperialistic vision and served to suggest that we could "take on the political destinies of the entire world." The fact that Burgess presented the modern constitutional state as the apotheosis of the form simply indicated to Willoughby that he could not, or did not, separate the concept of the state from particular forms of government. Willoughby concurred with Burgess's rejection of the idea of the "indestructibility and immutability" of the American states, on the grounds that they were becoming less important than a sense of national identity, but he was also contradicting Burgess's claim that the state was a people that existed before, and created, institutions of government.[73] And Burgess's position contained what Willoughby considered to be other contradictory or ambivalent elements regarding the relationship between national and state government. Although Dunning also distanced himself from Burgess on political issues such as colonialism, they both, despite dedication to the Union, were severe critics of the social, and racial, effects of Reconstruction, which was the principal object of Dunning's historical scholarship. Burgess maintained that slavery was wrong and secession a political blunder, but he argued that Reconstruction had been too harsh and that fortunately, by the turn of the century, "the white men of the South need now have no further fear that the Republican Party, or Republican administrations, will ever again give themselves over to the vain imagination of the political equality of men."[74]

By the time that the *American Political Science Review* (*APSR*) began publication in 1906, the theory of the state was no longer very visible in the

---

73. Ibid., 68, 71, 83. In *Social Justice* (266–67), Willoughby had already noted his agreement with Burgess on the propriety of "higher nations" exercising compulsion over "less civilized" races.

74. Burgess, *Reconstruction and Constitution, 1866–76* (New York: Charles Scribner's Sons, 1902).

discourse of the discipline, but, at the same time and consequently, the basis of democracy and popular sovereignty was being called in question. As Leacock's *Elements of Political Science* suggested, legal sovereignty was ascertainable but political sovereignty was obscure.[75] The presidential address to the third annual meeting of the APSA, with an attendance of 400 members, noted that the work of the Association was "not partisan" and that it was "not a body of reformers," but was instead devoted to providing education and advice in an age in which there was "a powerful determination to make use of the State, that is to say, of governmental power and agency."[76]

It is easy, in retrospect, to imagine how the concept of the state and the intellectual pedigree that attached to it constrained and limited political theory in the nineteenth century, but it is equally possible to interpret it as an enabling language that allowed theorists to address persistent issues in a novel manner. Both of these interpretations, however, suffer from the assumption that there is some neutral way in which to assess the theory of the state and its account of American democracy, to decide whether it was descriptively and normatively adequate. All that can be said with assurance is that the theory of the state eventually gave way to another theory of American democracy. One might suggest that the concept went into decline because the existence of an American people was becoming increasingly questionable. Robert Wiebe has suggested that "during the 1890s, as class alignments began a thirty-year transformation, the plates beneath American public life shifted" and the result of the process was the "dissolving of the people."[77] After "the disappearance of the People," the power of the modern state began to emerge to fill the vacuum, as collective democracy was replaced by individualist democracy. But, as I have stressed earlier, although there may well have been a correspondence and interaction between what was happening in politics and in political theory, the logic of this claim could reasonably lead to the assumption that the concept of the state should have been waxing rather than waning. A more interesting question than that regarding the fit between state theory and the American political system is that of why there was such a great consensus surrounding the theory. Part of the reason was surely, as some would occasionally remember in later years, that the search for the state, despite its grounding in esoteric German philosophy, was an attempt to find "the

75. Leacock, *Elements of Political Science.*
76. Albert Shaw, "Presidential Address: Third Annual Meeting of the American Political Science Association," *American Political Science Review* 1 (1907): 181.
77. Wiebe, *Self-Rule,* 162, 172.

nature of social and political unity," which, many continued to believe, "democracy must today discover or risk perishing."[78] But this is the consistent democratic paradox, and others would hold to the Madisonian notion that such unity need not exist, or could be replaced by a virtual or functional substitute. The theory of the state, despite its German origins, was adapted to the American republican tradition and its assumption that popular government must be grounded in a people, but there was at least one crucial divergence from that tradition. This was the *Federalist* idea of separate government and the relinquishment of the idea of virtual representation. Government was in some respects viewed as the organized form or persona of the state or people, but increasingly as their agent and instrument and as something dislocated from the ultimate seat of sovereignty. As the distinction between state and government began to fade, however, the latter was left conceptually suspended. It is indeed strange, given its practical impetus, its concerns with civic education and moral philosophy, and the volatile subject matter, that of all the emerging social sciences, political science was the least affected by ideological divisions. In nearly every era in the evolution of political science, theory has triumphed over ideology. Although there may be reason to suggest that, for various reasons both contextual and genetic, political science was from the beginning a particularly conservative discipline, the fact remains that even after the turn of the century and the creation of the APSA, there was little of the overt acrimony that characterized the professionalization of economics and disputes such as that between Ely and Sumner about the role of government in social policy. Part of the explanation was surely that for the most part political scientists decided to study the state rather than politics. The latter was a divisive and dangerous business—dangerous both for the profession of political science and to the authority of the discipline, and eventually even economists learned that the market was a safer terrain for investigation and relinquished political economy for pure economics. As the idea of the state disintegrated, so did the older ideological unity of political science, but in many respects the basic commitments of the discipline continued to override these differences.

There has always been an anomaly attaching to the relationship between the apparent "conservatism" of Burgess's work and the political tendencies associated with the next generation of students who came from Columbia. To some extent it was the impact of individuals such as James Harvey

---

78. Thomas I. Cook and Arnaud B. Leavelle, "German Idealism and American Theories of the Democratic Community," *Journal of Politics* 5 (1943): 214.

Robinson, the founder of the "new history," who, having studied first at Harvard and then in Germany where he received his doctorate at Freiburg, was viewed as safely conservative when he was hired at Columbia in 1895. But, on the whole, the metamorphosis at Columbia was a more internal affair. In addition to various circumstances relating both to the individuals and to the wider political context, which may have contributed to this divergence, there were some less apparent factors. First of all, the concept of state was easily transformed to serve different ideological purposes. Second, Burgess was deeply committed to validating political science as epistemologically equal to natural science both in general and in the context of Columbia, and there were two dimensions to his image of science. One involved an identification of science with history, which reflected his German education and Hegelian philosophical commitments.[79] History was, in his view, a science both in that it was dedicated to an inductive accumulation of fact and in that it was governed by principles such as universal laws of progression. Another aspect of his scientism was his embrace of statistics. Lieber had stressed "statistik" as well as history as a way studying social phenomena, the developing and static forms respectively, and Burgess championed statistics as a basis for legitimizing political science as a science at both Columbia and in the American academy in general, and as a way of establishing the uniqueness of the Columbia School among the emerging social sciences.[80] The third factor was Burgess's insistence that political science was a science designed to study "national popular sovereignty." This, he claimed, entailed that "liberty," as both a subject matter and normative commitment, was "the most fundamental principle of modern political science."[81] What would prevail over particular political differences among practitioners at Columbia was the grounding of the discipline in the ideas of science and democracy and even a continuing commitment to the term "state," and some of the attributes of the old theory, even if the word eventually came to refer to a new concept.

79. Burgess, "Political Science and History," *American Historical Review* 2 (1897).
80. See Charles Camic and Yu Xie, "The Statistical Turn in American Social Science: Columbia University, 1890 to 1915," *American Sociological Review* 59 (1994).
81. Burgess, "Political Science and History," 406.

3

THE DISCOVERY OF AMERICAN PLURALISM

The American people, however, are no
longer one in the same sense in which
the people of Germany or the people of
France are one, or in which the people
of the American Revolution were one.

— *Horace M. Kallen*

The great task in the study of any form
of social life is the analysis of these
groups. . . . When the groups are
adequately stated, everything is stated.

— *Arthur Bentley*

When Albert Bushnell Hart, who would soon be chair of the new
Department of Government at Harvard, claimed that "the most distinct
American theory of government is not to theorize," he was, in effect, repeat-
ing Tocqueville's assessment of the American unity of theory and practice.
He was also concurring with political theorists such as Dunning, and he

could be construed as having anticipated the arguments of certain historians and political scientists of the 1950s such as Boorstin. After presenting an exhaustive account of the evolution of theories of popular government in the United States, Hart concluded that, in the end, Americans "have furnished no political creative mind, furnished no accepted philosophical basis for their government" and that "in view of the rapid changes of the last thirty years, it is hard to say precisely what are the present theories of American government." He noted that contract theory was indeed dead, and even though the idea of the state as popular sovereign seemed to still hold sway, it represented a kind cultural lag, since it really did not fit the present circumstances of American politics. Hart suggested that Bryce was correct when he claimed that "Americans have had no theory of the State, and have felt no need for one," since "the nation is but so many individuals." Although he expressed faith that America was a democracy, he could not, any more than most of his contemporaries, adequately account for it theoretically. American government was, he finally analogized, like the "manufacture of Bessemer steel" in which carbon is totally eliminated and then judiciously restored. In the same way, he claimed, "American democracy restricts and limits the authority of public officials, and then bestows on them the powers necessary to national life." But as in the case of making steel out of iron, Hart could not describe the exact process.[1] To explain such political alchemy became the task of pluralist theory as it took shape and evolved during the first third of the twentieth century.

One of the ironies of the Civil War was that although it served to consolidate a large portion of the society and although it was fought in part to validate the unity of the American people, both the war and its aftermath, as in the case of the Revolution, also tended to bring to the surface just how diverse the society was and how many interests of various kinds there were to be reconciled. And indigenous differences were compounded by the effects of immigration. In the intellectual world, many of those touched by the war and who were important in shaping the philosophical and intellectual perspective of the first quarter of the century (such as Oliver Wendell Holmes, C. S. Peirce, and William James) came away suspicious of unalterable principles such as abolitionism as well as abstract universals, and developed a great tolerance for various interests and beliefs. Actions were viewed as prior to ideas, which were considered as instrumental, adaptable, and secondary to experience. The growing acceptance

---

1. Albert Bushnell Hart, "Growth of American Theories of Popular Government," *American Political Science Review* 2 (1907): 531–32, 557.

of theories such as that of Darwin reinforced a sense of contingency, randomness, and diversity, which contributed to the demise of the vision of homogeneity in both politics and the universe at large and to a greater concern about mechanisms of adjustment. There were, indeed, close connections between pragmatism and pluralism. As one commentator of the period noted, "pluralism is a metaphysic of pragmatism," and both developed in part "against what might seem to be the spirit of the German philosophy."[2] This was the period in which there was an Americanization of both philosophy and political science. While, however, it is tempting to think of philosophical pragmatism as giving rise to the concept of pluralism, James's metaphysical pluralism and his wish to embrace opposites such as religion and science preceded his formulation of pragmatism as a distinct philosophy, and while many people would refer to the manner in which he equated political pluralism with a wider "pluralistic universe," he began with the political metaphor of a "federated republic," which he extrapolated to the character of the world in general. In political theory, a nascent pluralist vision was emerging that was often quite at odds with the ideological position associated with individuals such as Burgess, but there continued to be a considerable affinity between his theory and that of many social scientists who came to prominence in the early part of the century. The fundamental transformation in the concept of democracy was not effected by the representatives of what is often characterized as Progressive political science and individuals such as Burgess's student Charles Merriam.

Although by the end of the 1920s the new generation trained at Columbia would begin to embrace certain dimensions of the new vision, the continuities with the past dominated their early work. While these individuals may, like Willoughby, have increasingly identified "state" with government, they still clung to some of the most essential attributes of state theory such as the assumption that government was, or should be, the instrument of a public—even if it were necessary to search for, and even create, that public. There was less an immediate theoretical shift than an ideological one, and it is not difficult to see how the theoretical premises of someone such as Burgess could be, and were, put into the service of a quite different political agenda. We have become so accustomed to thinking of this period in terms of analytical categories such as the "revolt against formalism" or some other broad characterization of the intellectual

2. Jean Wahl, *The Pluralist Philosophies of England and America* (London: Open Court, 1925), 273–74.

transformation that we often fail to see the continuities. Among both those who have defended and those who have criticized mainstream political science, there has been the persistent perception that the early part of the century was distinguished by a turn away from what nearly all have characterized as a legalistic and scholastic formalism and toward the embrace of realism and science. While Progressivism might be accurately characterized as involving a rejection of many of the attributes of nineteenth-century political science, this should not be allowed to obscure the fact that the Progressive attachment to national purpose and the idea of a democratic public was part of the nineteenth-century heritage.[3] Whether they believed in the existence of a democratic public or believed that it was necessary to create one, or its functional equivalent, it was not those usually classified as Progressives who created the image of democracy that would dominate political science by the end of the 1920s and that, arguably, became the core of a more general public philosophy. It was the pluralists—but pluralist theory, like the nineteenth-century theory of the state, was not ideologically univocal.

The Progressive image of a democratic public pushing aside corrupt politicians and plutocrats and taking back the power that properly belonged to it and using the state, now conceived as federal government, to curtail the actions of state governments and local political regimes, as well as to overcome the use of the Fourteenth Amendment as a legal barrier, could easily be accommodated to Burgess's basic theory. This was not unlike the manner in which social Darwinism was employed to support both conservative and Progressive positions such as those of Sumner and the sociologist Lester Frank Ward (*Dynamic Sociology,* 1911) respectively. One reason why there was so little direct confrontation with Burgess's arguments on the part of individuals such as Merriam and Dewey was the fact that they all shared some basic assumptions about the nature of democratic society. The principal textbooks of the day had maintained that the state was the subject of political science, and it was assumed by many that since "the state develops in accord with definite laws and principles," it was natural that "progress comes therefore by the purposive modification" of social life "through a governmental policy based on scientific knowledge."[4]

3. See, for example, Morton G. White, *Social Thought in America: The Revolt against Formalism* (New York: Viking, 1949). Many important studies of Progressive intellectuals still do not recognize the continuities. See, for example, Eldon J. Eisenach, *The Lost Promise of Progressivism* (Lawrence: University Press of Kansas, 1994); Leon Fink, *Progressive Intellectuals and the Dilemmas of Democratic Commitment* (Cambridge, Mass.: Harvard University Press, 1997).

4. James Quayle Dealy, *The Development of the State* (New York: Silver, Burdett & Co., 1909), 3.

Goodnow argued that while natural law and contract theories were both obsolete and incorrect, they had become the principles upon which the American constitutional system operated. The courts had utilized these principles to make the system static rather than dynamic and to inhibit democratic social reform. The interpretation of the Constitution and the method of interpretation employed by the Supreme Court functioned, he claimed, as a "bar to the adoption of the most important reform measures which have been made points of the reform program of the most progressive people of the present day." What he was referring to were policies of government ownership, regulation, and aid.[5] The decline of the theory of the state as a rationale for limited government did not diminish the commitment to the state, conceived as government and representing a public interest, by those political scientists who struggled with the facts of American diversity, which, at this point, remained for them more a problem than a virtue. But from the beginning, the commitment to an interventionist government was predicated on the assumption that there was a public whose interest was served and on whose authority the government acted. The eventual acceptance of a pluralist ontology would, by the 1960s, make it difficult to sustain the idea of a public interest and the legitimacy of positive government.

Although in seeking the genesis of the pluralist vision it is tempting to attribute considerable influence to the work of philosophers such as James, with his emphasis on pragmatism, empiricism, and a plural universe,[6] it was probably more a situation, as with a number of other thinkers who became implicated in the conversation, in which his work provided philosophical justification for the emerging paradigm. Similarly, it is necessary to be cautious about assuming that Arthur Bentley's work was the basic source from which pluralism issued. Although often credited, and maybe properly in some respects, with being the seminal thinker in the American pluralist tradition, Bentley and his early work had minimal direct and immediate impact on the discourse of political science. Furthermore, his focus on groups was not quite as innovative as often implied. Although Lieber propagated an organic image of the state, he emphasized the multiplicity within the system, and Bryce, like Tocqueville, called attention to the associational diversity within American politics. Peter Odegard, who wrote one of the important early studies of group

5. Frank Goodnow, *Social Reform and the Constitution* (New York: Macmillan, 1911), v.

6. William James, *Pragmatism* (1907; reprint, Cambridge, Mass.: Harvard University Press, 1975); *Essays in Radical Empiricism* (1912; reprint, Cambridge, Mass.: Harvard University Press, 1976); *A Pluralistic Universe* (1909; reprint Cambridge, Mass.: Harvard University Press, 1977).

politics, noted, in his introduction to the 1967 edition of Bentley's book, that when he first read the work as a graduate student at the University of Washington, he was not surprised by the claims, since his teacher, J. Allen Smith, had, before both Bentley and Charles Beard, described the creation of the Constitution as a product of conflict between interest groups. Before Beard's famous and, at the time, notorious challenge to the sanctity of the Constitution and the hallowed image of the founders (*An Economic Interpretation of the Constitution of the United States,* 1913), Smith had pointed to what he claimed was the "conservative" and antidemocratic vision embodied in the Constitution as well as what he perceived as the contemporary alliance between centralized government and big business. Contrary to Burgess's story, the founding, Smith claimed, was a reactionary movement that rejected the spirit of the Revolution.[7]

Bentley, who had been a student of Ely at Hopkins and studied with Georg Simmel and Wilhelm Dilthey in Germany, did not conceive his own work primarily as a contribution to the discipline of political science. He had been an instructor at Chicago and in contact with Dewey and George Herbert Mead, and he presented his work as a study of sociology and the foundation of economics. He had enunciated his basic perspective more than a decade before the *Process of Government* was published and had claimed that all social action must be viewed in the context of "social formations," that each "group of formations" was the basis of "a distinct field for a separate social science," and that the purpose of such sciences was to find a "better art of social control" and "a more perfect social philosophy."[8] Political scientists, and sociologists, were already beginning to seek the identity and domain of political science less in terms of an autonomous and preconstituted object such as the state or any other given configuration than, as even Willoughby urged, in terms of certain analytically constituted entities that could be factored out and studied empirically. Groups and conflict seemed amenable to this approach as well as constituting a salient matter of public concern.

Bentley argued that society itself is nothing other than the "complex of the groups that compose it," and the "raw materials" of "political life" consisted of "the differentiated activities of groups" and that there was nothing "more mystical, no more mysterious, no more fundamental." In his

7. Peter Odegard, introduction to *The Process of Government,* by Arthur Bentley (Cambridge: Belknap Press, 1967); J. Allen Smith, *The Spirit of American Government: A Study of the Constitution: Its Origin, Nature, and Relation to Democracy* (New York: Macmillan, 1907).

8. Arthur Bentley, "The Units of Investigation in Social Science," *Annals of the Academy of American Political and Social Science* 5 (1895): 941.

view, an "interest . . . is the equivalent of a group," and interests were manifest in the activity of groups. Among the various groups that an observer
could factor out of the mass and process of society, political groups were
the most prominent, or what he described as closer to the "surface," but
he also saw them as "the underlying groups" that moved mass activity.
There was, in his view, no fixed or natural distinction between political,
economic, and other types of groups. What was political or governmental
was a functional matter. Groups, he claimed, were defined largely in terms
of their relationship to other groups, and their search for domination
through numbers, intensity, and technique, and there was, at least in the
fluid and complex conditions of modern society with its almost infinite
variety of interests, no natural or fixed classification of groups. Bentley
noted that the concept of government could be construed generically as a
process equivalent to politics or the interrelation and adjustment between
groups, but more narrowly, it referred to particular structures that performed a certain function. There was also a third, more common-sense, use
of the term, which referred to the institutions that had traditionally
belonged to the study of the state, but Bentley pointedly rejected the concept of the state as something other than government, as well as the traditional idea of sovereignty, which he took to be a metaphysical entity with
no descriptive meaning. By calling into question the idea of sovereignty,
however, he implicitly called into question the dominant theory of democracy. If there was no such thing as sovereignty in the traditional sense, it
was difficult to make a case for popular sovereignty.

For Bentley, politics was largely a matter of "force" or what he preferred,
in the context of his discussion of government as group activity, to call
"pressure," and the constellation of groups and the existing equilibrium
or order that emerged from "groups pressing one another" was, at any
point, the constitution of society. Such a conception, however, raised severe
intellectual and professional questions about what political scientists had
attempted to circumscribe as their "domain." Elements of formal government such as the executive branch, the legislature, and the legal system
were not, Bentley argued, to be understood as the organized form of a sovereign public, but as the focal points of the interests brought to bear on
and expressed through them, and government was basically a mechanism
for "the adjustment of interests." Bentley claimed that traditional ideas of
the people ruling and the public interest were not really intelligible and
that normative or formal distinctions between despotism and democracy
were of little use, since governments were always animated by, and representative of, the existing structure of group interests. Although Bentley

tangentially indicated certain things that spoke to issues of democratic theory, such as his claim that "we see these manifold interests gaining representation through many thousands of officials," he did not really present any thorough answer to the problem of theorizing democracy that had been posed by Hart.[9] It would fall to the successors of and commentators on Bentley to transform a description of how government represented into a theory of representative government.

Even individuals such as Francis Coker, a student of Dunning and an instructor and Fellow at Columbia, who would never fully reconcile himself to pluralism even after moving to Yale, wrote a scathing critique of organic theories of the state in which he charged that there was a "failure of the theorists," from Johann Fichte and Hegel to Auguste Comte and Spencer, "to give rational basis to their thesis."[10] When Bryce became president of the APSA, he, like so many of his contemporaries, endorsed a new realism that would turn away from the abstractions of past scholarship, and he embraced a renewed emphasis on the practical purpose of political science. He endorsed an epistemology based on the assumption that "the Fact is the first thing," but, like Beard, he rejected the idea of the unity of science that, despite different ideas about what constituted scientific method, had been accepted by political scientists from Burgess onward. Although he argued that the goal of political science should be to generalize, he claimed that such principles as it might derive were predicated only upon general characteristics of human nature, which were contextually manifest in diverse ways. Such a science could not attain, and should not emulate, the nomothetic predictive achievements of natural science. For Bryce, political science was suspended between past and present and between history and politics. And while knowledge must be based on the facts of history, the discipline's concern, he argued, should be with the present and with producing "influential" knowledge. He did not, however, claim that this knowledge could or should be imparted to the whole community. While Bryce continued to be an advocate of democratic values, he concluded that despite some dissemination through teaching and writing, the policy-makers, the most direct receptor of knowledge, must be the elite of the "educated classes" and that, in the end, there was really only one form of government—"the Rule of the Few"—since the multitude had neither the capacity nor the interest.[11] In this elitist sentiment, he joined

9. Bentley, *The Process of Government: A Study of Social Pressures* (1908; reprint, Bloomington: Principia Press, 1949), 183, 204, 208, 210–11, 214–17, 222, 258, 262–64, 269, 453.

10. F. W. Coker, *Organismic Theories of the State* (New York: Longmans, Green, & Co., 1910), 201.

11. James Bryce, "The Relation of Political Science to History and to Practice," *American Political Science Review* 3 (1909): 5, 10, 18.

not only the nineteenth-century theorists but the new generation that would be represented by Merriam. There was, however, some question of who constituted the "few." In his presidential address to the APSA, Hart took the opportunity to express his disillusionment with the leadership of an "ephemeral" United States President such as Taft, who, he claimed, had asserted that a "government of men" was superior to a "government of laws,"[12] but what such a government of laws entailed was still unarticulated.

Another commentator from outside the United States who contributed to the emerging image of interest politics was Moisei Ostrogorski. His study of the American party system led him to a more general view of the "extra-constitutional forms" that underlay the political system and defined the nature of democracy in America. He concluded that the founding fathers "did not anticipate the flood of Democracy rising above the gates erected, nor the all-pervading development of Party, nor the coming of . . . Plutocracy" and political "bosses," which all together meant that "popular government has slipped away from the people" as they turned to economic pursuits and away from public life.[13] Although Bentley's more theoretical subversion of the old paradigm did not immediately dominate or change the character of the conversation, it was not unnoticed. Beard, for example, praised it for its "realism," even if he considered it a bit harsh and somewhat excessive in its rejection of the significance of ideas as forces in social activity.[14] Although Beard's study of the economic interests involved in the American founding was probably more directly informed by the work of the Columbia economist E. R. A. Seligman, Bentley could reasonably be construed as an influence on Beard's thesis that what was really at work in the founding was a conflict between interest groups. Beard's work did not, to say the least, receive a friendly reception in the discipline. Although really less intellectually revolutionary than Bentley's treatise, its review in the *APSR* characterized it as "a deliberate attempt to upset all our traditional ideas" and "reduce everything to a sordid mass of self-interest."[15] The work of Bentley and Beard, however, was only part of a continuing transformation in the vision of political reality as many social scientists, sharing in the Progressive muckraking spirit, rejected what Bentley called "soulstuff" in favor of focusing on the realities of power and

12. Hart, "A Government of Men," *American Political Science Review* 7 (1912).

13. Moisei Ostrogorski, *Democracy and the Party System in the United States* (New York: Macmillan, 1910), 398.

14. Charles Beard, review of *The Process of Government,* by Bentley, *Political Science Quarterly* 23 (1908): 739–41.

15. John H. Latane, review of *An Economic Interpretation of the Constitution of the United States,* by Beard, *American Political Science Review* 7 (1913): 697, 700.

interest. Their concern, however, was to awaken what they believed was a latent democratic public and majority voice. Bentley was distinctly part of this tradition, but by the time that he completed his book, his growing theoretical focus on social process and on generating a novel method of social scientific explanation had begun to overshadow both the original substantive concerns about groups and interests as well as the normative emphasis. It was this theoretical concern, however, that was often either misunderstood or neglected, even in the 1920s, as political scientists were drawn toward a vision of politics as group activity and of group activity as a democratic process.

The work of individuals such as A. Lawrence Lowell, a lawyer who joined the Harvard faculty in 1897 and succeeded Eliot as president in 1909, contributed significantly to undermining the nineteenth-century vision of democracy. Lowell insisted that in a popular government, public opinion should be in control, and this, rather than institutional or constitutional forms, was the essential criterion that distinguished such government. But although he argued that this required a certain cultural "homogeneity," he viewed modern society as so complex that public opinion now amounted to little more than the expression of a fluid "effective majority" on diverse issues through various mediums such as the legislature, lobbies, primaries, and recall. Contradicting Ostrogorski, he argued, like Ford, that it was only the activities of parties and political brokers that aggregated interest and enabled voters to act to any degree as a mass. Given this situation, there was, he claimed, a need for more experts in government and more control from the top.[16] Neither Bentley's analysis nor Lowell's account of popular government, however, reflected the dominant image of democracy embraced by most Progressives, including the author of what many would come to view as the leading tract of the period, which spoke directly to the concerns and possibilities of political science. While Dewey's colleague at the University of Michigan, the sociologist Charles Horton Cooley (*Social Organization: A Study of the Larger Mind,* 1909), held to the idea that there was a public that had an opinion and that such opinion was a rational expression of something more than the sum of individual interests, Herbert Croly was not so sure of its existence but was determined to create at least its functional equivalent.

When Croly, who in later years would be categorized as the quintessential "liberal," described what he took to be the "promise of American

16. A. Lawrence Lowell, *Public Opinion and Popular Government* (1913; reprint, New York: David McKay, 1961), 14, 35.

life" based on the "realization of the democratic ideal," he did not locate that promise in American diversity but rather in the traditional image of a national and popular sovereignty, which he argued could only be expressed by a national government. The word "state" may have played only a small part in his discussion, but the core of the nineteenth-century concept was very much present in his defense of a national "purpose" that would replace a prior, but now waning, "homogeneity of feeling." Although "democratic institutions" had always been predicated upon "economic independence and prosperity," the time had come, he argued, when this was no longer either a matter of "destiny" or a natural product of individual initiative. It had to be "planned and constructed" so as to raise "the entire body of a people to a higher level."[17] This required, in his view, a synthesis of the traditions of Hamilton and Jefferson as well as Republicans and Whigs in order to join the "democratic idea" to a "national principle" that would transcend "extreme individualism." He argued that the "contemporary situation" was marked by a "gradual disintegration" of an "early national consistency." The leaders of society and lawyers were no longer public figures. They had been replaced by the "business specialist" or "captains of industry" and the "political specialist" or "bosses," and this created a situation in which "American democracy was divided politically into a multitude of small groups" and "special interests" ranging from corporations to labor unions. Instead of constituting a public, "the vast incoherent mass of the American people is falling into definite social groups." This "social problem" demanded as "a counterpoise a more effective body of national opinion, and a more powerful organization of the national interest." Since the earlier "instinctive homogeneity" had declined, it was necessary to establish "another such solidarity" in the form of "a conscious social ideal" and put it into practice.[18]

Although some reformers such as Theodore Roosevelt were, from Croly's standpoint, better than others such as Randolph Hearst, he believed that the various goals and perspectives on "moral awakening" and "purification" among reform movements were too diverse to establish any "unity of action" and that they tended to represent various partisan interests. Since the American system was not capable of taking care of itself, what was required was not so much reform from below as "reconstruction" through national government "interference" in the cause of a democratic "public interest." In order to prevent dissolution of the "social bond" and achieve

17. Herbert Croly, *The Promise of American Life* (New York: Macmillan, 1910), 3, 6, 9, 11, 15, 21, 63.

18. Ibid., 104, 117, 121, 131, 138–39.

a "higher level of associated life," the "national government must step in and discriminate . . . on behalf of equality and the average man." Much like the nineteenth-century state theorists, Croly argued that "the American people possessed a collective character even before they possessed a national organization; and both before and after the foundation of a national government." Croly claimed that this aspect of "American political practice" was now, however, in decline, and an intensification of national life as a purposive community and the existence of a "nationalized political organization" were required if the public interest was to gain precedence over private interests and to realize popular sovereignty. Much like Burgess, Croly claimed that the "modern nation, particularly in so far as it is constructively democratic, constitutes the best machinery as yet developed for raising the level of human association" and achieving the "democratic ideal."[19]

Ford commented that Croly's book was an "indication that the democratic spirit in this country is beginning to work out of its eddy to join the main current now flowing throughout the modern world."[20] While Ford was sympathetic to the Progressive position, he argued that individuals such as J. Allen Smith should pay less attention to the Constitution and the past and, instead, focus on the democratic procedures that had developed within contemporary American politics.[21] Ford, who was a close associate of Wilson and wrote a book about him, like Wilson sought a closer connection between public and academic discourse in both action and language. What Wilson advocated in his presidential address to the APSA was a "statesmanship of thought," which would look at the "facts" of political life and, by discovering the common interest behind the partial interests, advance the "statesmanship of action." And he preferred the term "politics" rather than "political science," because he viewed it as encompassing both forms of statesmanship and implying a bridge between theory and practice.[22] This was his hope for the department at Princeton, but naming it the Department of Politics brought it no closer to political practice. A similar worry about the inefficacy of the academician was voiced by Lowell, who noted that "surely students of politics do not lead public thought as much as they ought to do." This, he suggested, was a consequence of the fact that they were too "theoretical" and did not devote

19. Ibid., 146, 152–53, 190, 204, 208, 266–67, 271, 274, 279, 284–85.

20. Ford, review of *The Promise of American Life*, by Croly, *American Political Science Review* 4 (1910): 616.

21. Ford, review of *Spirit of American Government*, by J. Allen Smith, *American Political Science Review* 3 (1909).

22. Wilson, "The Law and the Facts," *American Political Science Review* 5 (1911).

enough attention to the "actual working of government." His solution to the problem of gaining authority over political practice was, however, the traditional one of achieving scientific status by an objective analysis of political phenomena, and he claimed that this entailed studying, like biologists in their domain, the facts and forces involved in the "physiology of politics." Although he stressed that it was not necessary to be a political actor to have political effect, becoming involved in public affairs was helpful in the study of politics.[23] What Lowell propagated, much like Wilson, was the idea that popular government must be supplemented by expert administration.[24] The assumption was not only that democracy was enhanced by education, but also by expertise, and that "the achievement of efficiency is thus a fundamental chapter in the history of public morals."[25] Although the political attitudes and policy recommendations of individuals such as Ford and Wilson were significantly different from those of Burgess, their political ontologies were, in the end, similar; and while in telling the story of political science so much attention has been placed on Merriam, the latter's agenda and prescriptions were not only widely shared but often more fully developed by others. There is no denying Merriam's influence as an impresario of political science, but in many respects, he was less a theorist than an organizer.

Burgess's protege, Butler, now president of Columbia, complained that these new intimations of democratic theory indicated that the United States was moving from a representative republic to a socialist democracy.[26] If this had actually been true, it would have been quite acceptable to Walter Lippmann. Although not a political scientist, Lippmann, like Croly, had much to say both to and about political science, and his ideas were not only reflected in the work of individuals such as Merriam, but infiltrated the emerging conversation about democracy. In Lippmann's view, Butler, who after his passionate defense of constitutional government had supported the machinations of "Boss Barnes" at the Republican convention, typified the hypocrisy of many academic intellectuals and the persistent gap between theory and practice. Although he viewed Butler as only "a caricature of the typical university professor," Lippmann believed, like Beard, that his work represented the fact that "the more systematic works on politics by American university professors are useless" and had lost contact

23. Lowell, "The Physiology of Politics," *American Political Science Review* 4 (1910): 4, 6.
24. Lowell, "Expert Administration in Popular Government," *American Political Science Review* 7 (1913).
25. James T. Shotwell, "Democracy and Public Morality," *Political Science Quarterly* 36 (1921): 8.
26. Nicolas Murray Butler, *Why We Should Change Our Form of Government* (New York: Charles Scribner's Sons, 1912).

with reality and political practice.[27] It is only fair, however, to note that, like Merriam as well as so many later academic political theorists, Lippmann's political enthusiasm was not ultimately matched by his enthusiasm for politics. After an early and short foray as assistant to the Socialist mayor of Schenectady, he would never again engage directly in political life.

Lippmann's work was deeply indebted to Graham Wallas, whose book *Human Nature in Politics* paralleled in many ways the changing trends in political science in the United States and whose course Lippmann had taken in 1910 when Wallas was a visitor at Harvard. In this period in which there was, and would continue to be, a turn away from German philosophy, the English literature on politics became an important part of the dialogue. Although there was little theoretical depth to Wallas's work, which consisted largely of anecdotal explorations of politics coupled with pleas for realism, the rejection of abstract images of politics and its foundations, and the application of modern psychology, it resonated with individuals such as Merriam. In this first book, written shortly after assuming his chair in Political Science at the London School of Economics, Wallas claimed that although representative democracy was increasingly accepted in theory and practice, there was wide dissatisfaction with how it performed. In his view, the key to improving the situation was to return to a concern with human nature. Although many of the past ideas about this matter, from Plato's to Mill's, had in his view properly been discarded, there had, despite advances in contemporary psychology by thinkers such as James, been an unfortunate turn toward studying institutions rather than "men." Although there were signs of an increased emphasis on effecting social change through pedagogy and the study of psychology, they were not, he noted, evident at places such as Oxford. Wallas pleaded for "change in the conditions of political science" that would produce a contribution to "political invention." In order to accomplish this, he argued, it was necessary to relinquish the notion that it was "intellectuality" that determined things in politics and to realize that, instead, it was instinct, emotions such as fear and affection, habit, and nonrational inference interacting with an environment mediated by symbols. In order to deal with such factors, it was necessary to employ experts and focus on "relevant and measurable facts" and quantitative and descriptive methods that could be the basis of an effective political science and better political reasoning. As in the case of Thomas Buckle's *History of Civilization in England,* and the philosophy of C. S. Peirce, he was influenced by Adolphe Quetelet's notion of the sta-

27. Walter Lippmann, *A Preface to Politics* (New York: Mitchell Kennerly, 1913), 72–73.

tistical *l'homme moyen* and the idea of determining the character of the "average man" as a basis of prediction, control, and management of public opinion. This, he claimed, could "transform the science of politics" and create a "new political force" by harmonizing "thought and passion" and establishing realistic "ideals of political conduct" that could inform the "structure of our political institutions."[28] Despite Wallas's numerous and specific references to politics, his general position was vague, but it was, by his own interpretation, inspired by and in part based on American work such as that of Jane Addams.

Lippmann also urged the necessity of "iconoclasm" in overcoming "drift" and destroying routines, taboos, and "herd politics" and embracing invention and the kind of creative statesmanship that would transform the state into a "producer" rather than "policeman" and, in turn, create a culture of democracy. He complained that political science had become an endeavor that neglected human nature and conducted research with "human beings left out." His study of the "history of political theories" and the "great philosophers" at Harvard had led him to conclude that they contained nothing "relevant to American life" and that contemporary efforts directed toward political change could not wait for scholarship to catch up. Although this was largely a critical work, Lippmann endorsed a variety of reformers such as Roosevelt and Addams. He contrasted his vision of democracy with "demolatry" or subservience to public opinion and, instead, urged a "new statecraft" that would focus on "human interests" and create a situation in which "every group interest should be represented in public life."[29]

Wallas's second book (*The Great Society,* 1914) was explicitly addressed to Lippmann and contained much of the material that he had presented at Harvard. He argued that while technology had created modern society, our social consciousness lagged behind from lack of adequate techniques of control.[30] Lippmann continued this line of argument and pursued similar themes in *Drift and Mastery,* but now that he concluded that some of constraints of the past had been breached, he more pointedly embraced the idea and language of social control. Society, in his view, was the scene of the irrational and required the reestablishment of "authority" and the substitution of "purpose for tradition," of "conscious intention for unconscious striving." Even the "new freedom" of Wilson was, he claimed, really just another instance of "drift" and a reiteration of the old freedom of individualism,

28. Graham Wallas, *Human Nature in Politics* (Boston: Houghton Mifflin, 1909), 18–19, 169, 198.

29. Lippmann, *A Preface to Politics,* 203–4, 262, 270, 290, 303.

30. Wallas, *The Great Society: A Psychological Analysis* (New York: Macmillan, 1914).

and while "muckraking" had its value, it was not positive enough to produce the kind of "mastery" that the times demanded. In the private sec-
tor, the ethos of professionalism and craftsmanship should replace the profit
motive, and in the public sphere, the answer was to combine state action
with popular control by seeking a general interest behind the diversity of
interests that characterized the "great society." The basic answer that
Lippmann embraced was science and the scientific method. This was the
key to the "exorcising of bogeys" that were "so intimate a part of the effort
of self-government," and he claimed that "the scientific spirit is the discipline of democracy" and the basis of "modern communion" and a "common method in public affairs." It was science that at once provided a basis
for intersubjectivity and an instrument of creative action.[31] Merriam was
still in the process of making the intellectual and professional transition
from Columbia and the study of the history of ideas to Chicago and a new
vision of social science, but it is not difficult to see from where much of
his inspiration derived.

In his presidential address to the APSA in 1914, Willoughby explicitly emphasized that social legislation was within the proper sphere of government, and he endorsed the goal of forging a national community in
which individuals would subscribe to general social values and where individual rights would be subservient to conformance to the duties of citizenship.[32] However, it was this kind of sentiment, the threat of the type
of policies that Croly and Lippmann advocated, and, more specifically, the
passage of the Sixteenth Amendment to the Constitution, that prompted
Burgess to once again tell his story of the American founding. Yet it was
given a new twist, and placed in the context of a still more detailed account
of the "historical development of the state" as manifest in both past and
present civilizations. His criteria for evaluating these other "efforts," ranging from ancient Asia to contemporary Europe, was the extent to which
they managed to achieve, first and foremost, an "organization of sovereign
power, the state, back of and independent of the Government; second, the
delineation by the sovereign of the realm of Individual Immunity against
governmental power; and, third, the construction by the sovereign of the
organs and procedures for protecting this realm of Individual Immunity
against the encroachments of Government."[33] Although Burgess's image

31. Lippmann, *Drift and Mastery* (1914; reprint, Englewood Cliffs: Prentice-Hall, 1961), 17,
111, 137, 147–48, 154.

32. Willoughby, "The Individual and the State," *American Political Science Review* 8 (1914).

33. Burgess, *The Reconciliation of Government with Liberty* (New York: Charles Scribner's Sons,
1915), 289.

of the United States was his model for judging the achievement of democracy in other countries, as it would be for every generation of political scientists for the next half century and beyond, he noted that subsequent to the creation of the Constitution, the remaining "fault" in the system had been the extent to which concerns about liberty were couched in terms of acts of the central government. This emphasis on the dangers of the federal action had allowed the states to condone things such as slavery, and consequently a "crisis" came in 1861. The full "vindication" of liberty was finally represented in the prohibitions against state action in the Thirteenth and Fourteenth Amendments, and the judiciary, he argued, then became the principal guardian of liberty. This resolution, however, was put in jeopardy with the establishment of the federal income tax in 1912. While his colleague, Seligman, had defended the amendment, Burgess argued that it signified that the state had been duped into "signing over to the Government the whole power of the sovereign, unlimited and unqualified, to take what it will and in any way it will from the Individual." This, in effect, he argued, produced a "new political system."[34]

Despite the ideological difference, Burgess's basic diagnosis was much like that of Croly and the Progressives. Modern society, they all argued, had produced a situation where vocal minorities, through devices such as recall and referendum and the actions of party bosses, had displaced the democratic people. According to Burgess, however, this situation had been endorsed and exacerbated by a wide range of sociologists, political economists, and intellectuals. The "Jingo and the Social Reformer" had joined in a new party that supported "Caesaristic paternalism." What was happening, he suggested, was the "passing of the republic"—and even "the passing of the Christian religion." Although he viewed the state as "the human organ least likely to do wrong," it could be led astray and abuse or relinquish its unlimited power and sovereignty.[35]

Wilson also worried about fragmentation in both government and society, and other prominent political scientists of the founding generation of the APSA such as Jesse Macy continued to see political science, through the state as government, as an answer to the problem of controlling proliferating and conflicting interests.[36] All of this assumed, however, the existence of something close to the nineteenth-century image of the state, that

34. Ibid., 373; Edwin R. A. Seligman, "The Income Tax Amendment," *Political Science Quarterly* 25 (1910).

35. Burgess, *The Reconciliation of Government with Liberty*, 380–82.

36. Jesse Macy, "The Scientific Spirit in Politics," *American Political Science Review* 11 (1917); *Jesse Macy: An Autobiography* (Baltimore: Charles C. Thomas, 1933).

is, a people or a public, but there was growing skepticism about the existence of any such entity. Individuals such as Brooks Adams, like his brother Henry, had begun to despair about the validity of the traditional democratic ideal and the assumption that America represented the "apotheosis" of democracy. If the latter implied the willingness of individuals to sacrifice for the communal good, such a spirit was, he claimed, actually much more evident in Germany and France, while in the United States the trend was toward a "complete subordination of the principle of unity to that of diversity, of order to chaos, of community to the individual, of self-sacrifice to selfishness."[37] In political science, however, the principal theoretical assault on the traditional idea of the state came less from those who worried about the demise of the public than from those who envisioned a very different idea of democracy.

Although various strands of pluralistic thinking would converge, there were some significant differences. Part of the "discovery" of pluralism was the recognition and valorization of the fact of increased cultural diversity, but it was also a somewhat belated recognition of American difference at a point at which there were strong forces pushing toward greater unity and homogenization. The year that Bentley published his work was the same year that Israel Zangwill wrote the *Melting Pot*. Horace M. Kallen, for example, had for a decade attacked organizations such as the National Security League and the Ku Klux Klan and criticized "Americanism," as advanced by individuals such as George Santayana and Theodore Roosevelt, and the idea of America as a "melting pot." It was Kallen and his friend Alain Locke who coined the phrase "cultural pluralism," and the concept was developed in Kallen's essay "Democracy Versus the Melting Pot" published in the *Nation* in 1915.[38] It is easy to forget that at this point racism was not confined to individuals such as Burgess. Pragmatists such as Peirce and James were attached to ideas of eugenics and the inferiority of Negroes and were dubious about allowing immigration. The eventually prominent sociologist Edward A. Ross had been fired from Stanford (by its only trustee, Mrs. Stanford) for criticizing the use of Chinese workers, but it was not the plight of the Chinese that concerned him. A student of Ely, and strongly attached to the work of Ward and to the idea of the scientific management of society (*Social Control,* 1901), Ross had always been a defender of the labor movement, which he believed was threatened by foreign workers, and he was also a eugenicist and a vigorous opponent of

37. Brooks Adams, "The American Democratic Ideal," *Yale Review* 5 (1916): 232.
38. Horace M. Kallen, "Democracy Versus the Melting Pot," *The Nation* 100 (February 1914): 25.

immigration on the grounds that racial inequality was a natural fact. Kallen wrote his essay as a response to Ross's *The Old World in the New* (1914) and, one might conclude, in part in opposition to the views of Woodrow Wilson, who had opposed the idea of America as composed of groups and even stated that anyone who saw himself as primarily a member of a group was not truly an American.[39]

Even Kallen, however, who moved in pragmatist circles, did not base his position on the more enlightened science of the anthropologist Franz Boas, who stressed the "plasticity" of race, but on the same assumptions as those of many of the anti-immigrationists, that is, that race determined character and that ethnicity was unalterable. His cultural pluralism assumed that people preferred their own kind and that this was a good thing, which should be recognized and defended. America was based on the principle of difference, not homogeneity, Kallen argued, and he maintained that "democracy involves, not the elimination of differences but the perfection and conservation of differences." Just as the structure of government was federative, so was the nation a "mosaic of peoples," a "cooperation of cultural diversities," and a "commonwealth of national cultures." On a more theoretical level, he claimed that the individual was "no longer seen as an absolute and distinct autonomous entity" but as gaining identity as a part of "groups," which were not "organisms" but "organizations" with "spiritual autonomy." Liberty in the end was not grounded in "like-mindedness" but in "freedom of association."[40] Although Dewey did not advocate assimilation to one strand of American culture such as the Anglo-Saxon, he continued to have reservations about pluralism. While he endorsed Kallen's metaphor that society was like an orchestra with many instruments, he wanted to achieve a true symphony rather than various solos played simultaneously. Dewey's student Randolf Bourne pursued the notion that it was possible, through cultural transformation, to build a transcendent, federative, cosmopolitan unity on a pluralistic base and go beyond both individualism and identity politics.[41] These ideas would find renewed expression in late-twentieth-century democratic political theory, but the conversations of the 1920s including people such as Kallen would

39. Edward A. Ross, *Social Control* (New York: Macmillan, 1901); *The Old World in the New* (New York: Century, 1914). See Louis Menand, *The Metaphysical Club* (New York: Farrar, Straus and Giroux, 2001), 406.

40. Kallen, *Culture and Democracy in the U.S.* (New York: Boni and Liveright, 1924), 11, 43, 58–61, 116–17, 199. See Olivier Zunz, "The Genesis of American Pluralism," *Tocqueville Review* 9 (1987–88).

41. See Menand, *The Metaphysical Club*, 400.

be largely forgotten. In both instances, however, they would precipitate questions about whether there could be democracy without a national community.

In England, by the beginning of World War I, there was already hostility toward theories of sovereignty such as that associated with Austin. Ernest Barker not only condemned German philosophy and the "worship of power" in the work of writers such as Friedrich Nietzsche and Heinrich von Treitschke, but criticized Austin's theory of sovereignty as never having fitted the reality of English "polyarchism."[42] After this period, the term "polyarchy" would not significantly reappear in the conversation of political science until it was resurrected more than a generation later by Dahl and Charles Lindblom. Barker, originally at King's College, London, before occupying the chair of Political Science at Cambridge (1927), was one of the first academicians in England to identify himself as a political scientist. Both his chair and that of Wallas at the London School of Economics were financially underwritten by the Laura Spelman Rockefeller Foundation, which did so much to sponsor the new wave of social science at the University of Chicago and which was committed to exporting this approach abroad. Although he was involved with the tradition of British idealism, he, like A. D. Lindsay at Oxford, also came to reject many of its premises and to acknowledge the growing emphasis on pluralism.

Lindsay also confronted the problem of the theoretical status of the state and the issue of the place of groups in the polity, which was at the heart of emerging American conversation. He noted that the later half of the nineteenth century had been marked, in both theory and practice, by a transition from "individualism to collectivism." He emphasized that as a consequence it was no longer possible to accept the kind of individualism that was represented by the early utilitarians, and he suggested that even the distinction between public and private domain advocated by Mill was no longer viable. "Society cannot be looked upon as an aggregate of individuals." He claimed that, after the turn of the century, the idea of the state as a corporate personality and as an "organic unity" had replaced contract theory and doctrines of legal and economic individualism. In Lindsay's view, this transformation in theory had been somewhat of a "reflex" response to increased practices of state "interference," but by 1914 he perceived, in both spheres, the beginning of "notes of discontent" and evidence that "the state itself is on trial." Whether it was by socialists,

---

42. Ernest Barker, *Nietzsche and Treitschke: The Worship of Power* (Oxford: Oxford University Press, 1914); "The Discredited State," *Political Quarterly* 5 (July 1918); "The Superstition of the State," *Times Literary Supplement* 2 (1915).

syndicalists, pacifists and internationalists, or pluralists, all of the traditional claims justifying the unity and supremacy of the state had been
called into question, and Lindsay found it safe to say that "the theory of
the sovereign state has broken down."

In his view, however, the new challenge was less from a reassertion of
classic individualism than from claims on behalf of other associations,
communities, and organizations such as unions, the church, and political
parties, which had, in the modern age, become an integral part of society.
Lindsay maintained that once the state had been accepted as a corporate
personality, it was impossible to deny such status to other associations. His
answer to this question was, first, to insist that neither individualism nor
collectivism were theoretically adequate to account for the facts of modern life. The state was neither an aggregate of individuals nor a "higher
personality" into which individuals were absorbed. Second, he argued that
what was required was a theoretical and practical resolution of the issue of
the relationship between the state and other associations. While he found
it necessary to relinquish all the traditional theories of state priority, he
did find some truth in the general idea that the state was, in the end, the
"organization of organizations" and that it was "special" in that it represented "men's sense of obligation to one another" and constituted a general ethical system of rights and duties grounded in common culture and
traditions. The extent to which the state should interfere through the
agency of government, however, was, he claimed, a situational matter with
respect to which no a priori principles were available; but in his view, such
action was clearly more necessary in contemporary society with its complexity and high degree of economic development.[43] In the same year,
Barker offered a very similar assessment.

Barker had advocated a juristic theory of the state as a legal personality, but not because of any attachment to institutionalism and formalism.
He urged the "rule of law" and the responsibility of government in opposition to the authority of the "mysterious," inviolable and invisible Crown.
Although he tended to still equate the state with a sovereign public and
to view government as its agent, he argued that despite the influence of
the ideas of Jean Bodin, Hobbes, and Austin, "the state had been generally discredited in England" as far as constituting anything possessing a
transcendent will and personality. Although, he claimed, this disposition
to deflate the status of the state was originally rooted in religious

---

43. A. D. Lindsay, "The State in Recent Political Theory," *Political Quarterly* 1 (1914): 128–30,
140.

nonconformity and the elevation of voluntary associations, a tradition with which he was generally sympathetic, the basic attitude had spread to classic political economy and was more recently represented in Marxism and the work of pluralists such as John Neville Figgis and Frederic Maitland. Barker maintained that it was important to resist a metaphysical image of the state and, instead, to see it, as well as all other associations, as consisting of individuals related by a common organizing idea and interest, which in the case of the state was "law and order." The problem was that of the relationship between the state and other associations. Barker rejected both Hegelian and Austinian theories of state authority and sovereignty. Instead, he argued that people who live in a "community must have an ultimate source of adjustment of their relations" as well as a way of preserving individual freedom in the context of the various associations to which they belong. This, he claimed, was the function of the state and the basis of its special status. England was marked by "polyarchism" and an "unstable equilibrium" between associations, and it was the task of the state, with its instrument of law, to mediate as needed. He suggested that, paradoxically, the state was often discredited when it was doing well (and appeared not to be needed), and credited when it was doing badly (and appeared to be needed). In a footnote, Barker remarked that his assessment had been written in May of 1914 but that by the time it was published, in January of 1915, the facts had changed. Suddenly the state was "having its high midsummer of credit."[44] By the end of the war that credit would be withdrawn.

In the United States, Dunning held on to the view that German idealism, from Kant to Hegel, had a profound and beneficial effect on the "form and method of political philosophy" and had produced a "refined psychological analysis" whereby the "classification of political ideas assumed great scientific precision." Yet, he argued, "like all other idealists, the German philosophers in fact achieved little more than to clothe certain institutions and aspirations of contemporary politics with the sanctifying garb of mystic form and nomenclature." While idealism had initially sought to defend the individual, Hegel's glorification of "the State," in its "Bacchic frenzy," threatened the very ethic of individualism.[45] Dewey attacked German idealism and its evolutionary philosophy of history in favor of a critical and "experimental philosophy" that, he believed, could undercut the kind of nationalism that led to the war. Although Dewey maintained that politics

44. Barker, "The 'Rule of Law,'" *Political Quarterly* 1 (1914); "The Discredited State," *Political Quarterly* 2 (1915): 101, 118, 120–21.

45. Dunning, "The German Idealists," *Political Science Quarterly* 28 (1913): 493–94.

was the "controlling factor in the formation of philosophical ideas," such ideas also "served to articulate and consolidate" politics, and this was the case in Germany where "an apriori and an absolutist philosophy has gone into bankruptcy."[46] Yet Dewey argued that there was a "coincidence in the development of modern experimental science and democracy" and that what was required was a philosophy such as that of William James explaining and implementing this connection. He charged that up until this point political science had been a "recluse from the world of affairs and alternates between a pedantic conservatism and a complacent acceptance of any brute change that happens."[47]

Willoughby, too, joined in the attack on German philosophy, but one significant aspect of Willoughby's essay was that he pointedly did not attack the German state but the government and the philosophy of the state that, he argued, had given rise to both the particular form of government and the cultural attitudes that supported it. He was already pressing further his contentious nonsubstantive "juristic conception" of the state "as an instrumentality for the creation and enforcement of the law."[48] Willoughby began by stressing that a state is different from a government in that the former is simply "a group of individuals *viewed* as a politically organized unit, as an entity or corporate being possessing superior authority over the individuals constituting its body-politic."[49] All states, Willoughby once again stressed, were "essentially alike" and differentiated only by their forms of government. In his treatment, the concept of the state functioned as an analytic juristic category, something "formal" and a "convenience of thought," and a state qua state could not, he concluded, be criticized or defended since the concept was largely something that belonged to the language of political science and its virtual images rather than representing an entity in the real world. The problem in Germany, Willoughby alleged, was in part that German philosophers such as Fichte, Kant, and Hegel had used the concept of the state to refer not only to something actual, but to something "divine" that possessed an "exalted supernatural and mystical character" and had "interests and ends of its own." Much as Anglicans and Catholics believed the church to be something

46. Dewey, *German Philosophy and Politics* (New York: Henry Holt & Co., 1915), 123–25.

47. Dewey, "Philosophy and Democracy" (1919) and "Political Science as a Recluse" (1918), in *The Middle Works, 1899–1924* (Carbondale: Southern Illinois University Press, 1982), 11:48, 53, 95–96.

48. Willoughby, "The Juristic Conception of the State," *American Political Science Review* 12 (1918): 192.

49. Willoughby, *Prussian Political Philosophy* (New York: D. Appleton, 1918), 51, emphasis added.

"abstract and metaphysical" and more than its body of adherents and its organization, this organic philosophy of the state had, Willoughby argued, aided and abetted a *Weltanschauung* that both informed and justified an absolutist regime that contradicted every basic principle and institution of American politics and government.[50] Willoughby, however, left in abeyance the issue of exactly how the values of American government were to be justified.

Giddings, a radical Spencerian, stepped in and stated the case most dramatically. He charged that the "Teutonic philosophy" and its image of the state were nothing less than the product of a "demoniac imagination" and an attempt to justify "diabolic collective conduct."[51] Even Giddings, however, unlike Willoughby, continued to hold on to a traditional concept of the state, which he maintained was the "noblest expression of human purpose." The problem was the idea of sovereignty advanced by "metaphysical theorizing" and the claim, of the "Treitschkes and Kaisers," that the state was "absolute" rather than "finite and relative."[52] It was Harold Laski, however, who most consistently pursued the theme of the "discredited state" and who, during his relatively brief residence in the United States at Harvard, both introduced the word "pluralism" into the conversation and advanced a normative theory of pluralist democracy.

Laski argued against both the idea of the omnipotent state as the source of law and the notions of philosophical absolutism with which it was allied,[53] but, at the same time, he systematically turned to pluralism not only as an alternative account of social reality but as a theory of democratic society. His early work represented a constant attack on idealism, the monistic theory of the state, the idea of state sovereignty, and the Austinian-inspired emphasis on formal legal aspects of the state as the subject of social science. Most of this work, largely in the form of collected and poorly edited essays, was published while he was a visitor at Harvard (from 1916–20), and much of his philosophical inspiration or justification came from his reading of Dewey and James. What he initiated, and left behind, was a debate about the state that played a large role in precipitating a new theory of democratic society and contributed significantly to a transformation in the identity of political science.

50. Ibid., 53, 60, 62.
51. Giddings, *The Responsible State* (Cambridge: Riverside Press, 1919), 48.
52. Ibid., 46.
53. Harold J. Laski, *Studies in the Problem of Sovereignty* (New Haven: Yale University Press, 1917); *Authority in the Modern State* (New Haven: Yale University Press, 1919); Leon Duguit, *Law in the Modern State,* trans. Frida and Harold Laski (New York: R. W. Huebsch, 1919).

Laski ridiculed the "exaltation of unity" that had evolved in political theory from Dante to Hegel and that was represented in German politics and philosophy. He excoriated the "mysticism" attending attempts at "monistic reduction," which presented the state as a holistic "personality" and which sublimated and subordinated the social elements that composed it. Laski in some ways did not initially so much reject the underlying onto-logical assumptions on which the theory of the state had been predicated as displace them to other associations. According to Laski, each church, town, university, and labor union had its own distinct reality, "group-life," and "will." The image of the state in "political theory," and the concept of sovereignty as its "instrument," was simply the counterpart, and conse-quence, of philosophical idealism's notion of a metaphysical "absolute" as the basis of human judgment. Laski countered with James's image of the pluralistic universe, which, he suggested, led to a "pluralistic theory of the state." What constituted the state that he now conceived as plural was, however, less than clear, but he argued that, as a philosophical principle, the whole is not known before its parts and has no moral superiority. The parts are in themselves distinct, not part of a seamless web in which their reality derives from their relationship to something greater. Consequently, he claimed, the "State is but one of the variety of associations and groups to which the individual belongs" and to which allegiance is paid. The source of law was, in fact, not a command of a sovereign, as Austin had claimed, but in reality something sociologically generated from the "opin-ion" of individuals and instances of their consent or "fused good-will." The only reason that the state was supreme on occasion was that it managed to "obtain general acceptance" of the "constituent wills from which the group will is made" and "prove itself" (as Dewey suggested) on an "experimen-talist" basis. Any real disagreement among its parts rendered it impotent and the assumption of sovereignty meaningless.

Somehow for Laski the state was both a "whole" and one association among many, and his new metaphysics was not immediately more impres-sive than the old. Laski also sought support for his arguments in Aristotle's idea of mixed government and suggested that this conception of the polity constituted "a pragmatist theory of the state" in which progress came not from uniformity but from variation and conflict. Yet he rejected what might also be understood as Aristotle's claim that the state was more important because its concerns were more comprehensive or that it had a larger moral purpose. He argued, already prefiguring what would become his Marxist position in later years, that in fact it usually represented only a portion of society, and its purposes were in principle no more superior than those of a church or trade union. Even though the British Parliament, for example, might be the formal seat of authority, its dictates were in the end the result of a "vast complex of forces," and the public acceptance of those dictates was a "pragmatic" affair.[54]

These ideas were explicitly formulated in the context of Laski's associations with Croly as well as Roscoe Pound, who led the way in introducing the concept of interests and group representation into the theory and practice of law (e.g., *A Theory of Social Interests,* 1921), Felix Frankfurter, and Oliver Wendell Holmes Jr.[55] In his presentation, however, Laski more explicitly drew on the work of Maitland, Figgis, and Otto Friedrich von Gierke and their research on pluralism in medieval society.[56] He also attempted, through his studies of the Reformation and other instances of religious dissent, as well as by reference to more modern examples such as syndicalism in France and the guild socialism of G. D. H. Cole, to give historical and rhetorical depth to his idea and defense of pluralism and to his animadversions against the worship of the state and the dogma of its moral superiority. While the modern state had sought its independence from religion, it attempted, he claimed, to appropriate for itself that same kind of universality. Laski's primary concern, like Tocqueville, was actually his homeland. It was England and the conservatism of Parliament and the common law that bothered him, and he found in the United States what he believed was in many respects an exemplification of his theoretical claims about the "moral insufficiency" of the idea of the unitary state. He claimed that the very fact of the American Revolution, as well as the nature of the government of the United States manifest in the principles of federalism and the separation of powers, demonstrated the "absurdity," and the practical abolition, of Austin's theory of sovereignty and Albert Venn Dicey's image of a unitary and omnipotent state such as that supposedly represented in Parliament. Laski's metanarrative of the founding of the United States was considerably different from that of Burgess. He argued that the founders had taken the states for granted as a "foundation to be built upon" and did not attempt "to create a complete system of government" at the national level. And this, he argued, was still sociologically

---

54. Laski, *Studies in the Problem of Sovereignty,* 1–25.

55. For a discussion of pluralism in the law, see Morton J. Horwitz, *The Transformation of American Law, 1870–1960: The Crisis of Legal Orthodoxy* (New York: Oxford University Press, 1992). See also Daniel Ernst, "Common Laborers? Industrial Pluralists, and the Law of Industrial Disputes, 1915–1943," *Law and History Review* 11 (1993).

56. For a representative selection of some of this literature, see Paul Hirst, ed., *The Pluralist Theory of the State* (London: Routledge, 1989).

apparent in the "fundamental diversity of circumstance" in the country, "in the variety of its group life, and in the wide distribution of sovereign power," which promised the "guarantee of its perennial youth" and the "preservation of liberty." The eminent, imminent, and immanent danger, however, was, as in all modern countries, that of "centralization" and the loss of local autonomy. This position led Laski to label himself a "frank medievalist."[57]

Although one might be tempted, including Laski himself, to say that he developed a pluralistic theory of the state, he actually did not so much offer an alternative theory of the state as attempt to destroy every attribute of the state as conventionally conceived and, through concrete case studies, to demonstrate the absence of any historically persistent essence. In his successive essays, he moved more and more toward the thesis and logical conclusion already so evident in the work of Willoughby that "what we term state-action is, in actual fact, action by government." And this, in turn, amounted to little more than what was functionally accepted by groups in society and made operative.[58] And since there was never any ultimate assurance that government would be obeyed, as history seemed to so clearly demonstrate, the traditional idea of sovereignty was a myth. But while his primary target was the idea of centralized authority and the myths that sustained it, his work also served to undercut the notion of popular sovereignty, and democracy, as traditionally conceived. During the same period, Mary Parker Follett's work was an interesting and intellectually challenging move in the discussion about state and pluralism, but even though it must be counted as contributing to the transformation of pluralism into a normative theory of democracy, it did not become a major factor in the evolution of the conversation of political science. It was, however, an illuminating journey through the issues and arguments in its search for synthesis, and what might be considered its analytical and practical failures could be construed as outweighed by its ingenuity.

Follett focused on the group as the essence of political life, but her concern was less to depreciate the concept of the state than to reconstitute it in terms of a theory of group democracy. Follett's image of the group was hardly that of parties and interests that, she believed, tended to constitute the reality of contemporary government—masked by a fictional image of democracy. Neither representative government nor attempts at direct government were working, and when collective unity was achieved, it often

57. Laski, *Studies in the Problem of Sovereignty*, 268–82.
58. Laski, *Authority in the Modern State* (New Haven: Yale University Press, 1919), 30.

meant, she argued, the assimilation of the individual, which she considered the basic "unit of politics," into the "crowd." She urged that the "twentieth century must find a new principle of association" and that this should be "group organization," which would also entail a "new method in politics." Democracy could work and achieve a common good only if political life was revitalized by, and defined in terms of, "the organization of non-partisan groups" such as those represented by neighborhoods and occupations. Follett argued that although "pluralism was the most vital trend in political thought," it had not developed an adequately positive political theory that answered the questions of what was to be done with diversity and how to move to "a true Federal State" and eventually a "World State." In her view, "the organization of men in small local groups" provided the basis for a "continuous political activity which ceaselessly creates the state" as a wider collective community. Despite ideological differences, Follett did not sound much different than Lieber.[59]

Follett, like Laski, transferred James's image of the plural universe to politics, but she stressed the manner in which pluralism also contained the "secret of collective life" and of the "many becoming one"—unity without uniformity. What would be achieved would be a genuine "collective will" and a situation in which "we can never dominate another or be dominated by another; the group-spirit is always our master." Here would be a "new individualism" and true freedom found by participation in the whole. Follett, also like Laski, found inspiration in Pound's idea of sociological jurisprudence, where law and right were conceived as flowing from and serving the variety of interests in society, rather than standing above it. Democracy could no longer be conceived in terms of majoritarianism, natural rights, and individualistic notions of liberty and equality, but rather in terms of the "collective will of the people" embodied in the state. But this collective will was to be forged by learning a "technique" of "spontaneous association" evident in local groups—by "training for democracy" at this level and moving from "neighborhood to nation" and then all the way to world organization. All this assumed, however, the possibility of a "unifying state," and Follett's quarrel with pluralism, in the forms in which it was being conceived and propagated, was that in its reaction to monism, it tended to deny both the value and possibility of unity. She believed that those who drew on James's ideas failed to see that his plural universe implied a "unifying principle" and "a compounding of consciousness,"

59. Mary Parker Follett, *The New State: Group Organization, The Solution of Popular Government* (New York: Longmans, Green, & Co., 1918), 3, 7, 11, 13, 295.

which could find expression in a reconstituted political federalism that was based neither on centralization nor states's rights, that was "unifying" rather than unified. There had also, she believed, been an misunderstanding of Hegel, although Hegel, she suggested, had "misunderstood himself" as well when he defended the Prussian state, which did not grasp the manner in which he allowed for diversity within unity and for a "collective sovereignty." She was also dubious about looking to the Middle Ages for answers to modern problems of pluralist democracy, but most of all, she was concerned that there had not been adequate attention paid to "the scientific study of group psychology" that could find a basis of compatibility between collective and group sovereignty.[60] Ford noted Follett's arguments were ultimately unclear even if a "portent of the times."[61]

With the publication of his second major book, Laski was moving in the Marxist direction of claiming that the state, or what in his formulation now seemed to be government, really was always, and had always been, controlled by only a segment of society and a dominant economic interest.[62] But historically it had also been subject to all sorts of limitations, including the conscience of the individual, institutional checks, group diversity, and popular resistance and revolution. The real question was that of political obligation or why people obey authority. His answer was basically that government was forced to gain support, and this "leads to a pluralistic theory of society" and to a definite distinction between state and society. Since "the State is only one among many forms of association" and neither more in harmony with the end of society nor morally and legally superior than a union or lodge, it had no special claim to authority. "The state is based upon will; but the wills from which its will is eventually formed struggle amongst each other for survival." This description, he claimed, was "realism," while the notion that the state can be identified with some general community was idealism. The state was simply mortals governing, and that was why it must be limited by democratic institutional means such as the separation of powers and representation.[63] Just as government was, or should be, rendered into parts, so was society "basically federal in nature." The great danger for Laski continued to be modern centralization, which, he claimed, tended to depreciate the principle and reality of consent and to obscure the fact that the state, like a

60. Ibid., 73, 141, 195, 202, 258, 265–67, 270, 311.

61. Ford, review of *The New State,* by Follett, *American Political Science Review* 13 (1919): 495.

62. This claim would be fully developed in Ford's *The State in Theory and Practice* (New York: Viking, 1935).

63. Laski, *Authority in the Modern State,* 65–69.

"Darwinian species," at least properly, only "summarizes a general social experience" and has no separate validation.[64] He continued to hold up the United States as a model, but at the same time suggested an impending crisis based on his assessment that "a political democracy confronts the most powerful economic autocracy the world has ever seen," while the separation of powers gives way to the decline of Congress and administrative centralization. Yet despite "its corrupt politics," the "withdrawal of much of its ability from governmental life, its exuberant optimism, and a traditional faith in its orthodox political mechanisms that may well prove disastrous," there was, he allowed, hope. This rested on the country's revolutionary and democratic heritage, the growth of organized labor, social protest and progressive experimentation, the rebirth of natural rights ideas, and legal decisions such as those of Holmes and Brandeis that held the state (government) subject to law.[65]

Laski pursued the same themes in yet a third volume, but by this point his argument was no longer just that the theory of sovereignty had "fallen from its high estate." The monistic state and the pluralistic states no longer represented simply different theoretical accounts. The monistic state was now presented as the characteristic structure of contemporary political power, and pluralism was offered as an alternative normative program in opposition to the "unified sovereignty of the present social organization." Pluralism involved the substitution of "coordination" for "hierarchical structure," and its goal was the "partition" of sovereignty and the creation of social "federalism." Laski continued to stress the manner in which government was controlled by dominant economic forces and how liberty was incompatible with power in the hands of "a small group of property owners."[66] Laski still sought his exemplars in the Conciliar movement of the Middle Ages, Edmund Burke, and early American federalism. He argued that in the Middle Ages, where unity was achieved "through a system of groups," sovereignty was "unthinkable," despite the universalistic claims of the Roman church to which the modern unified state was the successor.[67] While the Reformation broke this hegemony, religion once again allied itself with political power and underwrote the idea of sovereignty in the modern state. A study of the Middle Ages, however, revealed the existence of ideas of popular sovereignty, natural law, and group autonomy that had been suppressed in modern political thought from the time of

64. Ibid., 74, 109.
65. Ibid., 116.
66. Laski, *Foundations of Sovereignty and Other Essays* (New York: Harcourt Brace, 1921), v, 209.
67. Ibid., 1.

Hobbes and, in practice, fettered by the unified state with its emphasis on centralization. Laski went to great lengths, like Gierke, to demonstrate that corporations and similar entities were not just fictions and functions of the state but rather were "real" and had distinct "personalities" and "wills" of their own, which made them self-governing. This, he claimed, demonstrated that the state was not in reality sovereign and that it was not possible to "doubt this polyarchism."[68] For Laski, even the idea of popular sovereignty was a myth that tended, as in the work of Rousseau, to depreciate the value and necessity of representative government, while abetting the idea of state supremacy. The notion of the state as an organic people acting as one was, he claimed, at least in modern times, an impossible fiction that obscured the fact that society was composed of "different wills."[69] He argued that the idea of the modern sovereign monistic state as possessing a single and overriding will was originally a somewhat pragmatic invention of lawyers but that it had been amplified and embellished by philosophers who raised it to the level of an ethical principle in the service of centralization and economic privilege. Both the idea and the practice of centralization must be combated by fractioning power through social and political federalism and by returning to ideas of natural rights that recognized not only individual liberty but such things as the necessity of a living wage as central to citizenship.

Although the socialist dimension of Laski's arguments was apparent and could be expected to evoke reaction, his claims presented difficulties even for political scientists who might have sympathized with him ideologically. This denigration of the state could, for example, scarcely gain much support from political scientists such as Merriam, since the state, now conceived as government, remained, in the latter's view, the vehicle for achieving and representing a democratic society. Laski was not well attuned to the concerns of professional political science in the United States and to such issues as disciplinary identity and the American setting of the relationship between public and academic discourse. Neither was he particularly sensitive to the degree to which the idea of democracy in the United States had been tied to the idea of state. Although Laski was not the only source of the basic ideas that would contribute to a pluralistic theory of democracy, his work did galvanize the conversation and contribute to some of the main constituents of the empirical and, particularly, normative dimensions of that theory.

68. Ibid., 169.
69. Ibid., 230.

One political scientist of the period who was involved in this conversation was Walter J. Shepard of the University of Missouri and an alumnus of Harvard, Heidelberg, and Berlin, who later became a president of the APSA. He reviewed Laski's work favorably, as well as other critiques of the traditional idealist theory of the state such as that of L. T. Hobhouse, but at this point, like many of his colleagues, he saw no clear alternative emerging in this literature and worried about the implications for the authority of government and about how conflicts between groups could be resolved without the supreme will of the state.[70] While Laski presented a rather benign and romantic image of group life, there was a continuing, and growing, sense among many that groups were, in fact, little more than aggregations of self-interest. Henry Adams claimed that what was called democracy had been, from the time of Andrew Jackson, degenerating and turning into a scene of "self-interest and greed" and was actually "an infinite mass of conflicting minds and of conflicting interests which, by the persistent action of such a solvent as the modern competitive industrial system, becomes resolved into what is, in substance, a vapor which loses in collective intelligence energy in proportion to the perfection of its expansion."[71] Although Adams's application of biological theories and the laws of thermodynamics as an explanation for the "degradation of the democratic dogma" was unique and bizarre, the general problem of how to find or conceive democracy in the midst of a universe of group self-interest was widely acknowledged. For political scientists, the new vision of political reality also raised the problem of the authority of political science.

With the decline of the state as the basis of a theory of democracy, Merriam and others, like later generations of political scientists, began to seek the identity and authority of political science more in its method than its subject matter. And many even claimed, or at least assumed, that there was or could be a symbiotic relationship between scientific and political rationality.[72] Such notions of methodological identity and authority were not, however, without their problems, and this in part explains the manner in which the controversy about the state and pluralism developed. Those who argued against pluralism as both a descriptive and normative

70. Walter James Shepard, review of *Studies in the Problem of Sovereignty,* by Laski, *American Political Science Review* 11 (1917); review of *The Metaphysical Theory of the State: A Criticism,* by L. T. Hobhouse, *American Political Science Review* 13 (1919); review of *Authority in the Modern State,* by Laski, *American Political Science Review* 13 (1919).

71. Henry Adams, *The Degradation of the Democratic Dogma* (New York: Macmillan, 1919), 85, 109.

72. See, for example, Macy, "The Scientific Spirit in Politics," *American Political Science Review* 11 (1917).

thesis may in some instances have been ideologically motivated, but what was also at stake was the professional, cognitive, and practical status of political science. Studying groups and interests was all too mundane and lacked the grandeur represented in attaching the profession to something as sublime and invisible as the state.

First of all, pluralism provided little basis for distinguishing political science from sociology, psychology, and economics—and, in fact, seemed to threaten subservience to these fields, which characteristically had more to say about such phenomena as groups. The domain of political science and the nature of political theory, whose boundaries had been carefully and assiduously circumscribed prior to World War I by Willoughby and others, were called into question. Second, if political science did not have access to the deeper scientific subject matter of the state, its claim to knowledge and authority was in jeopardy. Finally, pluralism undercut the notion that there was, after all, a "people," and this called into question the very idea of democracy as it had been characteristically conceived. As in the case of behavorioralism a generation later, it was less the empiricism of the new science of politics, advocated by individuals such as Merriam, that bothered the critics than the interdisciplinary character and rejection of the conceptions of political reality and democracy that had been represented by the idea of the state and that undergirded professional and theoretical identity. In some instances, ideological and philosophical differences were behind debates about method, but often concerns about the authority of the discipline and profession continued to override such differences.

Laski's arguments, in principle and perception, contributed to the subversion of a century of academic discourse devoted to giving substance to the concept of the state and, in turn, to the emerging image of political science. This was certainly not Laski's purpose, and one of the great accidents in the history of political science, which cannot be retrospectively rationalized as part of some general historical development, was Laski's presence in the United States. He was not the first to call attention to the ideas of individuals such as Léon Duguit and the implications for political theory, but he did bring this literature to prominence in the discourse of political science.[73] If it had not been for his voice, the issue would not have crystallized in the manner in which it did. Although the names of many individuals and different varieties of political thought and practice would be dragged into the discussion, it was largely through Laski's work,

73. Dewey had called upon Duguit's ideas in his critique of Austin, and J. M. Matthews had discussed Duguit's attack on the traditional theory of sovereignty in "A Recent Development in Political Theory," *Political Science Quarterly* 24 (1909).

and discussions of his work, that they surfaced. Many, including, for example, Dunning, praised Laski's repudiation of unitary sovereignty, but the path forward was not clear.[74] For instance, the philosopher Morris Cohen applauded Figgis, Duguit, and Laski for having "shaken political philosophy of its torpid or somnambulant worship of the State as the god on earth" and for resisting trends toward centralization of authority, but he cautioned that they failed to recognize that groups could be oppressive and that the state might have to intervene on behalf of the individual. And from a theoretical perspective, he worried about the tendency to transfer notions of "organism" and "personality" from the state to groups on other than a legalistic basis.[75]

Ellen Deborah Ellis of Smith College, a Ph.D. from Bryn Mawr, where she eventually returned, was the first woman to play a major role in the conversations of political science and the first person to attempt to give a definite self-conscious articulation of the controversy about pluralism and indicate how it had developed up to this point. She noted Laski's dependence on a long list of thinkers including Gierke, Maitland, Figgis, Duguit, and Barker as well as on ideas of guild socialism and syndicalism, and she stressed that what emerged was an increasingly distinct theory of pluralism that could be juxtaposed to monism—the "long accepted state theory of political science."[76] The latter, she pointed out, represented the state as a unitary and absolute sovereign association standing behind government and as the creator of liberty and rights. Ellis perceived accurately that the pluralist challenge to these assumptions often sprung less from a factual disagreement than from the normative claim that the state should be limited. But what exactly was to be limited was unclear in her discussion as well as in most of the literature. If the state was an associational unity behind government, the limitation would be on popular sovereignty, but if the state was another word for government, it was, as Burgess claimed, popular sovereignty that placed limits on it. The conversation was in the midst of sorting out these contradictions as the paradigm shift evolved during the 1920s. Ellis suggested that pluralist theory leavened some of the more dubious elements of traditional statism, such as the excessive emphasis on authority exemplified in German philosophy, and it called

74. Dunning, review of *Studies in the Problem of Sovereignty*, by Laski, *Political Science Quarterly* 32 (1917); review of *Authority in the Modern State*, by Laski, *Political Science Quarterly* 34 (1919).

75. Morris R. Cohen, "Communal Ghosts and Political Theory," in *Reason and Nature: An Essay on the Meaning of Scientific Method* (Glencoe, Ill.: Free Press, 1931), 396–97, originally published as "Communal Ghosts and Other Perils of Social Philosophy," *Journal of Philosophy* 16 (1919).

76. Ellen Deborah Ellis, "The Pluralistic State," *American Political Science Review* 14 (1920): 394.

"attention to the present bewildering development of groups within the body politic, and to the fact that these groups are persistently demanding greater recognition in the governmental system." However, the difficulty, she argued, was that pluralism offered no solution to this problem and tended to "lay the way open to a very disorganized and casual political organization," which would be a threat to both order and liberty and which disguised the inescapable fact that, in the end, any real and true state must be a "unitary state" in which there is "one supreme loyalty and political sovereign."[77] What was evident in Ellis's analysis, however, was that what she often meant by "state" was "government," as in the case of Laski as well. The equation of state and people was receding, but for Ellis and others the theory of democracy, as well as the identity of political science, was endangered by this transformation.

Coker perceptively questioned whether pluralists such as Duguit and Laski really advanced the same kind of ideas as Gierke, Maitland, and Figgis. He was sympathetic to Duguit's attack on Germanic images of the state, but he also suggested that some of the new pluralists had created a straw man and that, apart from syndicalism, recent ideas such as Emile Durkheim's emphasis on occupational groups, regionalism, interest group representation, and guild socialism all really neither grasped the practical implications of pluralist theory for legal doctrine nor actually required "any abandonment of the essential features of the conventional theory of state sovereignty." Some of the recent writers were, he noted, quite clear that their concern was largely with more diversity in the "initiation and execution of state policy." He argued that the dichotomy between monism and pluralism was somewhat artificial, and the state could reasonably be conceived as a coordinator of the relationship between groups.[78] But it was clearly the state qua government that he had in mind, and this notion of the role of government would be central to the theory of pluralism.

Apart from the attacks on German philosophy, leading political scientists of the period had given limited attention to the European conflict, but many began to applaud what they believed was the appearance of democracy in postwar Germany. The influential legal theorist and constitutional scholar Ernst Freund, for example, undertook a detailed examination of the Weimar constitution and concluded that Germany was now a republic: "The power of the state is derived from the people."[79] The

77. Ibid., 405–7.
78. Coker, review of *Law and the State,* by Duguit, *American Political Science Review* 12 (1918); "The Technique of the Pluralist State," *American Political Science Review* 15 (1921): 195, 211.
79. Ernst Freund, "The New German Constitution," *Political Science Quarterly* 35 (1920): 184.

assumption that democracy was becoming increasingly universal, however, as the case would be once more at the end of the twentieth century, simply made the task of articulating a theory of democracy more urgent, as well as that of demonstrating that the United States was the model of democracy. Questions about what actually constituted democracy and whether or not it was working were increasingly posed.[80] Bryce had defined democracy as the "rule of the whole people expressing their sovereignty by their votes," but such a claim was now fraught with ambiguity. The historian Carl Becker suggested that Bryce actually painted a very bleak picture of the gap between the real and ideal, and he wondered what such a definition meant in practice.[81] Not only was the place of pressure groups gaining attention, but there were also increased concerns about the implications of immigration and the appearance of ethnic groups and classes. It seemed to many as if the principal players in the "great game of politics" were interest groups, bosses, and machines rather than individual citizens and a sovereign democratic public.[82] What was emerging from many quarters was an image of an irrational pluralistic society, propelled by self-interest and, at best, acting through the vagaries of an amorphous public opinion. For many, such as Arnold Bennett Hall, who along with Merriam did so much during the 1920s to advance the cause of establishing a more rigorous science of politics and to provide an institutional base for such an endeavor within the profession and discipline of political science, the answer was not to embrace the techniques of Progressive democracy but to gain control over public opinion and improve the character of representation.[83] The search for a science of politics was in part the consequence of a concern about the intellectual inferiority of political science when compared with fields such as economics and sociology, but despite the lack of direct discussion about democracy, the driving force behind a series of reports by the APSA Committee on Political Research and three National Conferences on the Science of Politics was the sense, enunciated by individuals such as Merriam, that scientific control was the answer to a disin-

80. See, for example, Alleyne Ireland, *Democracy and the Human Equation* (New York: E. P. Dutton & Co., 1921).

81. Carl Becker, "Lord Bryce on Modern Democracies," *Political Science Quarterly* 36 (1921); Viscount Bryce, *Modern Democracies* (New York: Macmillan, 1921). See also Becker, *The United States: An Experiment in Democracy* (New York: Harper, 1920).

82. Rodney L. Mott, "The Political Theory of Syndicalism," *Political Science Quarterly* 37 (1922); Frank Kent, *The Great Game of Politics* (Garden City: Doubleday, 1923); review by John R. Commons of several books dealing with immigration and assimilation, *Political Science Quarterly* 37 (1922): 147–49.

83. Arnold Bennett Hall, *Popular Government* (New York: Macmillan, 1921).

tegrating and increasingly undemocratic society, that is, a society in which the sense of a public was fading.[84]

At this point, Lippmann offered the most systematic critique of the idea that public opinion was the expression of a specifiable body of people, and he anticipated, at the very least, Merriam's arguments about both the possibilities and need for manipulating public consciousness and speaking truth to power. Lippmann claimed that individuals lived in a world of competing symbols, which formed a fictional "pseudo-environment" that inhibited "direct acquaintance" with the real environment. Since the world was ultimately and inevitably too complex to be rendered directly, perceptions of reality were always mediated, and they coalesced in something that had been called public opinion or a "National Will, a Group Mind, or Social Purpose." But, Lippmann claimed, "traditional democratic theory . . . never seriously faced the problem which arises because the pictures inside people's heads do not automatically correspond with the world outside." He argued that citizens at large could not have "a competent opinion about all public affairs," partly because society was too complex and partly because they were neither directly involved in nor in possession of the necessary expertise. Therefore representative government required "an independent expert organization for making the unseen facts intelligible to those who have to make decisions." This task, he argued, was properly that of "political science," which had the capacity to grasp the "unseen event" and the "common interest" behind diversity and which should be the "formulator, in advance of real decision, instead of apologist, critic, or reporter after the decision has been made."[85] What Lippmann stressed was the degree to which, for better or worse, opinions could be formed and manipulated by elites and "how he who captures the symbols by which public feeling is for the moment contained, controls by that much the approaches of public policy." He claimed that we can no longer "believe in the original dogma of democracy" and must realize that government, and "group life" in general, is always a matter of elite rule through persuasion.

According to Lippmann, democracy was not based on either the "self-sufficient individual" or some "Oversoul," but rather on the creation of consent and public opinion.[86] He was clearly disenchanted with both muckraking and the press as a means of making the invisible world more

---

84. See the "Progress Report of the Committee on Political Research," *American Political Science Review* 17 (1923) and 18 (1924); "Reports of the National Conference on the Science of Politics," *American Political Science Review* 18 (1924), 19 (1925), and 20 (1926).

85. Lippmann, *Public Opinion* (1921; reprint, New York: Macmillan, 1961), 15–17, 3–31.

86. Ibid., 228–29, 248–49, 261, 310.

visible. What was required were "institutions" and "organized intelligence," but although society had turned to experts in many areas, it had
been "slow to call in the social scientist," who had been caught in limbo
between theory and practice. What would give the social scientist authority with respect to providing facts for decision-makers and providing
"expertness between the private citizen and the vast environment in which
he is entangled," Lippmann suggested, was a "method" that could yield
"a body of data which political science could turn into generalizations, and
build up for the schools into a conceptual picture of the world. When that
picture takes form, civic education can become a preparation for dealing
with an unseen environment." The problems, however, were that political
theorists, such as Plato, had turned away from politics and that "reason"
about politics was still "too abstract and unrefined for practical guidance."[87]
It might seem that Lippmann had written the libretto for Merriam's performance, and there can be little doubt that the "behavioralism" that is
often proleptically projected backward onto Merriam as well as accounts
of his empiricist commitments often fails to take account of the normative
agenda behind his work.

Ford also continued to push his hopes that political science could provide an answer to the "Crescendo of censure" that had been heaped on representative government and even on the Constitution, not only by Marxists
but by individuals such as Tocqueville, Bryce, and Ostrogorski, who had
questioned whether representative institutions really represented or whether
they were controlled by special interests. The discipline's relationship to
the body politic could, he suggested, potentially be like that of the vocation of medicine to the individual if only there were a way to deliver
knowledge about such things as the proper relationship between the legislative and executive branches of government.[88] For individuals such as
Lippmann, Ford, and Merriam, groups were still a problem to be overcome, but some, such as the sociologist Harry Elmer Barnes, who was
closely associated with Merriam and political science in general, were
beginning to see possibilities for democratic political theory in the realities of group politics.

In his analysis of the pedigree of the "group interpretation," Bentley
had noted that "the starting point for all practical purposes, is, of course,
Karl Marx."[89] And Barnes initially fastened on Durkheim's treatment of

87. Ibid., 364, 368, 371, 373, 378, 408, 414–16.
88. Ford, "Present Tendencies in American Politics," *American Political Science Review* 14 (1920): 4.
89. Bentley, *The Process of Government,* 465.

"occupational groups" and suggested that "all in all, the concept of political representation based on *interests* seems to be one of the most desirable and promising of proposed political innovations."[90] He then argued that Bentley's work as well as that of the pluralist theorists whose work had found its way into the conversation of political theory via Bentley and Laski (Figgis, Duguit, Maitland, Albion Small, Ludwig Gumplowicz, Gustav Ratzenhofer) both elevated the concept of group above that of "lobby" and avoided the radical implications of positions such as syndicalism and guild socialism. Willoughby, however, in reviewing Duguit's work claimed that the pluralists were simply "tilting at windmills." What they were really concerned with, he argued, was certain "acts" rather than the state itself, and they failed to see the difference between legal and political sovereignty—a distinction that he now pressed more strongly than ever as an answer to the theoretical quandary about the state. For Willoughby as for Ellis, part of the problem continued to be that the turn away from the state toward a focus on other types of organizations threatened the identity of political science.[91]

In the same volume of the *APSR* that Merriam issued his well-known call for a reformation of political science along more scientific lines, Barnes extended his survey of the "contributions of sociology to modern political theory" and focused again on the work of Giddings and Bentley's teacher at Chicago, the sociologist Albion Small, which he found complemented the general trends represented in the pluralist and realist approach of individuals such as Pound, Duguit, Wallas, Laski, Hugo Krabbe, Lippmann, and Beard. Barnes offered what was, at this point, a remarkable and relatively elaborate account of pluralism as *both* a description of social reality and a theory of democratic government—as well as what can arguably be designated the first depiction of pluralism as such. He suggested that the emerging theory of pluralism was the confluence of a number of intellectual contributions and that the bottom line was that although political institutions were "the highest manifestation of association," in terms of both scope and degree of voluntarism, they were ultimately the "product of a number of corporate groups." The function of the state, by which Barnes now unequivocally meant the government, was that of "adjusting the relations of groups to each other and to the state." Pluralist theory, he claimed, penetrated "beneath the surface of things" and grasped "the real

90. Harry Elmer Barnes, "Durkheim's Contribution to the Reconstruction of Political Theory," *Political Science Quarterly* 35 (1920): 252.

91. Willoughby, review of *Law and the Modern State*, by Duguit, *American Political Science Review* 14 (1920).

nature of social and political processes," and this involved "contesting interest groups seeking a realization of their aims and reaching an adjustment
with the continuing aspirations of other groups." Although some, such as
Gumplowicz, might view the state as legalized oppression and the instrument of an economic minority, it could, Barnes argued, be best construed
as an "umpire" that maintained order and prevented anarchy and undue
exploitation.[92]

Names such as Ratzenhofer and Gumplowicz did not, and would not,
have much currency in the discourse of political science. They had been
introduced by Bentley in his discussion of the development of group theory, just as Figgis and others came to attention through Laski. And
Barnes's interpretation of Bentley pushed a step beyond anything that was
explicit in Bentley's book. The difference between despotism and democracy, Barnes claimed, was that in the former, it is either the one or the
few who settled social antagonisms, while in the latter "every interest
group can express itself and secure representation for itself in a fair and
equitable manner." This is largely what would be meant by liberalism in
the next decade, and Barnes stressed that the role of the government in a
democratic political order was "to furnish the necessary restraint upon
this conflict of interests and to insure that the process will be beneficial
rather than destructive. Government is the agency and avenue through
which these groups carry on the public phases of their conflict and realize their objectives, or effect a temporary satisfactory adjustment of their
aims with the opposing aspirations of other groups." Barnes realized very
well that the incipient pluralist account had created a crisis in the theory
of democratic representation, but he maintained that ideas about the state
based on geography or notions of a general will were myths and that "representative institutions must be brought into harmony with the real purpose and function of government."[93]

In 1922, George Sabine, who had taken his degree in philosophy from
Cornell and was now in the philosophy department at Missouri, and his
colleague in political science, Shepard, participated in the translation and
introduction of Krabbe's work, *The Modern Theory of the State,* which along
with the work of Duguit would begin to gain increasing attention.
Although Sabine still associated political theory with the philosophy of

92. Barnes, "Some Contributions of Sociology to Modern Political Theory," *American Political
Science Review* 15 (1921). See also his contribution in *History of Political Theories: Recent Times,* ed.
Merriam and Barnes (New York: Macmillan, 1924) and the still more extended treatment, *Sociology
and Political Theory* (New York: Alfred Knopf, 1924).

93. Ibid., 377, 380–81.

the state, he had criticized idealism and the theory of the state as power, and he applauded Krabbe's work as offering a new conception of state sovereignty free from organic images of authority and as resting on a sense of political obligation based on a general consensus about right, embodied in law.[94] Merriam's own work as well as that of Beard, who had extended his earlier thesis about economics and politics, was drawing increased attention to the activities of interest groups in American politics. In his review of the Krabbe volume, Merriam suggested that Sabine and Shephard should advance their own views more directly.[95] Sabine would shortly take that advice, but although his pluralist and pragmatist sympathies were evident, he attempted to mediate some of the controversies of the day. As is often the case when faced with dichotomous choices at a point of theoretical change, he suggested that monism and pluralism were less competing theories than different "points of view"—one looking at legal structure and the other looking at process.[96] But his conciliatory approach obscured the increasingly deep-seated intellectual division.

By this point, political science textbooks were beginning to reflect elements of the pluralist image of society, but individuals such as Ellis continued to press the failure of pluralism, and particularly ideas such as guild socialism, to distinguish adequately, both historically and analytically, between state and government and thereby to threaten to "overthrow the very citadel of the state itself."[97] And Coker continued to worry about the manner in which individuals such as Sabine contributed to disparaging the idea of the state and the role of state authority in preserving "liberal values."[98] And this was really in large measure what was at stake here—whether liberal democracy was grounded in the structures and processes of civil society or in something more transcendent. Some recognized that a basic issue underlying the debate was the amount of power that should be accorded central political authority and that both statists and pluralists tended to confuse the issue by focusing on sovereignty and where it

94. Hugo Krabbe, *The Modern Idea of the State* (New York: D. Appleton, 1922); George H. Sabine, "Liberty and the Social System," *Philosophical Review* 25 (1916); "The Concept of the State as Power," *Philosphical Review* 29 (1920).

95. Charles E. Merriam, review of *The Modern Idea of the State*, by Krabbe, *American Political Science Review* 16 (1922); *The American Party System* (New York: Macmillan, 1922); Beard, *The Economic Basis of Politics* (New York: Alfred Knopf, 1922).

96. See Sabine, "Pluralism: A Point of View," *American Political Science Review* 17 (1923).

97. See, for example, Arthur N. Holcombe, *The Foundations of the Modern Commonwealth* (New York: Harper & Brothers, 1923); Ellis, "Guild Socialism and Pluralism," *American Political Science Review* 17 (1923): 584.

98. Coker, "Pluralistic Theories and the Attack on State Sovereignty," in *A History of Political Theories*, ed. Merriam and Barnes.

resided.[99] Raymond G. Gettell, who consistently addressed issues involved in the study of political thought, stressed how the revision of the idea of state sovereignty that was taking place in the literature was a prime example of the general historical dynamics of political theory and of how theory changed in relationship to its context.[100]

Many manifestations of political diversity, from the Ku Klux Klan to the prosecutors in the Scopes trial, continued to be far from entirely congenial to Merriam's vision of national consolidation and social control. He may have been disillusioned with the Progressive belief in the existence of a latent public, but he was hardly willing to concede that the activity of interest groups in the world of "jungle politics" added up to democracy. What was required, in his view, was a social science that spoke to and through elites and that would foster democratic values by civic education and the manipulation of public opinion. He acknowledged that American society was fractured and that the lack of political participation, and even the failure to vote, signaled problems for both politics and the very idea of democracy.[101] Like many others, he came to accept the fact of pluralism, but this was not a reason to depreciate the state conceived as government, which was, he maintained, the solution to the problem. Although by the end of the decade those defending a more traditional notion of the state would associate scientism with the enemy, the relationship between scientism and statism was a complicated one. Some believed that pluralism as a political philosophy required a more scientific approach and that what was needed was a new psychology and new view of human nature grounded in a theory of group behavior. Thus Kallen asked, "So, then, if political science is not psychology, what is it?"[102] Merriam's persistent concern, as well as that of his student Harold Lasswell and others, with bringing psychology to bear on the study of politics was in part a consequence of his belief that this field carried greater scientific authority and promise, but it was also tied to his image of political reality as consisting of group activity.[103] For Merriam, however, pluralism was not a normative thesis even if it had descriptive significance.

99. See, for example, S. A. Koff, "The Problem of Sovereignty," *American Political Science Review* 17 (1923).

100. Raymond G. Gettell, "The Nature of Political Thought," *American Political Science Review* 17 (1923).

101. Merriam and Harold F. Gosnell, *Non-Voting: Causes and Methods of Control* (Chicago: University of Chicago Press, 1924).

102. Kallen, "Political Science as Psychology," *American Political Science Review* 17 (1923): 203.

103. See Merriam, "The Significance of Psychology for the Study of Politics," *American Political Science Review* 18 (1924).

The nineteenth-century study of the state had not failed to pay attention to the particulars of politics and to the presence of various interests in society. This fragmentation was, in fact, what concerned theorists such as Lieber and Woolsey and prompted their concerns about democracy. They had cataloged and discussed a plethora of political diversity issues, while at the same time seeking unity in the idea of the state. By the 1920s, the search for unity was still a concern, and the fundamental problem was how to reconcile the facts of group politics with the theory of democracy. There was, however, already some indication in Merriam's work of the direction in which political science was moving. When Merriam reflected, in 1924, on "recent tendencies in political thought," the social features that he singled out as characterizing the period all amounted to indications of greater pluralism—the "development of industrialization and urbanism, the new contacts with diverse races or nationalities and the rise of feminism." And he saw one main line of theory as that initiated by Gierke, who, along with Dunning, had been the joint director of his dissertation, which he commenced in Germany. This was the view of the state as a conglomerate of economic and professional groups rather than as a geographic and ethnic entity. He designated this as part of a "theory of 'political pluralism,'" which included not only Gierke's analysis of medieval society but such contemporary perspectives as those of syndicalism and guild socialism. Assuming, like Dunning, that ideas were largely a product of social context, he concluded that in general, "pluralistic political theory may be looked upon as a rationalization of actually existing and developing group solidarity, and in fact can be interpreted and understood successfully in no other way."[104] If pluralism were such a rationalization, it had yet to achieve its full expression.

104. Merriam, "Recent Tendencies in Political Thought," in *A History of Political Theories,* ed. Merriam and Barnes, 1, 29–30.

THE THEORY OF DEMOCRATIC PLURALISM

Let us set briefly the problem with
which all modern political theory is
faced: the sphere in which autonomy
may be and should be permitted to
what English political theory has
termed voluntary associations.

—*William Yandell Elliott*

As what we today tend to refer to as the American state was taking shape,
the theory of the state was well on the path of declination, but what was
really involved was that the word "state" was beginning to become a synonym for "government." By the mid-1920s, the concept of the state as a
rational and identifiable public and the bearer of popular sovereignty had
been badly eroded. Lippmann asserted that the public was a "phantom"
and "abstraction" and that "nothing like the whole people takes part in
public affairs." And even government, as an institution, was not what it
had seemed. Governance was, he claimed, in fact, "a multitude of arrangements on specific questions by particular individuals," that is, something
that was seldom either visible to the individual citizen or subject to any
general public opinion. The idea of public opinion and the "dogma of
democracy," which had dominated from Aristotle to the nineteenth

century and which had continued to be manifest in progressive thought and socialist theory, really referred, he claimed, to things that did not exist. This notion of democracy was an "unattainable" and "false ideal."[1] What, then, was democratic government, if it was not the "direct expression of the will of the people," and what ideal of public opinion might be attainable? The image that Lippmann offered was remarkably similar to the plebiscitary account articulated by political scientists and by theorists such as Schumpeter a generation later. Democracy, Lippmann claimed, was a process of elections in which a majority of individual voters expressed, on the basis of numerous and unfathomable motives, either an acceptance or rejection of proposals and either support or opposition with respect to those who were governing. This, he suggested, was an ideal that could be realized—and taught. People could not be made rational in any full sense, but they might be taught to recognize individuals and policies that served their own self-interest. Society, he maintained, was not grounded in some basic underlying unity, but rather was characterized by a "deep pluralism" consisting of diverse groups acting in their own interest, and the task was, through education and open debate, to achieve "adjustment" between groups and prevent any one interest from gaining "counterfeit" strength and claiming to represent a general public interest.[2] The notion of a substantive public interest was not only false but dangerous.

Lippmann argued, as he claimed Laski had already demonstrated, that pluralism was not anarchy, and organic and monistic theories only obscured the real diversity in society and facilitated attempts to create centralized authority and "absentee rulers." The greatest danger was what he at this point called "liberalism" and its perpetuation of the myth that society consisted of some homogeneous body, and was more than an abstraction and the name of something other than "all the adjustments between individuals and their things." There was neither a people nor a public as an actor and no "organic unity and purpose" represented by terms such as "Society, the Nation, the Community." What democracy entailed, the "essence of popular government," was the recognition that in stable societies, there were not any great differences between those in and out of power at a particular moment, but rather a matter of deciding what policies best reconciled competing interests. If there seemed to be disturbing problems, it was simply a sign that it was time to kick the "ins" "out." Genuine public opinion was in effect "the voice of interested spectators of action" who

1. Lippmann, *The Phantom Public* (New York: Harcourt Brace, 1925), 17, 39.
2. Ibid., 41, 53, 77, 97.

had come forward and spoken up when they saw something that affected their interests and then returned "to their own affairs." Lippmann suggested that political scientists could aid in the process of governing by devising methods of sampling opinion and of defining criteria of judgment in matters of policy, and it was the "task of civic education in a democracy to train the public in the use of these methods."[3] Like Barnes's formulation, this was a remarkable prototype of later pluralist theory, but although Hall reviewed the basic thesis of the book favorably and even though it was much in accord with the kind of formulation that he and Merriam had advanced, he noted that, like most "political theory," it still fell into the category of "political literature."[4]

By this point, Willoughby had arrived at a concept of the state that would not be substantially different from that which political scientists would employ for the remainder of the century. The concept might be understood as inadequate by some, as in the case of behavioralism and theorists such as David Easton after mid-century, but less because it was in some basic way incorrect than because it was deficient as a universal tool for factoring out political phenomena from the general stock of social facts. Willoughby's image of the state and the later concept of the political system were, however, in many respects logically comparable. Willoughby repeated his dictum that political theory should be understood primarily as a "philosophical examination of the various concepts upon which the whole science of politics rests," and, in his view, state and government were the central concepts. His immediate purpose was to offer a textbook inquiry into the principles of "constitutional and popular government," and government was the subject matter.[5]

In this work, the concept of the state was presented largely as a term of art in political science for representing a "standpoint" from which to view society. This should not be confused with a claim such as Lieber's that the state is society perceived from a certain perspective, since in the case of the latter, the state as an association was conceived as a real entity and not a construct of the observer. More pointedly than ever, Willoughby asserted that the state is in fact "not a real thing" but an abstraction from concrete elements such as a circumscribed territory. Although the state might be considered "the thing in itself," as opposed to its parts, it was a construction

---

3. Ibid., 126, 145, 156, 172, 183–85, 197–99.

4. Arnold Bennett Hall, Introduction to the "Report of the Third National Conference on the Science of Politics," *American Political Science Review* 20 (1926): 199.

5. Willoughby and Lindsay Rogers, *An Introduction to the Problem of Government* (New York: Doubleday, Page and Co., 1925), v, 4.

"of the jurist or philosopher" for referring to a society that had a structure of governmental organization and a "supreme authority" for creating and administering law. A society was defined by the existence of a "common consciousness of mutual interests and aims," and when such an entity took on a governmental form, it became a "body politic" and could be called a state. Willoughby once again rejected various "organismic" accounts of the state based on metaphors drawn from biology, but society, conceived as the existence of a "feeling of unity of ideals and of identity of interests," was the fundamental datum, coeval with human life and although by definition inherently coercive, also the source of all freedom and rights. In Willoughby's work can be seen the roots of the turn toward the priority of society that both he himself had feared and to which later political scientists often subscribed—at the cost of drawing criticism from political theorists focused on the theoretical autonomy of "the political." Willoughby claimed that when the sentiments of a society were objectified in laws and institutions, one could say that a state had come into existence, but this prior society was not, he stressed, an actual actor on the political stage. Furthermore, the state was not a "moral entity" with "mystical and transcendental attributes" but a human "invention," and governments were but "contrivances" to be judged by the extent to which they fulfilled the purposes and performed the functions for which they had been created. The very definition of the state implied that its function was to further the welfare of the governed, and governments could be judged by the extent to which they succeeded in this task. Terms such as "people" and "nation" could be utilized, but they had no "fixed usage" even though one could reasonably speak of states that were based on nationality as well as nations that had not achieved the status of a state.[6]

What Willoughby meant by popular or constitutional government, republic, and democracy was the presence of attributes such as suffrage, legislative representation, the rule of law, and various sorts of institutional limitations on the exercise of power, but above all democracy involved a government that was, as Bryce had suggested, in some way responsive to "Public Opinion." He argued, however, that there were "no *a priori* grounds upon which any particular form of government . . . may be given preference." He maintained that "the vast size and the extreme complexity of existing political systems make the real rulers of a society undiscoverable" and that the idea that the people as a whole could be represented was

---

6. Ibid., 2, 14 n. 16, 28–29, 34. See also Willoughby, *The Government of Modern States* (New York: Century, 1919), 7.

largely a "fiction." From a legal or juristic standpoint, sovereignty was, he claimed, relatively easy to isolate, but the discovery of "political sovereignty" was more difficult and "one of the most important tasks of political science."[7] This ambiguity or dislocation of political sovereignty, which had been recognized by so many at this point, signaled the crisis of democratic theory. When, at mid-decade, Shepard, now at The Brookings Institution, turned to the issue of the history and future of political science, he relied very largely on Merriam's earlier assessment and noted that there had been recent "progress toward a really scientific character" for the discipline as well as an advance in normative concerns and that there was now a "close relationship between political thought and action." More substantively, he claimed that what marked the present stage of the discipline was a distinct decline in the traditional idea of sovereignty—including popular sovereignty—and a swing in "a pluralistic direction." Sovereignty, he argued, was meaningful only as a legal concept, and "to attribute to the mass of the population the character of sovereign, is to disregard this essential quality of sovereignty."[8]

Since it was Laski who had first redeemed pluralism, it was principally in response to his claims, and to the ideas of those he implicated in his arguments, that the debate about the state was generated and that pluralism as both a descriptive and normative theory of politics was invented. By the mid-1920s, the concept of pluralism and the idiom of pluralistic theory were common currency, while a decade earlier they had been absent from the literature. For the most part, however, pluralism was still viewed as a "critical political theory" directed against the "conservative political theory" of state monism.[9] More than anyone else, it was William Yandell Elliott who, even before the discourse of pluralism had become prominent in political science, took it upon himself to attack those who he believed were in one way or another undermining the idea of the state and, consequently, the concept of democracy. Elliott was a complex figure and his defense of the state was not simply a retreat to the barricades of nineteenth-century theory, and his influence on the discipline of political science and on the subfield of political theory has not been sufficiently recognized.

After a brief period at Berkeley, Elliott was hired by Lowell at Harvard where, from 1923 to 1964, he taught thousands of undergraduates and

---

7. Ibid., 10–11, 109, 167.

8. Shepard, "Political Science," in *The History and Prospects of the Social Sciences,* ed. Barnes (New York: Knopf, 1925), 426–27, 434–35, 438.

9. See Gettell, "Pluralistic Theories of Sovereignty," in *History of Political Thought* (New York: Century, 1924).

directed and served on the dissertations of many of those who would stand on both sides of the barricades during the behavioral revolution (e.g., Easton and Sheldon Wolin). Whether they came away from his tutelage supporting or condemning his views, few escaped the discursive context he created. Probably no political scientist since Lieber had been, or would be, so deeply involved in both the overt and subterranean dimensions of American public policy while remaining in the academy. In fact, his students often claimed that he was so frequently away in Washington that they seldom saw him. In recent years, he has become the *bête noire* of idiosyncratic intellectuals such as Lyndon Larouche, as well as the target of many on the left—in part because of his role as an academic and political mentor of Henry Kissinger and Samuel Huntington and his involvement in some of the clandestine aspects of American foreign policy.[10] Elliott was born in Murfreesboro, Tennessee, in 1896, and his father had been a supporter of the Union. He attended Vanderbilt, where he became a lesser member of the Fugitive Poets, a group that included Robert Penn Warren and John Crowe Ransom, and that has often been associated with a romantic, and sometimes conservative, Southern exceptionalist agrarian tradition and reaction against progressive liberalism. He was a Rhodes scholar, and his principal teacher during his graduate work at Oxford had been Lindsay, who was not only a formidable figure in political studies in England but a significant public intellectual and democratic socialist. But Lindsay, who focused considerable attention on the case of the United States, had developed a somewhat unique role in the conversation.

Lindsay noted that the issue of sovereignty had become "a storm center of political theory" and although it might seem that it admitted of "no answer," he argued that some confusion was involved in the controversy. He maintained, first of all, that Austin's concept of law, as habitual obedience to the command of a determinate person or persons who possess a monopoly of force, was based on an obsolete absolutist model and was not applicable to "modern constitutional government" such as that of the United States or England. And attempts to locate sovereignty in the state, the people, or some other abstract entity also failed. Lindsay's alternative was to advance a theory of the sovereignty of the constitution, and a version of this idea was adopted by Elliott. Lindsay claimed that what was behind law was a consensus among citizens about the basic "interests" and "principles" regarding methods for the "legal or constitutional settlement

---

10. See the eulogy by Elliott's son as well as a brief biographical sketch, available online at http://govt.claremontmckenna.edu/welliott/teachers/elliott.htm.

of differences" and about the government as representing the paramount "purposes" that must be safeguarded. In the case of the United States, this was what was involved in the creation of the Constitution as well as in the Civil War. The issue for Lincoln, Lindsay claimed, was not so much slavery as whether the Constitution and its interpretation by designated authorities were decisive in settling disputes. Second, Lindsay focused his criticisms on arguments such as that of Bernard Bosanquet (*The Philosophical Theory of the State*, 1899) and his Hegelian resurrection of the idea of a general will. Although Lindsay agreed that law is based on social solidarity, he rejected the notion that there should, or could, be "in the minds of the citizens of a state some general conception of the whole multifarious life of the society" that stood behind the law and the constitution. Bosanquet had advanced his theory in opposition to Austin, but Lindsay argued that the two were not dealing with same question. What Austin was concerned about was a juristic issue, and while political theory should "take some specific account of the juristic side of the state," Bosanquet was addressing the question of what constituted the unity of society that lay behind the law. For Lindsay that unity was simply the functional one of "the adherence of the great mass of the people to a definite principle for settling differences," a principle that would play a central role in American pluralist theory.[11]

Although Elliott would fasten on this idea of constitutional sovereignty, he was less inclined than Lindsay to view the unity of society as predicated merely upon tacit agreements about procedure. Elliott claimed that "pragmatic" and "romantic" theories, such as that of Duguit, which posited plural authorities and described law as the product of fear and force, undermined the democratic belief in a substantive general will behind government. The philosophies of James and Henri Bergson had, Elliott argued, not only intruded into the discourse of political science and threatened traditional democratic theory, but had become an inspiration for leaders such as Mussolini. He claimed to have found a theme in the "varied currents of contemporary political theory which seems to have set against the conception of unitary sovereignty as the basis of the structure of the state."[12] The views of pragmatists, realists, and pluralists were inviting social chaos

---

11. Lindsay, "Sovereignty," *Aristotelian Society Proceedings* (1924): 235–36, 248, 252–54.

12. William Yandell Elliott, "The Pragmatic Politics of Mr. H. J. Laski," *American Political Science Review* 18 (1924): 251. See also "The Metaphysics of Duguit's Pragmatic Conception of Law," *Political Science Quarterly* 37 (1922); "The Political Application of Romanticism," *Political Science Quarterly* 39 (1924); "Sovereign State or Sovereign Group?" *American Political Science Review* 19 (1925); "Mussolini, Prophet of the Pragmatic Era in Politics," *Political Science Quarterly* 41 (1926).

and were out of place "in so closely knit a unity as is formed in the modern state." Although Elliott claimed that pluralism was closely allied to syndicalism and such dangerous doctrines as those of Georges Sorel, his principal target at this point was Laski, and he characterized him, accurately, as not only following Barker's attack on the idea of the state but as a "disciple" of James and as an advocate of Dewey's experimentalism.[13] While ideological issues were involved in this emerging debate, the differences did not break neatly along these lines. What in part bothered Elliott were the implications of pluralism, and the methods attaching to its study, for sustaining the autonomy of both political science and its subject matter, for establishing the practical authority of the discipline, and for maintaining a special place for political theory within political science. These issues were, however, deeply entwined, and although he did not directly confront Merriam, the latter's position clearly represented much that agitated Elliott. In his review of the book edited by Merriam and Barnes in honor of Dunning, Elliott acknowledged that Merriam was "the dean of American theorists," but he questioned his use of the term "political theory" to refer to "the methodology of research" and found "the tone too largely sociological," and he was "astounded" by Merriam's suggestion that Bergsonianism and pragmatism had exercised little impact on the field's development. This, he claimed, was contradicted by the very content of the volume with all the references to Laski and other pluralists and socialists who were "pragmatic in the extreme."[14] It is important to stress once more, however, that Merriam was not the architect of the theory of pluralism, and despite their philosophical differences, the concerns of Merriam and Elliott were in many respects quite similar. They were both, in their own way, concerned about the existence of a democratic community and social solidarity.

With the publication of *New Aspects of Politics* (1925), it was evident that Merriam was leading the way in advocating an interdisciplinary approach in political science that would pay more attention to the "actual observation of political processes" and "political behavior." The purpose of this redistribution of emphasis was to achieve an "intelligent understanding of human behavior" that would both facilitate social control in an increasingly diverse society and combat the kind of "political fundamentalism" that led to a "suppression of liberty of speech or inquiry."[15] In his

13. Ibid., 275.

14. Elliott, review of *A History of Political Theories,* edited by Merriam and Barnes, *American Political Science Review* 19 (1925): 178–79.

15. Merriam, "Progress in Political Research," *American Political Science Review* 20 (1926): 2, 3, 7, 12; *New Aspects of Politics* (Chicago: University of Chicago Press, 1925).

approving review of *New Aspects,* Gettell emphasized the practical purpose of such a science and noted that "in a democracy in which public opinion is supposed to shape governmental policy," there is a need for accurate information and trained leaders and administrators.[16] For Merriam, as well as for Lasswell and others who emerged from the Chicago School, the task of political science was in part to create a public opinion even if there was not a public, in order to provide a virtual surrogate for a community of the people that seemed to have dissolved along with the theory that posited it. This was the basis of Merriam's extensive involvement in revitalizing civic education, which, in turn, was closely allied with a more general Progressive concern with community-building through education, which depreciated individual participation in favor of social conformity.[17]

As the debate about pluralism began to take on a life of its own, Laski became little more than a symbol. Neither his arguments nor those of figures such as Figgis and Maitland upon whom he putatively relied had been very carefully analyzed in the literature, and by the time that he wrote *The Grammar of Politics* (1925), his own focus had shifted away from the critique of monism toward a still more Marxist-inspired challenge to "the liberal theory of the state"—by which he meant classical liberalism. While he continued to affirm much of the pluralist critique, he no longer believed that pluralism had sufficiently taken account of "the nature of the state as an expression of class-relations."[18] In this "more positive" work, Laski announced that "a new political philosophy is necessary to a new world." This book was a rejection of Benthamite and Hegelian attempts to find some unitary principle of politics and a plea, instead, for the pursuit of "realism" and an attempt to account for the way things did and should work under the complex conditions of modern society. He continued to attack traditional theories of sovereignty that implied that "unlimited and irresponsible" power was located in some organ. "In the theoretic sense . . . the United States has no sovereign organ," since power is shared among the branches and levels of government. But, to the surprise of some of his erstwhile critics, Laski now claimed that "the State is the keystone of the social arch." He was, however, basically talking about government. Although he spoke about the (capitalized) "State" as some kind of a whole and a "fellowship of men" and an "association," this was largely the conventional use of the term for distinguishing territorial, social, and legal

16. Gettell, review of *New Aspects of Politics,* by Merriam, *American Political Science Review* 20 (1926).

17. See Julie Reuben, "Beyond Politics: Community Civics and the Redefinition of Citizenship in the Progressive Era," *History of Education Quarterly* (1997).

18. Laski, *The Grammar of Politics* (London: George Allen and Unwin Ltd., 1925), iii, xi.

units. He stressed the "difference between State and Society," because, like Willoughby, he wished to demonstrate that the state was an instrument of society and responsible to the individuals and groups that composed it. In effect, "the will of the State is the will of government," and "a theory of the State . . . is essentially a theory of the governmental act," which views the State "in administrative terms." The state was not the embodiment of some mysterious will of the whole, but a "morally neutral" functional entity to be judged in a "purely pragmatic" manner in terms of its results. The "State is obviously a public service corporation." But he nevertheless asserted that it was necessary to "differentiate sharply between State and government," because, he claimed, "to define the function of the State is not to define the powers of government; it is to define only the purpose it is the end of government to secure" and to ensure that government is responsible to those it serves.[19] In Laski's formulation, the ambiguity surrounding the concept of the state persisted. It seemed, in the last analysis, to be identical with government, but the shadow of the earlier holistic image persisted.

Elliott was more sympathetic to this work, which, he claimed, represented a "new Laski" and was not only the first attempt of a pluralist "to state an adequate basis for political reconstruction," but "may well be the most important contribution that has been made to recent political theory."[20] For Elliott, pluralism was, at least theoretically, more dangerous than Marxism. Elliott's claim that the theory of democracy was in danger was bolstered somewhat by the lack of focus on the concept in the discourse of political science. Shepard noted that all trends were away from ideals and toward pragmatic judgments, and "democracy, the cardinal ideal of nineteenth-century politics, has well-nigh ceased to cast its spell."[21] But while much of the discussion centered on state sovereignty and the issue of the unity of sovereignty, the underlying concern was the status of popular sovereignty.

The changing image of the state was apparent in the work of R. M. MacIver, who, while seeking something of a middle way in the controversy, contributed to undermining many of the assumptions that were crucial to earlier state theory. MacIver argued that the "theory of the state has too long been dominated by the legislative conception of sovereignty" and that political thought today recognizes the "limited and relative character

19. Ibid., 9, 19, 21, 26, 28, 35, 37, 41, 49, 61, 69, 70.

20. Elliott, "An Ethics of Politics," *Political Science Quarterly* 41 (1926): 259.

21. Shepard, review of *The Moral Standards of Democracy,* by Henry Wilkes Wright, *American Political Science Review* 20 (1926).

of sovereignty." It was necessary, he argued, to look at the state as a product of "social evolution" with no "perfected form" and to understand that it is only "one of the organs of the community" and that "the great associations are as native to the soil of society as the state itself."[22] Exactly what he, as well as many others of this period, referred to as "the state itself" was not clear, but his point was that legal absolutism had no special status and that it was no different than the manner in which ecclesiastical law was dominant in its particular sphere. The state was essentially one of many social "corporations" and less the source of law than its guardian. MacIver claimed that behind the state was a society or the "community," which constituted the unity or "solidarity of men," but the state was only a limited agent. Yet even if it were in no special way the "home of man," it was more than the product of clashing associations and represented, especially in its democratic manifestation, the most extensive and fundamental type of membership and provided a "form of unity to the whole system of social relationships."[23] What MacIver had done, in effect, was to identify the state as government while retaining the original image of the state as a national community, and this kind of ambivalence would be common in this era of the dissolution of the old paradigm. MacIver was critical of William Ernest Hocking's analysis for failing to achieve a clear notion of the state in his attempt to find a resolution of the relationship between groups and the state,[24] despite Hocking's insistence on the need for a sense of an overriding identity in the polity, but MacIver's own formulation was still not satisfactory to Elliott. Elliott applauded MacIver for a "fine restatement of the basic concept of democracy" and for not confusing the state with society and with the national community of which the state is an agent, but he was correct in noting that MacIver did not make explicit how "the ultimate sovereign, the general will for the state, gears itself to the control of the legislative sovereign, or more simply, the government," and maintains control over social groups.[25]

Elliott was further agitated by the intrusion into the conversation of European theorists such as Roberto Michels, whose sociological analysis of political parties added both to the sense that political science lacked a distinctive identity and to the image of politics as an arena containing the

22. R. M. MacIver, *The Modern State* (London: Oxford University Press, 1926), 468, 475.

23. Ibid., 479, 482, 485–86.

24. MacIver, review of *Man and the State,* by William Ernest Hocking, *American Political Science Review* 21 (1927).

25. Elliott, review of *The Modern State,* by MacIver, *American Political Science Review* 21 (1927): 432–34.

struggle of groups for power. Michels claimed that "democracy is of a massive nature" in that parties contend for the support of the masses, while the masses need parties, and the elites that lead them, to articulate their interests.[26] The belief that the state possessed some distinct "ethical basis" was waning,[27] and this raised questions not only about democracy but also about the status of political science. Ellis argued that after attempting to extricate itself from "a supernatural or metaphysical theory" and from the field of law and a formal juristic analysis of the state, political science was now besieged by disciplines such as sociology, economics, and ethics. It was at a "crossroads" where it was necessary to ask the question, Was it any longer possible to "attempt to reestablish it as a distinctive discipline?"[28] The pluralist and sociological accounts of Krabbe, Duguit, Cole, and Laski, as well as the work of individuals such as Merriam and Barnes, might, she suggested, have attempted to reach the "realities" behind the idea of the state, but they also tended to eliminate any distinctive political reality or meaning of sovereignty. In her view, Willoughby did not adequately distinguish what she called "the political" and establish a perspective on the "purely political character of the state."[29] Not only did the theory of democracy appear in jeopardy, but the very essence of the subject matter of political science seemed to be elusive.

Although perhaps Willoughby had done more than anyone to empty the concept of the state of its original meaning, and despite his criticisms of Burgess and German philosophy, he was among those who criticized the position of Krabbe, Duguit, and Sabine. His principal concern, however, about the critique of sovereignty was once again that it threatened the identity and domain of political science and obscured the "fact" of legal sovereignty upon which much of political analysis was predicated. He also attacked the critics on the same grounds that he had criticized Burgess, that is, for failing to distinguish between legal and ethical validity—between fact and value or political science and politics. Although he concluded that Krabbe placed the state on a higher plane than Duguit, in that he viewed it as more than just embodied power, he claimed that Krabbe and his translators still failed to see the difference between the "state in

26. Roberto Michels, "Some Reflections on the Sociological Character of Political Parties," *American Political Science Review* 21 (1927).

27. See, for example, Coker's review of *The Ethical Basis of the State,* by Norman Wilde, *American Political Science Review* 21 (1927), in which Coker noted the difficulty in attempting to maintain a "monist" position and provide an argument for the superiority of the state among other institutions.

28. Ellis, "Political Science at the Crossroads," *American Political Science Review* 21 (1927): 773.

29. Ibid., 784.

which legal sovereignty inheres, and the governmental organs through which it operates."[30] Sabine, however, now at Ohio State, eventually explicitly defended Krabbe and argued that juristic formalism and the separation between ethics and law was too simple an approach for dealing with modern political developments. These concepts, he argued, were an arbitrary way of carving up the world, and the distinction between legal and ethical domains was not just a difference between two analytical points of view, but represented theories that had a history and rationale rooted in particular past political contexts. The idea of sovereignty emerged from a definite stage in the history of politics, and it might no longer fit modern political, or even legal, circumstances.[31]

Since pluralism as a distinct theory had not quite taken shape and since the basis of the old theory was no longer intact, the arguments, while directed toward each other, often did not quite connect. For example, just as most political scientists had a less than clear grasp of Laski's position, Laski had little sense of the difference between Willoughby and other American state theorists.[32] And although in all of this discussion Dewey was mentioned prominently, his work featured more as a touchstone than as a serious subject of analysis, and few seemed to grasp clearly his position on either science or politics.[33] Although Dewey continued to excoriate much of traditional state theory, in which the state was considered as the "keystone of the social arch" if not the arch itself, and the "intellectual ghosts" associated with it, his extended account of the place of the public in a democratic society in *The Public and its Problems* (1927) did not deviate significantly from the basic arguments of either Burgess or the Progressives. This work, maybe more than any other of the period, represented the crisis in democratic theory. What Dewey in effect did was to retain the core of the theory of the state while substituting a new philosophical foundation, and while he insisted that democracy required a real public, he was ambivalent about whether it was actually there, and merely required reawakening, or whether it had to be created.

Dewey rejected all general theories of the state, including not only the German or Hegelian types but also the claims that it was the site of class

30. Willoughby, "The Juristic Theories of Krabbe," *American Political Science Review* 20 (1926).

31. See Sabine, "Political Science and the Juristic Point of View," *American Political Science Review* 22 (1928).

32. Laski, review of *Fundamental Principles of Public Law*, by Willoughby, *Political Science Quarterly* 40 (1925).

33. For a careful analysis of Dewey's relationship to political science, see Farr, "John Dewey and American Political Science," *American Journal of Political Science* 52 (1990).

oppression, that it was only one among a plurality of associations and performed the function of arbitrating among interests, or that it served the minimalist function of preventing individuals from unduly harming each another. What Dewey rejected was any "archetypal" image of the state, that is, as a substantive universal that was manifest in particular instances in time and space. The state, according to Dewey, if understood "factually," was simply the "organized public." A public was defined functionally as simply the sum of all those affected by social interactions to the extent that the consequences required general attention, and a government consisted of the officials and institutions designated to deal with those consequences. While differing temporally and spatially, states evolved from human activity as a way of dealing with the necessarily transactional character of the relationship between individuals and the results of their acts. Although he insisted that the "government is not the state," he claimed that the "external mark" of a state was indeed the "existence of officials" and that a state could be evaluated in terms of the degree of its organization and the extent to which it cared for the "public interests" that gave rise to its existence. A state was, in short, an integral combination of a public and a government. With respect to the thorny issue of the relationship between government, state, and society, Dewey seemed to be caught in the same conceptual quandary as his predecessors, also insisting that they were both identical and different. His solution, however, was to view them in functional and analytical terms with no a priori lines of demarcation. The government was not the state, he claimed, because the state included the public, of which the government (officials and institutions) were the representation. The public was the preeminent human association, because it included all those who were affected by transactions that had general consequences and involved interests shared by all. When it added political organization (government), the "public is a political state." This was, on the surface, the same argument made by the nineteenth-century theorists, but the crucial difference was that Dewey insisted that the state was not an entity with "will" and "reason," but rather the name for a kind of thing that emerged when human life became complex and required the performance of certain functions.

Since Dewey maintained that a state was inclusive of other associations, there was, he acknowledged, a certain affinity between his views and that of the "pluralistic conception of the state," but he stressed that his doctrine was not one that "prescribes inherent limits to state action."[34] In fact,

34. Dewey, *The Public and its Problems* (1927; reprint, Athens: Swallow Press, 1954), 8, 26, 33, 78.

it was quite clear that his goal was to expand those limits. Much like Burgess, Dewey claimed "that not until recently have publics been conscious that they were publics," and thus "states are a recent development" and democratic states a yet more modern form. Dewey stressed the ontological primacy of individuals, but viewed the public as something that comes into existence at a certain stage in the evolution of society and democracy as an aspect of that development involving the public becoming consciousness of itself and doing such things as electing officials. But, he argued, the conditions and "forces" of contemporary society that brought about the characteristics of the democratic state also inhibited "the social and humane ideals that demand the utilization of government as the genuine instrumentality of an inclusive and fraternally associated public."

The "new age," Dewey argued, did not yet have "political agencies worthy of it," and "the Great Society created by steam and electricity may be a society, but it is not community." A truly "democratic public is still largely inchoate and unorganized."[35] While originally the "American democratic polity was developed out of genuine community life," the contemporary national state had not achieved a comparable community, and thus there had been an "eclipse of the public." While community might still exist at the local level, the contemporary national continental state went far beyond the New England town meeting and required a public of commensurate magnitude. The "Babel" of signs and symbols that made shared experience impossible must be overcome by science and education. Dewey concurred with Lippmann's assessment, and claimed that the public was either "lost" or "bewildered," and neither philosophers nor political actors had been able to find it. What had taken its place, he argued, were pressure groups, parties, and other "factions" that had left the public "so confused and eclipsed that it cannot even use the organs through which it is supposed to mediate political action and polity." The relationships between individuals and between groups required constant adjustment, and in order to create a "genuine" democracy, a moral dimension with the appropriate "habits" and symbols must be added to the physical foundation of society. Since the public had become "diffused and scattered," and the role of citizens had been displaced by the narrower concerns of group interest, Dewey suggested that modern communication and science, and especially social science "experts," were the answer to reconstituting a public by creating, sustaining, and controlling a genuine and knowledgeable public opinion. But "till the Great Society is converted into the

35. Ibid., 77, 98, 109.

Great Community, the Public will remain in eclipse" and democracy would remain unrealized.[36]

What Dewey did was to begin with a functional definition of the public, but in the end he transformed it into a substantive and self-conscious community nearly indistinguishable from the "archetypal" entity he had criticized. Given this emphasis on the public and community, it was in some respects strange that Dewey was chosen as one of Elliott's principal targets, but Elliott did perceive the underlying affinity between pluralism and the kind of empiricism and experimentalism championed by Dewey and Merriam. If the stuff of politics and government, and even democracy, was in fact groups, and if sovereignty was fungible, then it was necessary to account empirically for the existence of these phenomena and the character of their activity. Democratic theory and an empirical science of politics seemed inseparable, and this was a conclusion that would emerge in much more articulate form as the theory of pluralism evolved. Furthermore, if the domain of political science was not substantively identifiable and universal, as theorists of the state had deemed it to be despite its invisibility, it was necessary, as even Willoughby emphasized, to carve out analytically what class of empirical phenomena was political. There was also a connection between scientific experimentalism and the ideology of liberal interventionism, since the lack of a definable and self-conscious public seemed to invite and require action from the top, and to assume many of the characteristics of plurality.

Another Dewey, the political scientist A. Gordon Dewey, offered an extended examination of this emerging congruence between social scientific methods and group theory. He presented a Bentleyan analysis of politics as a relationship between pressure groups and government and defended an inductive factual study of such phenomena. Since public opinion was not something that was simply there to be "discovered" but was "made," and since it existed not as a "homogeneous mass" but as a "heterogeneous complex of ingredients," systematic empirical methods of inquiry were required.[37] This kind of argument was pursued at length by Stuart A. Rice, who claimed that "politics and sociology must be made behavioristic" and must employ quantitative methods, which could reach the "intangible subjective elements of political activity," that is, the "purposes and attitudes" that were represented in the "conduct" of political groups and individuals. In a yet more methodological vein, Stuart Rice's

36. Ibid., 111, 113, 116–17, 121, 137, 142.
37. A. Gordon Dewey, "On Methods in the Study of Politics I," *Political Science Quarterly* 38 (1923): 65; "On Methods in the Study of Politics II," *Political Science Quarterly* 39 (1924).

influential book *Quantitative Methods in Politics* was published in 1928. Rice had studied under Giddings, and he viewed politics as part of group life in general and within the province of sociology—a position that, on all counts, irritated Elliott.[38]

The two most articulate interlocutors in the conversation about the connection between pluralism as an account of social reality and the nature of political science were Elliott and G. E. G. Catlin. Catlin attended Oxford before and after World War I, but both his politics and his devotion to a view of science such as that of Wallas (who he counted as his mentor), led him, despite the offer of a scholarship, to flee the "rules and judgments" of that "academic cloister" and head for the United States. Although he was offered opportunities at Harvard and Minnesota, he accepted a faculty position at Cornell, where he also wrote a dissertation (which was published as *The Science and Method of Politics*) and remained for a decade before returning to England. He found in America, in the company of individuals such as Merriam, Lasswell, and Beard, the kind of dedication to a *"scienza nuova"* with a practical end that he sought, and he viewed Bentley as nothing less than "a veritable Grandma Moses of American political science." In his autobiography, he noted that "we found political science a chaos. We left it tidied up," and along "with the Pluralists, we deposed the sovereign national state to the study of the politics of Society itself."[39]

Catlin declared that "politics is concerned with a field of human behavior characterized by the recurrences of specific behavior patterns," particularly group processes, which can be defined psychologically and measured by various quantitative and statistical means.[40] He applauded the pluralist position and its attack on the "absolute state" as well as its embrace of factual realism, but like Willoughby, he complained that it was still an "ethical philosophy," which treated politics from a "liberal" perspective, rather than a "dispassionate study of actual human behavior." Although he wished to hold to pluralism as an empirical claim rather than a normative theory, he left no doubt that the purpose of social science was social control just as the purpose of natural science was control over nature, and he clung to the inherent logical and practical complementarity of science and democracy. He argued, however, that it was first necessary, as in the relationship between biology and medicine, to find some "basal principles of

---

38. Stuart A. Rice, "The Behavior of Legislative Groups," *Political Science Quarterly* 40 (1925): 60.

39. George E. G. Catlin, *For God's Sake, Go!* (Gerrards Cross: Colin Smythe, 1972), 27, 54, 58, 60, 66.

40. Catlin, "The Delimitation and Measurabililty of Political Phenomena," *American Political Science Review* 21 (1927): 255.

political method" and establish "a behaviorist science of politics" that would allow sound diagnosis of political problems and administrative and legislative treatment.[41] History, Catlin concluded, "is not and never can be a science," but "it provides the data of the social sciences," which must be subjected to measurement and quantification and analyzed according to the deductive method. The historian may have critical impact, but "social therapy is not his affair." The latter is the responsibility of the political scientist, but at present, he asserted, political science, unfortunately, was only "a barren name." It was necessary to "go back to Aristotle" and imitate his approach by creating a comprehensive science with a distinct method based on empirical observation and generalization.[42] Catlin was a far more philosophically grounded spokesman than Merriam, and his work exemplified the manner in which the commitment to science and the commitment to social control and democratic values were two sides of the same coin.

Catlin's model among the social sciences was economics, and much like the rational choice theorists of "positive" political science in later years, he wanted to find the identity of political science by constructing abstract fictions called the "political man" (the power seeker) and the "political situation" (competing wills) that would lend themselves to a hypothetical, predictive, deterministic and causal, experimental science that derived data from history, form from economics, and substance from psychology.[43] Except for the work of Laski, Catlin was largely dismissive of most trends in political theory. He castigated Hegelianism, Comtean positivism and its philosophy of history, *Staatslehre* and its residue, and the inadequate scientific basis of Progressive tracts such as that of Lippmann.[44] It was now time, he claimed, for political science to carve out its domain among the social sciences, develop a theoretical structure to define and explore it, and put science in the service of democracy. This was the kind of program that had been advanced by Merriam, and Lasswell summed it up when he stated that "democracy has proclaimed the dictatorship of palaver, and the technique of dictating to the dictator is named propaganda."[45] A. Gordon Dewey's review of Catlin's book recognized how his methodological argument changed the focus of political science from an association such as the state to the group behavior of individuals.[46]

41. Catlin, *The Science and Method of Politics* (New York: Alfred A. Knopf, 1927), x–xi, 284, 295.

42. Ibid., 75, 81, 84–85.

43. Ibid., 93, 200–205.

44. Ibid., 143.

45. Harold D. Lasswell, "The Theory of Political Propaganda," *American Political Science Review* 21 (1927): 631.

46. A. Gordon Dewey, review of *The Science and Method of Politics,* by Catlin, *Political Science Quarterly* 42 (1927).

Merriam had placed his hope for the future progress of political science in the work of people such as Beard, "our distinguished colleague, the Connecticut Farmer," who was "still young." And Beard, after stepping away from academia following the turmoil at Columbia, did return in 1927 to become president of the APSA. Although he presented one of the most critical assessments of the discipline's capacity for creatively engaging contemporary issues, he did not really enter the debate about pluralism.[47] His early work added momentum to the pluralist persuasion, but in a review of Catlin's book he concluded that if Catlin were correct, "then darkness enshrouds all those who labor under the impression that politics is fundamentally concerned with the state and government."[48]

An article in the 1927 issue of the *APSR* was devoted to a long historical overview of the issues at heart of the controversy about pluralism. The author attempted to demonstrate that the contemporary debate was yet another engagement of the old questions about the relationship between de facto and de jure sovereignty and the relationship between political and ethical judgments. He argued that while there had always been a search for an overriding theory of social unity, both states and elements within the state had demanded a certain autonomy and recognition of their interests.[49] This was a reasonable assessment, but it failed to grasp the extent to which this was a new debate even if it resonated with the terms of former controversies. Pivoting on an essay by the Harvard historian C. H. McIlwain that distinguished between legal and political sovereignty, John Dickinson, an assistant professor at Princeton and ancestor and namesake of the revolutionary hero and author (*Letters from a Pennsylvania Farmer*), entered the conversation in a decisive manner.

Dickinson, specializing in law and political theory, agreed with Willoughby that while the formal or juristic idea of the state was essential to thinking about any particular political regime, it had been a longstanding mistake to seek some particular entity, whether an element of the government or an entity called the people, in which sovereignty was located as well as to project the idea of sovereignty into the sphere of international relations. The contemporary attack on sovereignty had served, he argued, to demonstrate that "it is not something in the nature of things." In his view, even Laski had not gone far enough in rejecting the traditional theory of sovereignty, since he held on to the concept even while claiming,

47. Merriam, "Progress in Political Research," *New Aspects of Politics*; Beard, "Time, Technology, and the Creative Spirit," *American Political Science Review* 21 (1927).

48. Beard, review of *Science and Method of Politics*, by Catlin, *American Political Science Review* 21 (1927): 653.

49. William Orton, "Social Theory and the Principium Unitatus," *American Political Science Review* 21 (1927).

illogically, that it could be divided. And while, despite Bentley's intima-
tion to the contrary, law was more than "interest-group facts," it was
important to distinguish between positive law and the "facts" of political
sovereignty. What lay behind legal sovereignty was always a manifold of
social, economic, and moral forces, and "government, if it performs its
function, is simply a great central coordinating agency" for "adjusting the
contrary aims and interests of competing groups and individuals."[50] Within
a short time, Dickinson would represent one of the most important voices
in articulating pluralist theory, but the most pointed critic continued to
be Elliott.

Elliott perceived a crisis when a president of the APSA could jettison
"traditional democratic theories" as unnecessary constraints on science and
the art of government, when a philosopher could treat equality as a pragmatic fiction, and when discussions of American democracy were increasingly "removed from the blood and sweat of any arena, political or other."[51]
The presidential address to which he referred was that of William Bennett
Munro. Munro had recently moved to the California Institute of Technology
after many years as chair of the Division of History, Government, and
Economics at Harvard, and he had recently brought together several of his
lectures challenging the traditional idea of popular sovereignty and other
concepts associated with democracy. He claimed that "all governments . . .
are subject to the pressures of invisible influences." What may in part have
agitated Elliott was that Munro was one of several political scientists during this period who had made favorable comments about fascist government, and however conservative one might construe Elliott to have been,
he was not sympathetic to the kind of authoritarianism that was emerging in Europe and Russia. Munro, invoking a version of Walter Bagehot's
nineteenth-century analogy between physics and politics, argued that just
as the study and subject matter of physics had changed since Bagehot's
book had been written (now embracing quantum mechanics and relativity), so had the conception of politics. Yet political science continued to
speak in the language of an old conception of political reality, which
included terms such as sovereignty, absolute rights, and the individual.
Just as physics had sought a reality deeper than the atom, it was time for
political science, if it were to explain politics and gain control over such
matters as civic education, to give up the "atomic theory" of politics and
look to the "imponderables" that constituted "invisible government" and

50. John Dickinson, "A Working Theory of Sovereignty," *Political Science Quarterly* 42 (1927);
"A Working Theory of Sovereignty II," *Political Science Quarterly* 43 (1928): 32, 42.

51. Elliott, review of *Democratic Distinction in American,* by W. C. Brownell, and *The American
Philosophy of Equality,* by T. V. Smith, *American Political Science Review* 22 (1928): 461.

to the underlying forces that determined individual action. For Munro, this entailed turning away from both juristic approaches and psychology and focusing on the "realities" of group life, since the basic problem of politics was "maintaining a fair balance between the groups to which individuals belong."[52]

Elliott finally brought together his strictures against "the pragmatic revolt in politics" and attacked both the empirical and normative versions of pluralism. Part of this less than well organized work had been written as a doctoral thesis just after World War I, but it incorporated later articles and reviews. The work as a whole lagged behind the main conversation about pluralism, but it reflected the continuing worries that surrounded the theory. The book was dedicated to Lindsay, to whom Elliott, in part through exposure to Kant and T. H. Green, attributed the most significant intellectual influence. Elliott designated Laski as his "greatest stimulant," who he still perceived as the principal formulator of pluralist theory, but Elliott, and the conversation about pluralism, had now moved beyond the views of Lindsay and Laski.

The latter individuals had recently crossed paths in a symposium on Bosanquet, in which the differences between them ultimately seemed negligible. Lindsay noted that it was ideas such as Bosanquet's theory of the general will that had prompted Hobhouse's attack on the *Metaphysical Theory of the State* as well as MacIver's critique of the idea of the state as a person, and he once again pointed out both the confusion involved in attempting to oppose such an idea to Austin's theory of sovereignty and how both theories were rooted in an obsolete model. He claimed that Austin's theory did, however, represent the juristic dimension of the state, and Bosanquet's argument, like that of Rousseau, did reflect the fact that the state was a kind of association that was neither a contract nor a product of instrumental reason, that in some basic way reflected the "moral life of society." Lindsay suggested that Bosanquet, as well as the authors of similar nineteenth-century images of the state, represented attempts to validate democracy (e.g., that Bosanquet had called Plato a democrat), but that these organic theories did not literally fit the modern state even though "we are becoming increasingly to recognize that democracy can be made a reality on a large scale" and that the individual can be viewed as part of a larger whole.[53] Laski largely accepted Lindsay's discussion of Bosanquet and seemed reluctant to challenge the "master of Balliol," but

52. William Bennett Munro, *The Invisible Government* (New York: Macmillan, 1928), 1; "Physics and Politics—An Old Analogy Revisited," *American Political Science Review* 22 (1928): 5, 7.

53. Lindsay and Laski, "Symposium: Bosanquet's Theory of the General Will," *Aristotelian Society Proceedings* 8, supplementary volume (1928): 39–40, 44.

although he did not deny that the state was "the great coordinating organ of society," he noted that it still "appears as a government issuing orders" and remains a fallible thing that did not represent any actual "common will" or "common good," but only the sum of competition between individuals. Such commonness was simply a function of fairness. He did not reject Lindsay's claim that there was something that could reasonably, by some functional criteria, be called the "common life" or "unity" of society, just as one could speak of international relations as a whole; but a national society, like the international sphere, was "not a One, but a Many," which was a "collection of men and women," and it did not become a one comparable to an individual because of the existence of the state qua government.[54]

Although Elliott was far removed from the ontology of someone such as Burgess, he could not visualize democracy without some sense of organic unity or commonality. Yet, quite differently from Lindsay, his work continued to represent an American professional and disciplinary concern. His book in many respects resembled works written a generation later attacking scientism and pluralist liberalism in mainstream political science— albeit often from a different ideological perspective. Elliott's opus made it clearer than ever that in his view the problem was not only that the pluralist vision of political reality threatened democracy, but that jettisoning the very idea of a distinct and autonomous political domain threatened the identity of political theory and the authority of political inquiry in general and that seeking the authority of the discipline in scientific method rather than the integrity of its subject matter was insufficient. Elliott argued that there was, "in practice as well as theory," a "modern tendency away from the dominance of rationalism in politics." This "revolt against political rationalism" was manifest in the contemporary attacks on "the constitutional and democratic state" in Europe by both "Capitalistic Fascism" and by the syndicalist and communist left wing of the Marxist movement. He claimed that the philosophy behind these attacks, which "gives them their ideology and their values," was pragmatism, but this was, ironically, basically an American intellectual product despite its tangential appearance in the work of individuals such as Sorel and Mussolini. Although such events as World War I and its aftermath and the "development of modern capitalistic industrialism" had undoubtedly created strains, a concerted critique of the foundations of liberal democracy had, in Elliott's view, been mounted. Part of what made pragmatism so dangerous, he claimed, more so than the dogmas of bolshevism, was that it

54. Ibid., 48, 50, 54, 57.

was so totally "skeptical of absolutes" and thereby threatened to undermine both political philosophy and political practice as well as possibilities for their conjunction.[55]

The political attack on state authority was, Elliott argued, a pervasive
one that was in evidence everywhere—from labor unions, dictatorships of
the left and right, and those seeking a world-state. While syndicalism
sought to discredit the state, fascism, in reaction, aimed at creating an
excessively and repressively organic one. Both, through instruments of force
and violence, subverted law, public discussion, the franchise, and other
characteristics of liberal constitutional society. Contemporary political science, however, had failed to discern what was happening, in part because
it was itself infused with pragmatism and focused on scientific descriptive
studies that made it increasingly politically irrelevant.[56] Elliott once again
directly attributed this revolt against the constitutional state, which had
now, he argued, reached "alarming proportions," to the philosophies of
James and John Dewey. As a consequence of their influence, "mainstream
American political science" had become "behavioristic in terms of psychology and positivistic in terms of philosophy." The result was that philosophy and political practice had become disassociated as scientists joined
politicians in an attitude of "pragmatic skepticism." Pragmatism, in the
narrow sense, had gained a strong hold on academic life, but it also represented a more general world-historical anti-intellectual trend that was
reflected in the theoretical "revolt against the sovereignty of the personal-
ized state and against parliamentarianism," which was manifest in a wide
variety of ideas including the "more chastened pluralism" of Laski, Duguit's
theory of *droit objectif,* and the "Fascist 'efficiency' gospel of Mussolini."

This repudiation of the state as "a moral agent and legal overlord" was,
according to Elliott, the result of a long intellectual decline that reached
from post-Kantian philosophy and the age of reason to Dewey and James.
The latter's ideas had infiltrated political practice and informed the "group
theory of the state." Despite their different practical manifestations, pluralism and fascism rested on the same intellectual foundation. It was the
idea of the "reality of group selves" that "forms the rock upon which
Idealism and pragmatism have alike gone aground with their ships of
state." While the former went to extremes with the notion of group
"unity," the other denied it altogether. Pragmatism treated all groups

---

55. Elliott, *The Pragmatic Revolt in Politics: Syndicalism, Fascism, and the Constitutional State* (New
York: Macmillan, 1928), viii.

56. Ibid., 4–5.

except the state as moral persons, and this led to an instrumentalist and functional attitude that eventually "re-enthroned" the state as a necessity and produced fascism. Elliott claimed that the pragmatic philosophy was visible in various aspects of what was called "modernism"—whether in education or politics. The traditional theory of the state had been dismissed as not fitting the facts—and the putative facts were groups. "The life of certain groups within the state, notably trade unions and professional associations, has become a more real thing in men's experience than the common political life represented by the state." According to Elliott, philosophical rationalism and the idea of state sovereignty were mutually entailed in that both emphasized the priority of an organizing reason over diverse parts, while pragmatism stressed instinct, will, and plurality. "If Hegel was the apologist of Prussianism, Duguit is not less that of Fascism."[57]

Although Elliott conceded that pragmatism made a reasonable point when it challenged Hegelian philosophical absolutism and idealism, it went too far. Its "anti-intellectualistic pluralism begins with individualism, goes through groups, and culminates in force as an abstract power in the organically absolute state of Fascist theory." When this philosophy was put into practice, it became, he claimed, "the mother of a brood of revolutionary theories" and provided no normative standards. Elliott argued that "constitutional government," on the other hand, represented the "same effort at political synthesis that conceptual logic does for thought synthesis. It must shun alike pluralism and absolutism" while providing an ideal and an "accepted rule fixing political responsibility." Such a political system provided, he claimed, a kind of unity that inhibited both the centrifugal forces of pluralism and the centripetal forces of dictatorship, while at the same time creating a kind of moral whole and a community of purpose in which popular sovereignty becomes a "reality." Elliott was not advocating a return to the Austinian view of sovereignty or to Hegelian images of universality, but he argued that such a juristic concept, even if something of a fiction, was a necessary part of the idea of constitutional government. Those such as Laski who had discredited the idea of the state had, Elliott claimed, moved in the direction of positing sovereign groups that raised the threat of corporatism and elevated, for example, freedom of religious sects above community interest.[58]

The ideological implications of this argument could, in principle, be variable, but Elliott, echoing earlier American theorists of the state, wished

57. Ibid., 31–32, 40, 43.
58. Ibid., 64, 75.

to stress that the federal government possessed only a limited or delegated sovereignty. The institution of government was the "creature of the political community" and the representative of "the federal state created by the Constitution." Elliott, influenced by Carl Friedrich, his German émigré colleague at Harvard, fell into the increasingly common belief that while other countries were abandoning liberalism and representative institutions, "the new Germany seems steadfast in its practice of parliamentary government under the benign moderation of Hindenburg." Although he could not accept the claim of Carl Schmitt, the German legal theorist who became a principal Nazi apologist, regarding the deficiencies of parliamentary decision-making, he sympathized with Schmitt's essentializing of "the political" and his attack on pluralist liberalism, and he saw much of what Schmitt called modern political romanticism in pluralist thought. and practice, especially in the work of Sorel, who, Elliott claimed, romanticized American life and its propensity for violence. He recounted at some length his experience as a young army officer at the May First demonstration in Paris in 1919, which represented for him the loss of reason and order and the type of anarchy out of which fascism emerged. Elliott was not simply an ideologue of conservative interests and an advocate of non-interventionist government. His concern was the loss of state authority, which he believed was manifest not only in the activity of labor unions but in events such as the surrender of Sid Hatfield to Baldwin-Felts detectives during the West Virginia coal mine battles. What Elliott found in all these varieties of pluralism was the "sublimation" of the political realm in subpolitical groups and the loss of any distinct idea of a political community. The alternative that he envisioned was a return to the tradition of liberalism represented by Green and by more recent works such as Norman Wilde's *The Ethical Basis of the State* (1924), which called for a "community of purpose" that stood above particular associations, an idea that sounded much like the claims of Croly. This image of political authority might, he admitted, be to some degree a "mythos," but it was a barrier to fascism. Pluralists, in their dismissal of anything approximating a general will and a political community in favor of force and habit, surrendered any such ground, and by positing groups as political reality, they provided "an apology for the Fascist ideal of a 'disciplined' national organism." While pluralists saw the state as government, and government as merely an instrument of group interest, Elliott insisted that the "constitutional state . . . is the political community" whose purpose and will was expressed in law.[59]

59. Ibid., 106–7, 247, 250, 298, 315.

For Elliott, the basic problem of "modern political theory" was the question of what authority was to be permitted to "voluntary associations," and his answer was to make political authority paramount without at the same time creating a "super-organism." His positive alternative was what he called a "co-organic," as opposed to an organic, theory of groups, and this in some respects resembled Lieber's image of institutional liberty as well as the ideas of Follett—and even formulations such as that of Croly. It recognized that a group consisted of an organic, largely economic, instrumental consensus, but was also properly identified in terms of a defining moral purposive consensus of individuals who, in the case of the political association or the state as a group, were the subject of political science. He claimed that the co-organic type of political association was historically manifest in the Anglo-American constitutional state and that both pluralism and fascism were aberrations. Coolidge's action in the handling of the Boston police strike, the issue over which Harvard University had sent Laski packing, seemed to Elliott an appropriate example of the co-organic constitutional state in action.[60] Elliott was not the only one who suggested that James was one of the "mentors" of Mussolini, and that this was evident in the manner in which he switched from left to right in following the "will to power,"[61] but even those such as MacIver—who proclaimed that Elliott "comes to redeem the long-continued neglect of political philosophy in the United States" and provide a much needed defense of democracy and constitutionalism—found this claim a bit over the top.[62]

Despite the intellectual distance between them, Catlin's response to Elliott's polemic was mild. This was in part because they were, in the end, united, as Americans would be during the next decade, in an increasing perception that whatever exactly constituted liberal democracy, it was present in the United States and largely on shaky grounds elsewhere in the world. Catlin claimed that Elliott's work was "indubitably the book of the year in political theory" and an important exposition of the "new liberalism"—which would actually be welcomed by those wishing a defense of the "old liberalism" with its emphasis on idealism and statism. Catlin suggested that Elliott stood to Laski like T. H. Green to Mill.[63] He did, how-

60. Ibid., 423.

61. William Kilborne Stuart, "The Mentors of Mussolini," *American Political Science Review* 22 (1928).

62. MacIver, review of *The Pragmatic Revolt in Politics,* by Elliott, *American Political Science Review* 23 (1929).

63. Catlin, review of *The Pragmatic Revolt in Politics,* by Elliott, *Political Science Quarterly* 44 (1929): 259.

ever, take serious issue with the notion that Mussolini could be best under-stood as a pragmatist, since, according to Catlin, he appeared closer to a Platonist. He argued that it was in fact the kind of idealist philosophy espoused by Elliott that threatened individual rights by its insistence that the "state is the good, the beautiful, and the true." Nationalism, Catlin claimed, was "one of the most dangerous social poisons of our age" and a danger to the rule of law and constitutional morality, and in this respect Elliott was "on the side of Mussolini." For Catlin, internationalism and respect for local rights offered a better hope.[64] Although he agreed with Elliott that "facts" did not yield norms, he maintained that knowledge of facts explains norms and illuminates what is possible for human purpose. Maybe, he suggested, his differences with Elliott rested "upon an irre-solvable diversity of aesthetic judgment on values," but he was pleased to note that Elliott also insisted on the difference between "scientific and poetical," or sociological and ethical, aspects of politics.[65] Harold Lasswell, while also obviously in disagreement with Elliott, reviewed the book cau-tiously and suggested that because it broadened the perspectives of stu-dents of government, it should be "welcomed with enthusiasm."[66]

In 1927, a book written as a dissertation at Cornell undertook a criti-cal survey and summary of the variety of literature associated with plural-ist theory, which it defined as an attack on the concept of the state and juristic monism. This work, like that of Ellis, contributed to making the controversy a distinct object of conversation, but despite its sympathy with the older perspective, Elliott suggested that the book took too broad a view of pluralism and suffered from the adoption of a Hegelian perspective. Ellis also suggested that maybe it went too far.[67] By this point, however, the principal conversation about pluralism was veering away from the kinds of arguments represented by Laski and Elliott. Political scientists were beginning to pay detailed attention to the action and ideas of pressure groups, and pluralism as an empirical thesis was taking more distinct form.[68] Although Laski's term "pluralism" was being applied, it now had little to do with the general context of Laski's concept and argument, and .

64. Ibid., 261, 263.
65. Ibid., 260, 265.
66. Lasswell, review of *The Pragmatic Revolt in Politics,* by Elliott, *American Journal of Sociology* 35 (1929–30): 134–35.
67. K. C. Hsiao, *Political Pluralism: A Study in Contemporary Political Theory* (New York: Harcourt Brace, 1927; Elliott, review of *Political Pluralism,* by Hsaio, *Political Science Quarterly* 44 (1929); Ellis, review of *Political Pluralism,* by Hsaio, *American Political Science Review* 22 (1928).
68. See, for example, E. E. Cummins, "The Political and Social Philosophy of the Carpenter's Union," *Political Science Quarterly* 42 (1927).

a new normative theory of pluralism was beginning to take shape in the work of individuals such as Dickinson.

The first major study in political science that can be construed as representing the new pluralism, or what might be called the group theory of politics, was Odegard's account of the activity of the Anti-Saloon League. As one reviewer noted, this would appeal to "the pluralist tracking down the activity of interest-groups."[69] Odegard had applauded Frank Kent's popularized account of politics as group competition. Although he concluded that it was not as thorough as the work of Ostrogorski, as penetrating as Bentley, or as profound as Michels, it was "too good to miss" and a contribution to the new emphasis on the realities of politics.[70] It was, however, Pendelton Herring who, in his book on groups and Congress, took the most decisive step in articulating the empirical thesis. Herring did not actually use the term "pluralism" in the original edition, but in a 1967 reissue, at the height of the behavioral era, he claimed "the strong infrastructure provided by well-organized groups makes a pluralistic society a reality and a representative system of government meaningful."[71] He noted that the Progressive movement had seen special interests as bad and had looked to a "somewhat disembodied public opinion and nebulous public interest." It was against this background and the intellectual context of the 1920s debate between statism and pluralism that he had written the book, originally his dissertation, while he was a graduate student at Hopkins. Willoughby was the director, and Elliott, reading the work in typescript, paved the way for Herring's position at Harvard. What this may indicate is that while Willoughby and Elliott were unrelenting critics of pluralism in the work of Laski, Duguit, and others, they did not fully recognize it in its new form. And at Harvard, Herring would be far more comfortable with Elliott than with Friedrich, to whom students referred as the other "eagle" of constitutionalism. Herring admitted that his acquaintance with Bentley's work had been very minimal. Although he viewed his own study as basically a descriptive account of an aspect of how "groups, active, coherent, organized, are rising to place of increased importance in the community," he claimed "the full significance of such a movement must be left to the political theorist and the public."[72] There was no

---

69. Paul Lewinson, review of *The Story of the Anti-Saloon League*, by Odegard, *American Political Science Review* 22 (1928).

70. Odegard, review of *Political Behavior*, by Frank R. Kent, *American Political Science Review* 23 (1929).

71. Pendelton Herring, *Group Representation Before Congress* (New York: Russell and Russell, 1929), xi.

72. Ibid., xvii.

explicit statement that this was intended to be a contribution to a new theory of democracy, but Herring did not altogether neglect the normative implications. What he was studying through his account of the recent expansion of groups and their activity was, he suggested, nothing less than recent developments in "national representation," a new dimension of the accepted idea of representation, and the key issue of how "public opinion" is expressed in a democratic society. He noted that Laski and others had seen in group life a new basis of democracy and a more representative and efficient form of government, and that it involved something more immediate to the individual and a new source of meaning and expression as well as a new form of representation and contribution to popular government.

Odegard also had initially largely avoided discussion of the implications of his study for democratic theory, but in a review of Herring's book he took the opportunity to claim that what was demonstrated was that as a society we "are organized" and "are not only political animals in the Aristotelian sense, we are factional animals as well." What American, he asked, does not belong to an organized group? And, he claimed, from the perspective of the political scientist, "the individual no longer counts." Politics was the activity in which group engagement takes place, and although "we may bewail this prevailing pluralism and cry out for the 'good old days' when America was not an organocracy, when there was an 'American people' equal under universal suffrage animated by a national consciousness," the fact was that "since the beginning of history we have been governed by groups," and "public opinion in any other sense than organized group opinion remains a phantom." This, however, he claimed, was a "healthy democratic development."[73] Within a short time, Odegard concluded that traditional parties could not adequately represent the public and that it was pressure groups that aided in performing this function. "It is through such organizations that the ordinary citizen finds true representation."[74] And by this point Lindsay had come around to a still more pluralistic image of the "essentials" of democracy, one that seemed far removed from Elliott's position regarding voluntary associations and the state.

Lindsay argued that the basic "purpose of democratic machinery is to represent differences" and that this required "a society of democratic nonpolitical associations." Formal politics, he suggested, was "a secondary matter" in which the role of the state was basically to take care of a "common

---

73. Odegard, review of *Group Representation Before Congress,* by Herring, *American Political Science Review* 23 (1929).

74. Odegard, *The American Public Mind* (New York: Columbia University Press, 1930), 168.

life" rooted in "voluntary non-political activities." The "essentials" of
democracy were not based on some "dogma," but consisted of "toleration
and recognition of differences," which allowed the kind of discussion that
sprung from "innumerable voluntary associations of all kinds which exist
in modern democratic society." He insisted that such discussion, however,
produced "a real unity of purpose out of differences," which in turn provided a kind of background consensus or "spirit of the whole" that placed
limits on difference. He noted that "in actual fact politics tends to be a
dirty business" involving interest and power and that the state was an
instrument of power and coercion, but ultimately "the best society is that
which increases spontaneity and life and variety; and that is not primarily
done by the state but by all this rich complexity of voluntary associations."
The role of the state was one of regulation and adjustment. The task, he
concluded, was to make our "non-political associations really democratic,"
since they were the training ground of citizenship.[75] Although written by
an English don, this was a précis of what was emerging as the pluralist
theory of liberal democracy in the United States.

By 1929, one political scientist noted that "we find ourselves . . . in a
difficult and very perplexing situation. During the past twenty-five years
every assumption of political theory, of the claims of democracy, of limitations on government, even of the right of the state to be, has been challenged," and there seem to be no "universally valid dogmas."[76] In
retrospect, it is clear that a new conception of politics and democracy was
in fact coming into place, and among the social sciences it was not only
psychology and sociology that gave theoretical support to the new paradigm. Robert H. Lowie's *The Origin of the State* (1927), which took its cue
from MacIver's *Community,* was noted as "anthropology's first avowed contribution to political theory and history," dealing "by direct implication
with all the issues raised for political theory by pluralism."[77] This was most
evident in the work of Dickinson, who, more than anyone else of this
period, provided an extended and theoretically integrated grounding for
both the empirical and normative dimensions of the new vision as well as
for their conjunction.

Drawing upon diverse anthropological sources and, in various ways, on
such different figures as Dewey, Willoughby, Simmel, and Gierke, Dickinson,

75. Lindsay, *The Essentials of Democracy* (Oxford: Clarendon Press, 1929), 1,8, 34, 37, 42–43,
46–47, 70, 72–74.

76. Jesse S. Reeves, "Perspectives in Political Science 1903–1928," *American Political Science
Review* 23 (1929): 10.

77. Paul Lewinson, review of *The Origin of the State,* by Robert H. Lowie, *American Political Science
Review* 22 (1928).

in a long two-part article, sought to demonstrate the vast "relativity" that characterized the social world but especially to describe the "nature and operation of what may be called the 'non-political' agencies of order" or groups that manifested the various interests in society. What was required, he argued, was a whole theory of group life and of how agencies of social control evolve in order to protect and regulate group interests. In more primitive societies, "custom" fulfilled this function, and later religion, but in less static modern societies, with larger "uniformities" of interest, achieving equilibrium required more. Although there was much voluntary adjustment of interest as well as the development of various "mediating agencies," both political anarchists and social theorists such as Sumner were wrong to believe that ethical and economic forces would, even in primitive society, sufficiently constrain and direct the pursuit of group interest.[78]

Dickinson argued that social theory had placed too much emphasis on individual interest and not enough on "group organization" and "an aggregate or group result." What was particularly important was the role of government in arbitrating disputes between groups and maintaining the integrity of the group processes that constituted and defined social life. He defined "political" authority as authority over the various types and levels of groups that constituted social reality, and the function of political authority, within and through law, was to act as an external and impartial adjudicator. Dickinson claimed that "government, like the human will, is motivated by the very forces that it governs; its function is to arrange them in a more orderly pattern." Through various formal and informal sanctions, government monitored, adjusted, and controlled group activity, and thus, in the end, was or should be a virtual "transcript of the relative strength of interests in the community." The essence of modern democracy and representative government was to be found in the fact that groups could pursue their goals and voice their concerns and opposition and that they possessed a variety of ways to gain access to government and make their voice heard. This prevented any majority from gaining a preponderance of power, but essential to this whole process of group "adjustment," which Dickinson described at such great length, was the existence of an underlying consensus or kind of virtual "general will" to which all parties subscribed.[79]

However, this emphasis on groups, and on a political science designed to study them, continued to make many political scientists uneasy about

78. Dickinson, "Social Order and Political Authority," *American Political Science Review* 23 (1929): part 1, 294.

79. Ibid., part 2, 593–94, 619, 623, 629, 632.

the future of the discipline and its relationship to what Edwin Corwin termed, in the idiom of the day, the "democratic dogma." Corwin argued that political science had been a "normative, telic" science and that, historically, "it sprang from the same matrix as the democratic dogma." Political science was at most an "exotic" in most countries such as England, because it was a creature of the particular form of eighteenth-century rationalism that took root in the United States in an intellectual context that stressed individual rationality and the capacity for self-rule. What, Corwin asked, would happen to the theory of democracy if political science substituted "laboratory science," devoted to social control and the manipulation of public opinion through propaganda, for its role as "crusader," and adopted "behaviorism" and economic models that entailed relinquishing the assumption that the human being is a "rational creature"? Both the democratic dogma and the traditional role of political science were, he claimed, under siege by "Groupist philosophers," psychologists such as Watson, and the ideas of individuals such as Wallas. Here the "intellectual preconceptions of nineteenth-century democracy are squarely challenged for the first time," and "both the professional and personal vanity of the political scientist were ministered to at one stroke."[80]

Corwin's answer, whether entirely serious or somewhat tongue-in-cheek, was not to resurrect and defend the old dogma and its philosophical foundation. Instead, he suggested that actually even individuals such as Wallas had apparently underestimated the "plasticity" of human beings that was so evident in modern advertising and government controls. The lesson of all this was not that political science could be a "real science" in the sense of natural science, but rather that it pointed to the "essential irrationality of popular thought and action" as well as to a certain idea of "education in democracy" based on the assumption of the "indefinite educability and even re-educability of the masses." The real rulers would become those who, as Lippmann suggested, "create consent." What the work of individuals such as Rice indicated was that political scientists wanted to be these rulers. The primary task of political science was "popular education, and therefore it must still retain its character as a 'normative,' 'telic' science" and not try to be a natural science, but it could "appear to be so" and consequently might return to the status that Aristotle envisioned. Americans would probably submit to its authority, so "the more of the scientific method the better."[81]

80. Edwin S. Corwin, "The Democratic Dogma and the Future of Political Science," *American Political Science Review* 23 (1929), 570, 581.

81. Ibid., 582, 586, 589, 591–92.

Given his account of pluralism and the role of government, it may not be surprising that Dickinson, who was now a professor of law at the University of Pennsylvania, would play a significant role in the Roosevelt administration when, one might argue, pluralist theory and practice came to complement one another. He once again echoed Elliott when he claimed that "the transformation of aristocratic Germany into a stable republic under the presidency of von Hindenburg is one of the spectacular miracles in the long story of democratic advance."[82] While individuals such as Karl Mannheim in Weimar Germany struggled with the issue of how rampant pluralism could be subdued, Americans saw diversity as a sign of democracy. Weimar seemed, for many Americans viewing it from afar, both physically and culturally to indicate success in grafting liberal democratic institutions onto a highly pluralistic society. This less than prescient view of the German situation, which was reinforced by events such as the creation of the *Hochschule für Politik* and which many viewed as the institutionalization of a form of American political science,[83] was quite widely shared, but what Dickinson's statement also indicated was the crystallization of a new theory of democracy as well as the articulation of the assumption that such a theory was to be found in an empirical examination of the practice of American politics. Much of the literature of political science was increasingly focused on international affairs and on disturbing developments in other countries that raised questions about the future of democracy, and in this context, more and more the assumption was that the United States was the outpost of democratic life and that to understand democracy, it was necessary to probe and grasp the character of the American political system. This was nearly the exact syndrome that would reappear in the 1950s.

The greatest impetus behind the idea of a science of politics was, first, to find democracy, and, second, to gain the cognitive and practical purchase necessary to sustain and enhance it. Dickinson claimed that it was necessary to be wary "when we seek to assess the supposed trend in recent years away from democracy." Even though both some prominent European literature and recent events might suggest such a direction, the larger historical picture indicated "progress." Those parts of the world where democracy actually was in decline should be no surprise, but on the whole, he argued, it was not declining. Part of the difficulty, he suggested, was that

82. Dickinson, "Democratic Realities and Democratic Dogma," *American Political Science Review* 24 (1930): 286.

83. See, for example, J. Eugene Harley, "The Hochschule fur Politik: A Significant German Institution for Teaching Political Science," *American Political Science Review* 24 (1930).

what people had in mind when speaking of democracy was an erroneous model. What was required was "a reassessment of what political democracy means." Not only, Dickinson argued, did people often construe democracy in other than political terms, but they had also, as Corwin noted, accepted a "democratic dogma," or "stereotype" and "theology," that was out of step with reality. This included notions that democracy involved, in some way, rule by the people as a whole, that there must be an identifiable popular will and a public opinion, and that there should be active participation by the electorate. All of these ideas, Dickinson maintained, were actually fictions and, when embraced, led to actions such as recall and referendum, which paradoxically only served to create a situation in which "more power is placed in the hands of special groups and interests."

Dickinson noted his agreement with Judge Learned Hand that all that the idea of a common will as the author of public policy meant was that something was "changed when it becomes irksome to enough powerful people who can make their will effective." The traditional image of democratic consent was a fiction. He concluded that "the larger number of members of any political society have no opinion, and hence no will, on nearly all the matters on which government acts. The only opinion, the only will, which exists is the opinion, the will, of special groups." Thus "the task of government, and hence of democracy as a form of government, is not to express an imaginary popular will, but to effect the adjustments among the various special wills and purposes which at any given time are pressing for realization." The legislature, he claimed, was really a forum for interest groups, and government in general should be conceived as an "arbitrator" over contending interests.[84]

What is "right" as a matter of public policy, Dickinson claimed, was totally "relative" to the decisions that government made at any particular time about which special interests should "win." In a society with many interest groups, there would always be those who would be dissatisfied. The criterion for democracy was whether the dissatisfied had an opportunity to pursue their case. It was not the electorate that moved the government but the pressure of interests, and the measure of democracy was the possibility of gaining access to the government. "Government by elected officials ordinarily affords opportunity for practically every interest of importance in the country to find somewhere in their respective assembly a spokesman to voice its claims." And "conflicting interests,

84. Dickinson, "Democratic Realities and Democratic Dogma," *American Political Science Review* 24 (1930): 284–92.

instead of standing apart and testing their numerical strength at the polls, are supplied with means for coming into contact, consultation, and adjustment in a way that can conceivably allow something to each." Dickinson claimed that "every representative is a potential mediator for the interest which has the strongest control over him in the face of other interests; and in this way opportunity is given for bringing interests into touch and convincing each of the advantage of accommodating itself to the others with which it has to live." This was what representative democracy was all about—and "not the realization of a supposed 'popular will.'" Dickinson clearly viewed the institutions of American government as less than perfectly designed for this new vision of democratic politics, since for the process to work well, there should be a "central organ to aid in making adjustments" as in the case of "cabinet government," and there was always a worry that there might not be a sufficient consensus on the rules of the game or cleavages of interest and geography that might hinder the operation of representation conceived in this manner.[85] If a Ph.D. student at Yale in the late 1950s or early 1960s had based an examination answer regarding democratic theory and practice simply on this account, the examinee would surely have covered all bases.

What was striking about this formulation of democratic theory was the manner in which its acceptance cut across both ideological and philosophical differences. For example, both Sabine, who quite consistently identified himself as a "liberal" and value relativist, and Francis G. Wilson, who would become a principal interlocutor in the conversation about political theory during the next decade and who would, when the label became available to him, identify himself as a "conservative," embraced what they took to be "pragmatic" perspectives on democracy and the practice of political science. Wilson believed that whatever had been the case in American politics, things had now changed, and this required rethinking democracy. "Political philosophy must be built upon the facts of political life." Voting was a privilege in political society and a way of protesting, and consequently it was a mistake to assume that actual and consistent participation in politics through suffrage or other means was a democratic indicator. The active citizens would always be few, and the actual business of bargaining between interests and with government would be conducted by elites. Like Corwin, Wilson suggested that maybe apathy indicated contentment, confidence in the system, and stability of opinion. Real public opinion was the deep consensus in society on such matters as the

85. Ibid., 295–97.

Constitution, not something that must be expressed in terms of day-to-day issues. What was called the "public interest" was in reality the sum of "competition and compromise of interests," and the "prime function of government" was the balancing of interests. Such interests were "real, not mere fictions," and "modern pluralism comes ultimately to a compromise theory of government. It is interests that count in the long run in politics, and it is interests that must seek a real expression, not opinions or ideals abstracted from their setting among interests. A working theory of government must assume that men generally know their own interests." Wilson argued that these "interests should have free access to the ear of the state; their representation should be recognized in order that they might write boldly across the pages of the statute book."[86]

Although Sabine ultimately found pragmatism "doubtful" as a general philosophical position espoused by individuals such as Dewey, its implications and what it represented "in action" and as an approach to social science were congenial to him. It was, he believed, the very opposite of "mechanistic behaviorism," but it also involved embracing a more experimental attitude and forsaking a search for "absolutes." It indicated that political science should move away from "formal legal studies which have issued in the theory of sovereignty and the juristic theory of the state" and, instead, look from an interdisciplinary perspective at the "purposes" and "habits" actually expressed in politics. It "may force us to get down to actualities," and although it would be utopian to believe that "social forces" could be completely controlled, it could aid in "inducing a strict realism in political theory" that would, in turn, provide "freedom from tradition, a deliverance from useless abstractions, and the possibility of harnessing logical operations—classification, deduction, and induction—to problems that will not let political theory get too far away from real situations."[87] Willoughby ended the decade by taking up the issue of the "ethical basis of political authority" that he had so often distinguished from "juristic" issues and allotted to the task of "final political philosophy." He once again criticized varieties of pluralism for failing to make this distinction and for not differentiating between legal and ethical validity. However, his answer to this question was, in effect, to suggest that there was no real ethical ground. After considering all the answers that had ever been advanced, from divine right to contract, he concluded that the "true basis" was that

86. Francis G. Wilson, "The Pragmatic Electorate," *American Political Science Review* 24 (1930): 16, 32–37.

87. Sabine, "The Pragmatic Approach to Politics," *American Political Science Review* 24 (1930): 865, 880, 884–85.

ultimately political authority in its various forms sprung from society and was not really different in kind from any type of social coercion. Popular government was simply one in which the individuals in various ways have, in some general manner, a greater say.

The articles by Dickinson and similar claims were, indeed, the most complete account of a group theory of politics that would appear before the 1950s, and, if combined with such texts as Barnes's statement a few years earlier, one would be hard pressed to find any essential element in the later versions that was missing from this formulation. In retrospect, one might very well ask what, after 1930, individuals such as Truman and Dahl had to offer as far as enunciating the basic principles of what would come to be called the group theory of politics or democratic pluralism. The answer is very little, yet these earlier authors had disappeared from the consciousness, or at least the literature, of mid-century political science as it sought its reference point in the work of Madison and Bentley. There was no indication that individuals such as Dickinson who formulated this new theory of democracy saw themselves as repeating or reconstituting the theory of the *Federalist* or the observations of Tocqueville. This was not something that was merely functionally equivalent to later articulations of pluralist theory or something that was "rediscovered," but rather a new vision of American politics and democracy that would persist at the core of the discourse of American political science through World War II and that political scientists would increasingly equate with the concept of liberalism. Its rearticulation in the 1950s took place, however, in a disciplinary and political context not unlike that in which it was originally formulated.

5

FROM PLURALISM TO LIBERALISM

An abstract word is like a box with
a false bottom; you may put in what
ideas you please and take them out
again unobserved.

—*Alexis de Tocqueville*

By the early 1930s, the nineteenth-century image of popular sovereignty as embodied in the invisible people designated by the "state" was still a picture that held captive the imagination of some conservatives and Progressives alike,[1] but the pluralist description of the American polity, along with the absorption of the concept of the state into that of government, had began to dominate the literature. It was at this point that the term "totalitarianism" first appeared in the discourse of political science as a label for political developments in countries such as Italy,[2] and pluralist imagery increasingly represented the alternate form of regime and became equated with democracy. As one political theorist noted, "the pluralism implicit in Gierke's thought makes it utterly foreign to the

1. See, for example, MacIver, *Society: Its Structures and Changes* (New York: Ray Long and Richard R. Smith, 1931).
2. Henry R. Spencer, "Political Development in Italy," *American Political Science Review* 23 (1929).

totalitarian ideal."[3] Gierke's work, however, actually had little to do with the content of the new pluralist vision in the United States, in part because the American discourse of democracy in all its forms had been, and continued to be, predicated on individualist assumptions rather the ontological priority of groups, but like other figures whose work had surfaced in the conversation, Gierke remained a symbol. Maybe the most elaborate engagement of the issues attached to the discussion of pluralism in the British literature, as well as of the role of political science, was Barker's long introduction to his translation of a portion of Gierke's massive study of the German *Genossenschaftsrecht* and the natural law tradition. He appended to the volume Ernst Troeltsch's 1922 lecture, "The Ideas of Natural Law and Humanity in World Politics," delivered at the *Hochschule für Politik* in Berlin, which juxtaposed the individualistic tradition of Western Europe to German romantic ideas, including those of Gierke, which Barker claimed had led to the "deification of superpersonal Groups" and especially the nineteenth-century idea of the state. Although Barker was sympathetic to many aspects of Gierke's study of groups and "the great school of Natural Law," he was consistently critical of key elements of Gierke's basic "conception of the group" and of how Gierke forced everything into the Procrustean bed of that concept.[4] Pluralism had by this point, however, become largely an American intellectual property. Little remained of Laski's original formulation as he began to stress individual liberty and the incompatibility of democracy and capitalism,[5] and ties to the classic texts of pluralist thought such as those of Figgis and Maitland had become vague and tenuous. Over the course of the decade, however, it was liberalism, rather than pluralism, that became the favorite encompassing generic term as the word migrated from the language of politics into the discourse of political science.

There is no simple one-dimensional explanation for the recession of the term "pluralism" during the 1930s, anymore than there is for its resurgence in the 1960s, but in both cases the changes were partially a function of perceptions of the fortunes and misfortunes of political liberalism. What brought the term "liberalism" to the fore was in part the New Deal

---

3. John D. Lewis, review of *Otto von Gierke's Staatslehre und unsere Zeit,* by Reinhard Hohn, *American Political Science Review* 30 (1936): 326.

4. Otto von Gierke, *Natural Law and the Theory of Society 1500–1800,* vol. 1, trans. Ernest Barker (Cambridge: Cambridge University Press, 1934), xi–xii.

5. Laski, *Liberty in the Modern State* (New York: Harper & Brothers, 1930); *Democracy in Crisis* (Chapel Hill: University of North Carolina Press, 1933); *The State in Theory and Practice* (New York: Viking, 1935).

politics of many of those who dominated the field and their insistence on the correspondence between this political version of liberalism and the concept of democracy. And on a practical level, the New Deal also contributed to a common identity for liberalism and pluralism, both by its emphasis on social diversity and by the particular political strategies that Roosevelt embraced. Liberalism was also the term used, both positively and negatively, by certain foreign publicists in speaking about democracy and about the United States. What is somewhat remarkable, however, is that while in some ways one might look upon the period of the 1930s, as did many of those involved in the discourse of political science at that time, as representing a crisis of democratic theory as well as a crisis of liberalism, there was very little in the way of attempts to articulate more fully a theory of democracy. There were some incremental emendations, but the pivotal paradigmatic shift had taken place in the 1920s. It was assumed that the counterpoint to totalitarian regimes and their ideologies was to be found in the practices and processes of American politics, and pluralism was accepted as the basic description of liberal democracy. The increasing concern of many within the discipline with establishing a systematic terminology and operational definitions was in part a consequence of attempts to be scientific, but it was also a way of dealing with the breakdown of old concepts, such as the state, and solidifying the new meanings.[6]

The distinction between political and legal sovereignty continued to be pressed, since many could not conceive of dispensing with the latter even though the tenets of what was increasingly referred to as the "democratic dogma" of popular sovereignty seemed untenable, both descriptively and normatively. But even the viability of sovereignty as a legal concept was challenged in light of the growing emphasis on the social and interest-based character of law by individuals such as Pound. It was argued that "modern society is more and more a federation of groups," such as those involved in business and religion, that interact with the state (now conceived as government) but are never exactly in harmony with either it or with each other and that, in effect, have their own spheres of law.[7] Odegard claimed that what was often called the "public mind" was in fact essentially the product of group activity, and Lasswell insisted that a "realistic political science" paid attention to the variety of groups and their psychological bases and that what constituted a "public" was, as Bentley had

6. See, for example, Charles H. Titus, "A Nomenclature for Political Science," *American Political Science Review* 25 (1931).

7. Walter Sandelius, "National Sovereignty and the Rule of Law," *American Political Science Review* 25 (1931): 4.

stressed, a fungible entity consisting of those groups that were involved in a particular issue at a particular time.[8] This, however, did not settle the question that had informed the concerns of someone such as Laski. If the state qua government was to be viewed basically as a coordinating agency, concerns such as Beard's about restraining such central authority from overstepping its role or favoring a particular segment of society became possible. If the idea of a general will, and even a notion such as that of the law of the constitution advanced by Lindsay, was not realistic, how was the activity of groups to provide a check on government?

One answer that would gain wide acceptance, and that would be incorporated even more explicitly in later pluralist theory, was that the functional relations characterizing the political process of group activity "should be linked directly with the structure of government,"[9] and many believed that this would be revealed to be the case by a more careful empirical analysis. A generation later critics would attack the theory and practice of pluralism for exactly such a liaison, but Herring became increasingly pointed in his claim that an account of the realities of American politics revealed the nature of democracy as a representative form of government. He argued that "the public interest cannot be given concrete expression except through the compromise of special claims and demands finally affected. Special interests cannot be banished from the picture, since they are the parts that make the whole."[10] Although political science textbooks tended to lag behind the new formulation and often still presented the state as a "community of persons,"[11] even when their descriptions of politics belied it, Sabine summed up the situation regarding the status of the concept of the state when he noted that not only was it "difficult to draw a clear line between state and government" but that the word "state" in fact "commonly denotes no class of objects that can be identified exactly, and for the same reason it signifies no list of attributes which bears the sanction of common usage." He claimed that the term now had no universal significance and that to grasp its meaning, it was necessary to examine how it

8. Odegard, *The American Public Mind*; Lasswell, "The Measurement of Public Opinion," *American Political Science Review* 25 (1931): 326; *Psychopathology and Politics* (Chicago: University of Chicago Press, 1930).

9. Lewis Rockow, "The Sovereignty of the Constitution," *American Political Science Review* 25 (1931): 584. For Beard's concerns about democracy, see Charles A. Beard and William Beard, *The American Leviathan: The Republic in the Machine Age* (New York: Macmillan, 1930); Charles A. Beard, "The Teutonic Origins of Representative Government," and Beard and John D. Lewis, "Representative Government in Evolution," *American Political Science Review* 26 (1932).

10. Herring, "Special Interests and the Interstate Commerce Commission," *American Political Science Review* 27 (1933): 917.

11. E.g., James Garner, *Political Science and Government* (New York: 1932).

was used in the context of particular past and present theories and forms of political practice.[12] In his presidential address to the APSA, W. W. Willoughby's brother, William, submitted a detailed prospectus for future research in political science that included reexamining "Popular Government" and its "Philosophy and Its Present Operation in the United States." Just how unclear such a philosophy was to some and what it involved in practice was apparent in the fact that as late as 1933, Friedrich claimed that "Germany will remain a constitutional democratic state with strong socializing tendencies whose backbone will continue to be its professional civil service."[13] This kind of optimism sprung not only from a faith in institutional structures such as those in the Weimar Constitution, but from the observation of German pluralism. Hugo Preuss, the Constitution's principal author, had written a biography of Lieber and had also believed that the basic features of "institutional liberty" could be replicated in other than the American setting.[14]

Although some such as McIlwain still defended the traditional idea of sovereignty against the pluralist critique and alternative, the dominant voices in the literature were now those of individuals such as Francis Wilson who continued to depreciate the notion of an organic public opinion as the core of a democratic theory. Wilson took it upon himself to sum up the decade of struggle between pluralism and monism, and he emphasized that pluralism had become less a critical perspective on state authority than "a general theory" based on realities of contemporary politics and the recognition that the state was "a coordinating agency." The problem all along, he suggested, much like Sabine, had been that both sides had been caught up in seeing the issue in terms of "universals," when in fact both doctrines were "relativistic" and applicable to a different range of facts and norms such as the difference between legal and political matters and the differences between historically and culturally diverse regimes. There was also, he noted, the "pragmatic" monism of National Socialism, fascism, and communism, which was really neither ethically nor legally based, even if something resembling such a claim had appeared in the work of Schmitt and the doctrines of Hitler.[15]

12. Sabine, "State," in *Encyclopaedia of the Social Sciences,* vol. 14 (New York: Macmillan, 1934), 328–29.

13. Willoughby, "A Program for Research in Political Science"; Carl J. Friedrich, "The Development of the Executive Power in Germany," *American Political Science Review* 27 (1933): 203.

14. Hugo Preuss, *Franz Lieber, ein Burger zweier Welten* (Hamburg: J. J. Richter, 1886).

15. C. H. McIlwain, "A Fragment on Sovereignty," *Political Science Quarterly* 48 (1933); Wilson, "Concepts of Public Opinion," *American Political Science Review* 27 (1933); "A Relativistic View of Sovereignty," *Political Science Quarterly* 49 (1934): 386, 390.

By this point, the pluralism/totalitarianism dichotomy had become so firmly entrenched that even Elliott moved further toward the pluralist side and concluded, in what was, on its face, a startling reversal of his earlier statements, that "pressures by freely organized groups upon the state are a necessary and creative factor in free government" and that the "state must fulfill the role of a responsible referee." He did not, however, come to this conclusion by the same path as many of its exponents and proponents such as Herring, who he mentioned by name. His position was more like that of Burgess's defense of corporate freedom. Elliott was concerned with the New Deal and its curtailment of group activity associated with capitalism, and he claimed that an attack on the "propertied and managing classes inevitably results in fascism." He charged that the government was not acting as a responsible referee and representing the "commonweal," but rather taking over the economic enterprise and, by its pursuit of economic equality, threatening "the soundest heritage of American character—*responsible individual initiative*." Elliott, however, was not advocating a return to the policies of Hoover, but rather a radical reconstruction of American government, through devices such as more centralization of presidential power (particularly in foreign affairs), the consolidation of local government in regional administrative areas, the establishment of an impartial bureaucracy, and a "brain trust," with more professors than traditional administrators. These ideas would gain him attention in Washington from this point through the Kennedy years. He claimed that, together, all this would produce greater authority and bring the government more into line with a parliamentary system.[16] Lurking behind this recommendation, in his case, was the lingering assumption that the government represented a national community.

In 1935, Shepard devoted his APSA presidential address to the transformation that was taking place in the concept of democracy, a transformation that he endorsed. He claimed that for a century and a half Americans had been under the "spell" of the "democratic idea," which included assumptions regarding both individualism and the will of the people. The notion of economic individualism had, he argued, now been discredited, and the "doctrine of political democracy," by which he meant traditional ideas of popular sovereignty, should likewise be relinquished. He claimed that it was clear that even "the state as a juristic or ideal person is the merest fiction. It is real only as a collective name for governmental institutions," which in turn are nothing but "behavior patterns"

16. Elliott, *The Need for Constitutional Reform* (New York: Whittlesey House, 1935), 8, 9, 11.

informed by "an ideology." Like the more familiar claims of political scientists two decades later, he argued that democratic theory and democratic practice had become two different things, and it was time not only to bring the former into accord with the latter but to remove the old theoretical constraints on democratic politics. This, he suggested, might even entail appropriating certain elements of fascism and communism as part of a new vision of democracy that would include achieving the "good life" through economic planning and depreciation of the electorate as a source of wisdom in favor of calling upon people with "brains."[17] This attempt to mold democratic theory not only to the general characteristics of American politics but to *Democratic* policies indicated the path through which the change within the theory of democracy associated with the concept of liberalism would occur.

By the mid-1930s, the conversation about democracy, that is, what it meant in principle and the extent to which it was realized in the American system, had largely stalled out as attention turned more and more to international affairs and to concrete matters of domestic policy. The basic tenets of pluralism as both an empirical and normative theory had, however, become deeply embedded in the language of political science. This was no longer the antistatist pluralism of individuals such as Laski, and there was general and growing support for the notion that democratic practice should become more "authoritarian," even if this entailed borrowing from its totalitarian antithesis. The dominant "politics" of voices in mainstream political science was clearly that of the New Deal. Coker, now Cowles Professor of Government at Yale, was still not reconciled to pluralism as an account of democracy, since he continued to view it primarily as a critical theory that failed to acknowledge adequately the need for the state to exercise general power, and in his presidential address to the APSA, he criticized Hoover's vision of "American Liberalism" and endorsed a moderate version of Franklin Roosevelt's policies. He wrote the entry for pluralism in the *Encyclopaedia of the Social Sciences* and suggested that "the pluralist doctrine is in part a rationalization of recent movements in actual society, tending in various ways toward a more decentralized application of social control," but that in the end it was forced to readmit many of the traditional functions of the state.[18] The issue was, in part, how to reconcile interventionist government with the pluralist image of the state as a coordinating

17. Shepard, "Democracy in Transition," *American Political Science Review* 29 (1935): 2–4.

18. Coker, *Recent Political Thought* (New York: Appleton-Century, 1934); "Pluralism," in *Encyclopaedia of the Social Sciences*, vol. 12 (New York: Macmillan, 1934), 171; "American Traditions Concerning Property and Liberty," *American Political Science Review* 30 (1936).

agency, an issue that would claim the attention of the next generation at Yale. But in sorting out political policies, Coker was one of the first in political science to appropriate the liberalism/conservatism dichotomy that was becoming part of the language of politics.

It has often been noted that the terms "liberal" and "liberalism" first appeared in nineteenth-century European politics, first in Spain, Italy, and France, and then in Germany around 1820. In England, they emerged in 1819 as a characterization of a political party and later, in 1847 and 1859, as the actual self-ascribed name of a party. Such terminology was, however, apart from some very generic uses, virtually absent from the language of political inquiry in the United States and appeared only rarely in American political discourse. Brownson, for example, had occasionally referred to himself in these terms, and there was a Liberal Republican Party in the 1870s as well as Liberal Republican reformers such as Carl Schurz, but seeking the early history of "liberalism" in political science and political theory is much like pursuing a null hypothesis. Discussions of liberalism prior to the 1930s were usually about English and Continental politics or involved international relations and such things as Woodrow Wilson's foreign policy. Wilson, once he entered the world of politics and gave up the role of "literary politician," was related to the virtual politics of the academy in a quite different manner. While in the 1920s there were occasional references to liberal democracy and sometimes an equation of the two concepts, there was no extended discussion of anything called liberalism.

When J. A. Hobson spoke in 1909 about a "crisis of liberalism,"[19] he was speaking about the Liberal Party in England, and it had nothing to do with what Americans would be referring to by this phrase a generation later. Although L. T. Hobhouse's account of Liberalism (with a capital "L") conveyed the sense that he also was talking about something concrete, he was already using the concept as a category to refer to a variety of liberties that had been won during the modern movement of Western civilization away from authoritarian government.[20] No one he discussed actually used the term "liberal" or "liberalism." After Hobhouse, the concept of liberalism began to take on something of a life of its own in academic discussion and increasingly referred less to historical specifics than to Hobhouse's formulation and interpretations of his work. Even when there were distinct allusions to British politics, the actual subject was often a certain "habit of mind."[21]

19. J. A. Hobson, *The Crisis of Liberalism: New Issues of Democracy* (London: P. S. King & Son, 1909).

20. Hobhouse, *Liberalism* (Oxford: Oxford University Press, 1911).

21. See, for example, W. Lyon Blease, *A Short History of English Liberalism* (New York: G. Putnam's Sons, 1913).

Croly, who for many years has been featured prominently in accounts of what is now so frequently and retrospectively labeled American liberalism, hardly used the word and certainly had not employed it in any significant sense in *The Promise of American Life*. In those instances in which the concept of liberalism was adopted, it was used in diverse, but usually positive, ways. H. L. Mencken, for example, attacked Theodore Roosevelt posthumously as having rejected "all the fundamental projects of Liberalism."[22] There was a Liberal Club in Greenwich Village, attached to the Washington Square Book Shop, that served as "A Meeting Place for Those Interested in New Ideals" and that was frequented by individuals such as Emma Goldman, John Reed, and "Big" Bill Heywood—not exactly individuals that political theorists would today be likely to designate as "liberal." On the other hand, an idiosyncratic critique of politics by the diplomat William Kay Wallace characterized liberalism as a kind of failure of nerve—actually a conservative "effort to reform existing institutions which are growing senile" and "at best a futile doctrine, a sort of social anesthetic."[23] Wallace would recommend a complete revision of the Constitution in the service of greater nationalization and central control of the economy.

When Dunning had reflected on the path of politics during the nineteenth century, he described the first fifty years as a long struggle between liberalism and conservatism, but he employed these concepts as categories for distinguishing things such as democracy and authoritarianism.[24] He was referring neither to specific political policies nor to distinct political theories. In the third volume of his *History of Political Theories,* which treated modern political thought up through Spencer, there was no mention of liberalism or the attachment of the label "liberal" to thinkers such as Locke. When Merriam, at the same time, updated his original Dunning-like account of the development of American political ideas to include the period after the Civil War, liberalism did not appear. And when he further expanded his account of politics and political ideas in "recent times" in the book of essays by Dunning's students, which was presented as the fourth volume of their teacher's magnum opus, the term "liberal" was used only in reference to party politics in Germany and England.[25] Gettell's

22. H. L. Mencken, *Prejudices* (New York: Knopf, 1920), 111–12.

23. William Kay Wallace, *The Passing of Politics* (New York: Macmillan, 1924).

24. Dunning, "A Century of Politics," *North American Review* 179 (November 1904).

25. Merriam, *A History of American Political Theories* (New York: Macmillan, 1903); *American Political Ideas: Studies in the Development of American Political Thought, 1865–1917* (New York: Macmillan, 1920); Merriam and Barnes, eds., *A History of Political Theory: Recent Times* (New York: Macmillan, 1924).

prominent text on the history of political thought, which was intended to succeed and compete with Dunning's project, did not, even in the concluding discussion of recent ideas, mention liberalism even though he referred to what he considered to be "liberalizing tendencies."[26] Pluralism, rather than liberalism, was a subject in Robert Murray's very comprehensive history of political science, *The History of Political Science: Plato to the Present,*[27] and although the book was written from a British perspective, even Mill was not categorized as a liberal. While Gettell's widely used text, *The History of American Political Thought,* focused on the development of democratic ideas, there was no discussion of liberalism, even though the term "liberal" was occasionally used as a contrast with "radical."[28] Another principal text on the development of American political thought, published in 1930, never referred to liberalism, and although the basic elements of what would be called "liberalism" were at the core of McIlwain's very influential study, *The Growth of Political Thought in the West,* the term was not applied.[29] During this period, there was no more detailed textbook in American political thought than that of J. Mark Jacobson,[30] but, again, it made no mention of liberalism.

One book that appeared prior to the 1930s did, however, adumbrate the subsequent discussion of liberalism, and it marked the threshold of the adoption of liberalism as an American political identity by both political actors and academic commentators. This was Vernon Louis Parrington's interpretation of American literature, a work whose themes would be reflected in Hartz's image of the liberal tradition in America. But the ideas of Parrington's senior colleague at the University of Washington, J. Allen Smith, resonated in the book. Although Smith actually made only limited use of the term "liberal," Parrington, by 1930, described the work as embodying "liberal thought." He characterized Smith as the first person to introduce "democratic liberalism" into the political science establishment, as a representative of the "new liberalism," and as perceiving the "decline of liberalism" in the postwar period. For Smith, the relevant polit-

26. Gettell, *History of Political Thought* (New York: Century, 1924).

27. Robert H. Murray, *The History of Political Science: Plato to the Present* (Cambridge: W. Heffer & Sons, 1926).

28. Gettell, *History of American Political Thought* (New York: Century, 1928).

29. William Seal Carpenter, *The Development of American Political Thought* (Princeton: Princeton University Press, 1930); McIlwain, *The Growth of Political Thought in the West* (New York: Macmillan, 1932).

30. J. Mark Jacobson, *The Development of American Political Thought* (New York: Appleton-Century-Crofts, 1932). It is significant that in a 1961 reprint, edited by Thornton Anderson, liberalism does appear.

ical poles had been "conservative" and "democratic," but in a book published posthumously, he altered the categories by claiming that "from the very beginning of our political history, there has been a constant struggle between conservatism and liberalism." "Liberal political philosophy" and the idea of "popular control" were the antithesis of centralization and conservatism, which Smith believed were responsible for the contemporary "decadence" of constitutional government.[31] Parrington, in his own work, used the concept of liberalism in two somewhat different ways. First of all, he noted, following Smith's categories, that his study was conducted from a "liberal" rather than a "conservative" perspective, and this was an indication of the extent to which the label "liberal" was beginning to displace "Progressive" in both politics and in second-order discourse. Second, Parrington defined his study as an account of how "liberalism," or the "liberal doctrine of natural rights," had been transplanted from Europe and developed in America. He claimed that it had first appeared in Puritanism and then had evolved in the "colonial mind." While the "soil" of Europe had been "inhospitable" to liberalism, it "flourished" in America.[32] It was in Parrington's work that the academic idea of a liberal tradition, later to be given full expression in the work of Hartz, first began to take on recognizable shape.

The *Encyclopaedia of the Social Sciences,* which was published in the mid-1930s, was to a large extent a project that stemmed from the New School of Social Research and involved European and émigré authors. Although it was here that the first systematic discussion of liberalism appeared, there was no mention of liberalism in the American context.[33] In his review of these volumes, Lasswell noted that "if sedition lurks within the *Encyclopaedia of the Social Sciences,* the subversive scimitar has been so deftly swung that patriots have not thought to shake their heads."[34] What he was referring to was not entirely clear, but the *Encyclopaedia* did, subtly, represent the beginning of the prodigious influence of European scholars who would play a significant role in changing the course of democratic theory in political science and who would contribute fundamentally to altering the attitude toward liberalism. But by the middle of the 1930s, the *Encyclopedia*

31. J. Allen Smith, *The Growth and Decadence of Constitutional Government* (Holt, Rinehart and Winston, 1930), 94, and "Introduction," by Vernon Louis Parrington.

32. Parrington, *An Interpretation of American Literature from the Beginnings to 1920* (New York: Harcourt Brace, 1927), i, vi.

33. Guido de Ruggiero, "Liberalism," in *Encyclopaedia of the Social Sciences,* vol. 9, New York: Macmillan, 1933).

34. Lasswell, "The *Encylopaedia of the Social Sciences* in Review," *International Journal of Ethics* 46 (1936): 396.

Britannica had not recognized liberalism as category or tradition of thought.

As late as 1937, in Edward R. Lewis's *A History of American Political Thought,* liberalism was not a topic,[35] but Sabine's paradigmatic work on the history of political theory, published in the same year, more closely reflected the place that liberalism was beginning to occupy in the discourse of political science and, particularly, the subfield of political theory. Sabine, who had come to Cornell as a professor of philosophy in 1931, included two entire chapters on liberalism, which he took to represent the major development of political thought in the modern era and whose roots, he claimed, were deeply embedded in Western political thought. Whether subsequent writers would applaud or condemn this "development," few would question its reality and the idea that there was a Western liberal tradition. Sabine, however, was still struggling with two concepts of liberalism—one referring to a general image of democratic ideas including attributes such as pluralism and one more closely tied to a certain ideological position in politics. Even Sabine had not yet "discovered" that Locke was a liberal. According to Sabine, liberalism as a distinct political theory began with Adam Smith and the philosophical radicals such as Bentham. "Political liberalism" was characterized as "a massive movement that made itself felt in all the countries of Western Europe and in America," but the essential ideas, he claimed, could be discerned as far back as ancient Greece. Since Sabine had long been a defender of pluralism and pragmatism, it is not surprising that what he found at the core of liberalism, and what distinguished it from communism and National Socialism, was communication across the boundaries between diverse social and economic interests. Although he noted that the relationship between group interests was "more or less antagonistic and always in need of mutual adjustment and readjustment," the requisite principles of negotiation, compromise, good will, and the like had "never since Aristotle been absent from liberal thought."[36] The concept of liberalism was still on the cusp between referring to an analytical and a historical datum, but Sabine's work both reflected and contributed to the institutionalization of liberalism as an essential category in political science and political theory. Can we say, then, that the concept of liberalism as we have come to know it in academic discourse was largely an invention that came into existence during a period of not much more than five years? The answer, in effect, is "yes," but the story is more complicated than this general assertion might suggest.

---

35. Edward R. Lewis, *A History of American Political Thought* (New York: Macmillan, 1937).
36. Sabine, *A History of Political Theory* (New York: Holt, Rinehart and Winston, 1937), 907–8.

Even though political science had not made much use of the term "liberalism" through the mid-1930s, the word had distinctly emerged in the universe of political discourse in the United States.[37] While some concepts, such as the political system, originated basically in academic discourse and found their way into the more general vocabulary, many, including liberalism (and conservatism), had their origins in the first-order activity of politics and migrated into second-order practices. Liberalism was appropriated by political scientists from the language of politics, often by those who favored the politics of the Roosevelt administration. It was then abstracted and equated generically with democracy, and reified and reapplied retrospectively to functionally or categorically similar ideas and modes of action before being further concretized as a description of American politics and ideas. While most of the earliest social scientific references to liberalism were either directly or indirectly to a self-ascribed political ideology and program, social science steadily emptied liberalism of its mundane political content and filled it with new meaning—a process that was largely complete by the 1950s when Hartz told the story of the "liberal tradition in America" and found its roots in Locke.

Publications such as the *New Republic* and individuals such as Croly and Lippmann had, by 1915, distanced themselves from the policies of Theodore Roosevelt by dropping the term "Progressive" and adopting "liberal." Woodrow Wilson was, for various reasons, also wary of being too closely identified with the Progressive label by the end of World War I. The term "liberal," both in America and Europe, was, however, relatively untainted and uncontested. Wilson introduced it in the context of international affairs with respect to advocating national liberation and self-determination, but it was employed more generally to indicate his political views both at home and abroad.[38] To refer in retrospect to Wilsonian liberalism, as many commentators do, either favorably or pejoratively, may nevertheless be misleading, since it might imply that there was some such distinct political tradition and ideology with respect to which Wilson took a particular stance. And, after all, by 1917 it was still democracy rather than liberalism for which he wanted to make the world safe. Progressives who disagreed with Wilson, such as Bourne and Harold Stearns, attacked Wilson's policies, as well as those of other Progressives who had supported the War such as John Dewey, by either denigrating liberalism or suggesting

---

37. For a thorough account of the concept of liberalism in American politics, see Ronald D. Rotunda, *The Politics of Language: Liberalism as a Word and Symbol* (Iowa City: University of Iowa Press, 1986); David Green, *Shaping Political Consciousness* (Ithaca: Cornell University Press, 1987).

38. See David Steigerwald, *Wilsonian Idealism in America* (Ithaca: Cornell University Press, 1994).

at least that it had taken the wrong path.[39] In doing so, they, and then in turn their opponents, increasingly infused, and confused, Wilson's political rhetoric with historical substance and contributed to the reification of liberalism in political language. Since liberalism, much like democracy, was for the most part still a term of approbation, there was a tendency less to reject it than to seek to appropriate it, and this trend was accentuated as competition for the concept continued into the 1930s. In the 1920s, even the arch-conservative academic Butler had called himself a "liberal,"[40] and Hoover sought to identify himself as a liberal. Hoover attacked opponents for not living up to the name. He claimed that out of our past "grew a great philosophy of society—Liberalism," from which in turn came the "structure of American Democracy" and the "American System" of politics. For Hoover, "democracy" was the less inclusive term and referred primarily to government, while "liberalism" was a tradition, a way of life, and a set of values. He claimed, however, that there were now many "perversions" represented in "National Regimentation, Fascism, Socialism, Communism, [and] Nazism" and that "true liberalism" was in danger of eclipse both in the United States and abroad. Hoover was far from an advocate of radical laissez-faire, but he maintained that American, as opposed to European, liberalism was not compatible with "collectivist philosophy" and the kind of "national regimentation" represented by Franklin Roosevelt, which in his view brought government into competition with its citizens. He argued that "it is a false liberalism that interprets itself into the government operation of commercial business" and that such a policy "poisons the very roots of liberalism."[41]

Although in the 1930s there was for a brief time a Liberal Party that was basically committed to what today would be called a libertarian position, and although journals such as the *New Republic* were using the terms "liberalism" and "conservatism" in much the manner that they are employed in political discourse today, it was Franklin Roosevelt who most distinctly succeeded both in fixing "liberal" in the vocabulary of politics and in winning the battle over the label. He even managed to make his opponents eventually accept as their identity what he designated as liberalism's opposite—conservatism. Although Roosevelt had at times called

39. Harold Stearns, *Liberalism in America* (New York: Boni and Liverwright, 1919); Randolf Bourne, *Untimely Papers* (New York: Huebsch, 1919).

40. Butler, *The Faith of a Liberal* (New York: Charles Scribner's Sons, 1921).

41. Herbert Hoover, *The Challenge to Liberty* (New York: Charles Scribner's Sons, 1934), 3, 5, 8, 23, 76, 204; Hoover, in *A Source Book of American Political Theory,* ed. Benjamin F. Wright (New York: Macmillan, 1929).

himself both a Progressive and a liberal in the 1920s, he was increasingly labeled a liberal even though some attempted to deny him the name. By the late 1930s, however, he aggressively and consistently adopted the liberal identity and thereby captured the future as well as the past. For Roosevelt, "Progressivism" carried certain liabilities both because of previous associations and because some old-line Progressives were dubious about certain aspects of both foreign and domestic interventionism. Roosevelt maintained that *he* was the "true" liberal, and liberalism served well as a concept that allowed him to avoid "socialism" and "radicalism" in his pursuit of the policies that defined the electoral realignment that he sought. "The Seventy-fifth Congress," he claimed, was elected on a platform that was "unambiguously liberal," and he stressed that by "the word 'liberal,' I mean the beliefs in progressive principles of democratic representative government and not the wild man who, in effect, leans in the direction of Communism."[42]

Representative government and party responsibility, Roosevelt argued in 1941, required two distinct parties and schools of political belief—"liberal and conservative"—and "I believe it to be my sworn duty, as President, to take all steps necessary to ensure the continuance of liberalism in our government" and "to see to it that my party remains the truly liberal party in the political life of America."[43] Although for a decade, politicians such as Robert Taft would still be reluctant to relinquish fully the liberal label, by the beginning of the 1940s Roosevelt had not only made liberalism part of the American political vocabulary, but convinced both political actors and academicians to accept the name "liberal" for the policies he advocated. When Dewey addressed the issue of liberalism, he now typically employed the concept very broadly to refer to a certain range of beliefs and attitudes that, even though more prominent in the modern era, "might be traced back to Greek thought," but he attempted to give liberalism a distinct contemporary historical identity.[44] The book was a major step in the reification of liberalism, and Dewey's argument for the application of intelligence to human affairs and his plea for a new liberalism, which would replace the laissez-faire variety, was, despite whatever reservations he had about Roosevelt, an unmistakable, though perhaps gratuitous, philosophical underwriting of the New Deal legislative program. One commentator

42. Russell D. Buhite and David W. Levy, *FDR's Fireside Chats* (Norman: University of Oklahoma Press, 1992), 125–26, 133.

43. Franklin D. Roosevelt, *Public Papers and Addresses,* vol. 1, ed. Samuel I. Rosenman (New York: Random House, 1938–50), 742–56.

44. John Dewey, *Liberalism and Social Action* (New York: Putnam, 1935).

would note that Dewey had done for liberalism intellectually what Roosevelt had done for it politically,[45] but the academic "discovery" of the philosophy of liberalism and of a historical tradition to support it was already well underway. And it was already a contested territory as everyone from Marxists to capitalists sought to identify themselves as liberal. In the same year that Dewey's book was published, the Godkin Lectures at Harvard consisted of a diatribe, equally thinly veiled, against the New Deal couched in terms of a defense of a venerable "liberal tradition."[46] Laski's account of the "rise of liberalism" was an attempt, much like that of Dewey, to demonstrate that liberalism had been a philosophy that provided a rational justification for the economic and political character of the modern age, and particularly capitalism, but, Laski argued, both as "a habit of mind" and a "doctrine" of freedom, liberalism had degenerated and was out of step with the policy needs of the time.[47] As the meaning of liberalism continued to be contested in both political and academic discourse, the consequence was further abstraction, but it was this abstract vessel that now became the receptacle for the pluralist vision of American politics, a vision that had not yet quite found a philosophical place to rest.

In 1935, the *APSR* explicitly identified "Liberalism" with "Democracy," but once liberalism had been accepted as the identity of American politics and as a democratic identity, it became an object of both defense and criticism, as well as an object for which a clear reference was still lacking. The mid-1930s might be considered, as Alan Ryan has suggested, the "high-tide of American liberalism,"[48] but it is necessary to clarify this metaphor. The high-water mark of liberalism as either a set of social policies or political attitudes had not been reached, and liberalism as a concept in second-order discussion was still rising. This period, however, did mark the full sea of liberalism as a term of approbation in the discourse of political science—a point at which certain eddies had already appeared, just before the current turned and the stream of liberalism began to ebb. Philosophers such as T. V. Smith at Chicago would continue to claim that "Americanism is liberalism,"[49] by which he meant largely attributes associated with pluralism, but it was precisely these attributes that would soon be called into

45. Virgil Michel, "Liberalism Yesterday and Tomorrow," *Ethics* 49 (1939).

46. Lewis Douglas, *The Liberal Tradition* (Cambridge, Mass.: Harvard University Press, 1935).

47. Laski, *The Rise of Liberalism: The Philosophy of a Business Civilization* (New York: Harper & Brothers, 1936).

48. Alan Ryan, *John Dewey and the Hightide of American Liberalism* (New York: W. W. Norton, 1995).

49. Smith, *The Promise of America* (Chicago: University of Chicago Press, 1936), 207.

question. By the beginning of the last half of the decade, there was a commonly acknowledged "crisis of liberalism," which, by now, was also understood as a crisis of democracy.

Although this sense of crisis was in part a reflection of certain contradictions in liberal theory and practice, that is, in philosophy as well as politics, it was most fundamentally pluralism that was at issue. When Lindsay wrote the preface for a new edition of his *Essentials of Democracy* in 1935, he apologized for having spoken in 1929 about "the new democracy of Germany," since what Germany really represented was the basic alternative to democracy—the absence of pluralism and its attending values— but it was far from clear that the realist accounts of American politics, such as that advanced by Lasswell, were, in an increasingly polarized world, matched by an adequate normative vision.[50] At this point, it was Francis Wilson, at the University of Washington, who presented the most expansive and focused analysis of political science and democracy. Although maybe less than the most creative contributor to the conversation, Wilson had been, and would continue to be, the most vigorous and persistent interlocutor, and in his journey from a tentative embrace of pragmatism to a self-styled conservatism, a central thread in the democratic discourse of political science can be traced.

The discipline of political science, Wilson suggested, was in somewhat the same situation as English political thought had been when it reacted to the French Revolution. It was in many ways less a science than a response to the contemporary growth of "political authoritarianism." What was now required of a "true liberal," he claimed, was a somewhat "conservative" interpretation of the "leading principles of republican political life," which had fallen to the status of unconscious assumptions.[51] Wilson still held on to the idea of the state as the subject of political science, and he still defined a true state as a "political community of free citizens occupying a territory of defined boundaries, and organized under a government sanctioned and limited by a written constitution and established by consent of the governed." But in his actual usage state meant government, and even though he considered public opinion central to democracy, he maintained that it was basically a concept of political analysis and denied that there was any such thing as a general will or a social entity to which "public opinion" referred. The purpose of the state was to achieve "a point

---

50. Lindsay, *Essentials of Democracy* (London: Oxford University Press, 1935). See also Lasswell, *Politics: Who Gets What, When, How* (New York: Wittlesey House, 1936).
51. Wilson, *The Elements of Modern Politics* (New York: McGraw-Hill, 1936).

of balance or of political equilibrium," and it was the idea of such a balance of plural interests that was the core of democracy as a social philosophy. He stated that "the general issue of pluralism is so important in modern political theory that we must consider it in detail," but, in his view, the "challenge of political pluralism" was to reconcile both realist political analysis with democratic theory and to make the state as lawmaker compatible with pluralist claims about group autonomy. But this challenge was, he suggested, mounted in the midst of a "crisis in the democratic and the liberal foundations of society."[52]

The crisis, as characterized by Wilson, first appeared after World War I, when democracy as a form of government began to be called into question in certain countries. Like Hoover, Wilson viewed liberalism as more fundamental than democracy and as a social structure and way of life that came into existence in the eighteenth century. It was distinguished by the dominance of the middle class, the values of individualism and freedom as well as toleration and a recognition of group claims, and the idea that "compromise and adjustment" can be achieved by constitutional means. Democratic government, he argued, emerged as an "appendage" to liberalism, but now that democracy had been challenged, liberalism was necessarily implicated. Part of the crisis, Wilson argued, had been a consequence of the fact that many liberals, while opposing fascism, had accepted communism, which was equally out of phase with liberalism. The basic problem was that political conflict in many societies seemed to be running deeper than the capacity of democratic constitutional machinery to deal with it. Although by this point Friedrich, like Lindsay in England, had admitted that after predicting that Germany would remain "a constitutional democratic state," the Nazis had made him "look like a fool,"[53] Wilson held on to the notion that it was really too early to judge the results of communism and fascism, and maybe all that National Socialism ultimately sought was basic liberal values. The challenge to liberalism qua pluralism, was, however, closer to home than Wilson seemed to recognize at this point. During this period, there was in the United States itself, he suggested, the beginning of a relatively sudden and unexpected assault on the very idea of liberal democracy as it had heretofore been conceived. Wilson himself, however, would eventually be closely involved with this assault.

After World War I and the decline of the theory of the state and entailed European ideas, American political science had been relatively isolated from

52. Ibid., 211, 221, 265, 478.
53. Friedrich, *Constitutional Government and Politics* (New York: Harper, 1937), xvi.

Continental thought. The appearance of émigré scholars in the United States, beginning in the late 1930s, adumbrated a sea change in the discipline. Before coming to the United States, many of these scholars, on both the left and right, had become committed critics of liberalism as both a political form and a political theory. Outside the United States, liberalism was hardly uniformly a term of approval. For example, totalitarian critics of Anglo-American institutions labeled them "liberal," and a general political and intellectual critique of liberal doctrines and institutions was beginning to appear in Europe. In the case of the émigrés, their critique of Weimar politics—which in their view was defined, politically and intellectually, by liberalism, pluralism, and relativism—was transferred to an analysis of American politics and the politics of the West in general. When, for example, Leo Strauss encountered Schmitt's sustained attack on liberalism, his principal reaction was that it did not go far enough.[54] Marxists had long criticized liberalism, and many of those touched by the philosophy of Heidegger found in his work the basis for a philosophical critique of liberalism. For many of the émigrés, liberalism was perceived as the threshold of totalitarianism. For some, liberalism was simply the hallmark of modern political decadence, while for others the problem was less that liberalism was inherently defective than that it had failed to be sufficiently antiliberal in defending its own principles.[55] Many of those in the first wave of émigré authors, such as Oscar Jaszi, Aurel Kolnai, and Hermann Rauschning, had looked for an underlying intellectual explanation for the rise of totalitarianism, and they concluded that it was in part the inability of liberalism to resist. Kolnai, a Hungarian educated in Vienna before coming to England, Canada, and the United States, claimed that the Nazi movement was not some accident of personality and circumstance, but rather a logical entailment of certain trends in German philosophy that could not be adequately countered by the tenets of utilitarian liberalism.[56] Rauschning, who before his disillusionment with National Socialism and immigration to the United States had been appointed president of the German senate by Hitler, argued that Nazi "nihilism" actually sprung from intellectual forces unleashed by Enlightenment values, and he advocated a new form of conservatism as a response.[57] This same theme of the self-

54. Leo Strauss, "Comments on Carl Schmitt's *Der Begriff des Politischen*," in Schmitt, *The Concept of the Political*, trans. George Schwab (New Brunswick: Rutgers University Press, 1976), 89–90.

55. See, for example, Gerhard Liebholz, "The Nature and Various Forms of Democracy," *Social Research* (February 1938).

56. Aurel Kolnai, *The War Against the West* (New York: Viking, 1938).

57. See Hermann Rauschning, *The Revolution of Nihilism* (New York: Longman's, Green, 1939); *The Redemption of Democracy* (New York: Alliance Book Corporation, 1940).

destructing tendency of liberal and Enlightenment values would also be adopted by theorists with a quite different political ideology and philosophical perspective such as Max Horkheimer, Theodor Adorno, and other members of the Frankfurt School after coming to the United States.[58]

For many Americans, this was a paradoxical argument—that totalitarianism was somehow an outgrowth of liberalism, since liberalism, as an American political identity, had been largely shaped in the process of attempting to distinguish democracy from such regimes and to provide some self-conscious theoretical account of democratic processes in terms of which to confront foreign doctrines. For these critics, it was not, as the émigré historian Hans Kohn would argue, that Nazism was the result of the eventual consequence of the historical failure of liberalism in Germany,[59] but rather that there was something internally pathological about liberal society and its pluralistic and egalitarian character that made the fate of Weimar a warning to the West. It is ironic that the New School of Social Research, founded in New York in 1918 by Progressives and social science dissidents from Columbia such as Alvin Johnson, Croly, Robinson, and Thorstein Veblen and which became a major venue for the Americanization of social science and social theory, was transformed into the principal institutional vehicle for the émigré attack on liberalism and the American vision of social science. But a somewhat similar reversal took place at Chicago under Robert Maynard Hutchins.

What in part propelled a sharper articulation of liberal values in the 1930s, and eventually a rearticulation of pluralism, was the chorus of critical voices that were joining the conversation. By the middle of the decade, the issue of whether liberalism, as a philosophy and as a mode of public policy, was sound or bankrupt was beginning to be part of the discussion. The underlying concern, which found philosophical and social scientific expression, was often the totalitarian challenge to liberal democracy and the domestic revision of liberalism represented by Roosevelt. Philosophers Charner Perry and T. V. Smith, as well as Merriam and Lasswell, were frequent participants in this conversation. There was a great deal of emphasis on the issue of whether the "liberal" view that values were subjective and experimental was preferable to some form of moral objectivism. Perry defended the former position and attacked natural law. He identified "political theory" specifically as the study of norms and the art of their con-

58. See Max Horkheimer and Theodor Adorno, *Dialectic of Enlightenment* (New York: Herder and Herder, 1972).

59. Hans Kohn, *The Mind of Germany* (New York: Charles Scribner's Sons, 1960).

struction and reconstruction by elites devoted to social control. He point-edly argued that the belief in the subjective character of value judgments led to useful moral principles that aid in settling disputes, while objec-tivism only created an atmosphere of contention and doubt.[60] And Merriam and Lasswell continued to press their program of social control through the conjunction of social science and political power as the answer to cre-ating democracy and democratic identities.[61]

By the early 1930s, the concept of relativism, which was at the heart of the critics' worries, was closely tied to the American image of liberalism. Although Beard never embraced the radical relativism sometimes attrib-uted to him, he did press his claim about perspectivism in writing history. The historian Carl Becker argued for relativism as a basis for criticizing establishment values and claimed that both liberal democracy and com-munism were only slightly different secular ideologies of progress that had been preceded by Christianity. These, he suggested, were all "useful social myths" but destined to be supplanted by "factual knowledge." For Becker, however, there seemed to be little doubt that the "Truth" of liberalism was somehow distinguished by its coincidence with the "matter-of-fact."[62] In a similar vein, Marten ten Hoor suggested that while fascism and com-munism represented a return to "dogmatism and medievalism," democ-racy rested on "a relativistic attitude toward all regulative ideas" and was the "practical expression of the philosophic doctrine of the relativism of political ideas." Thurman Arnold's *Folklore of Capitalism* (1937) sought to expose values as the historical reflection of interests that must be understood in order to be controlled.[63] The characteristic American position, most force-fully pursued by Dewey, was that in one way or another, the values and method of science and democracy were symbiotic, if not identical.[64] Others such as Jaszi, however, argued that the relativism inherent in scientism had undermined conceptions of "right and wrong" and had led to a theoretical

60. Charner M. Perry, "Bases, Arbitrary and Otherwise, for Morality: A Critique Criticized," *International Journal of Ethics* 43 (1933); "Knowledge as a Basis for Social Reform," *International Journal of Ethics* 45 (1935); "The Relation Between Ethics and Politics and Political Science," *International Journal of Ethics* 47 (1937).

61. Merriam, *Political Power* (New York: McGraw-Hill, 1934); *The Role of Politics in Social Change* (New York: New York University Press, 1936); Lasswell, *World Politics and Personal Insecurity* (New York: McGraw-Hill, 1934).

62. Carl Becker, "New Liberties for Old," *Journal of Social Philosophy* 1 (1936): 121.

63. Marten ten Hoor, "Medievalism in Contemporary Political Thought," *Journal of Social Philosophy* 3 (1938): 348–49; Thurman Arnold, *Folklore of Capitalism* (New Haven: Yale University Press, 1937).

64. See, for example, Marie Collins Swabey, *The Theory of the Democratic State* (Cambridge, Mass.: Harvard University Press, 1939).

and practical "breakdown of liberal democracy," which culminated in the "fatal collapse" represented by World War I and its aftermath.[65]

What began to emerge was a line of argument about the dangers of "pure tolerance" that would characterize the work of diverse émigré theorists such as Strauss and Herbert Marcuse. The claim was that "democracy and democratic tolerance had been used for their own destruction" in Weimar and elsewhere and that democracy would need to become more self-conscious and "militant," and, in effect, illiberal and "authoritarian" if it was to survive the universal threat of fascism.[66] Even for those who had identified with pragmatism and pluralism, there was a concern that liberalism was becoming too flaccid. Although Wilson was wary of some who recommended borrowing from totalitarian regimes, he continued to stress the lack of authority in liberal society and even suggested that the rise of National Socialism was "understandable" in terms of the modern "crisis in the economic, political, and social foundations of society." He did not condemn pragmatism, which he still believed represented the basic spirit of the American electorate, but he argued that during the "pragmatic age," liberalism and democracy had been "asleep" and that it might be necessary for liberalism to become "partially tyrannical in order to preserve itself from destruction at the hands of a greater despotism."[67] T. V. Smith, philosophically underwriting the social science of the Chicago school, continued to defend liberalism both with respect to the sphere of politics as the enlargement of economic regulation and with respect to political theory as a process of group competition. Merriam suggested giving up attempting to associate democracy with any particular institution or policy and embracing a functional definition that amounted to the existence of diversity and processes for making major decisions that in some way involved "the bulk of the community."[68] It was, however, precisely this kind of vague image, as well as the coherency of the pluralist account of democracy, that was being contested. Yet the controversy about liberal-

65. Oscar Jaszi, "The Good Society," *Journal of Social Philosophy* 3 (1938): 154–57.

66. Karl Lowenstein, "Militant Democracy and Fundamental Rights," *American Political Science Review* 31 (1937). See also, for a different ideological perspective, Max Lerner, *It Is Later Than You Think* (New York: Viking, 1939).

67. Wilson, "Prelude to Authority," *American Political Science Review* 31 (1937): 13, 25; "Political Suppression in the Modern State," *Journal of Politics* 1 (1939): 241.

68. Smith, "Political Liberty Today: Is It Being Restricted or Enlarged by Economic Regulation?" *American Political Science Review* 31 (1937); "The Democratic Process," *Public Opinion Quarterly* 2 (1938), special supplement on "The Challenge of Totalitarianism"; Merriam, "The Assumptions of Democracy," *Political Science Quarterly* 53 (1938); Odegard and E. Albion Helms, *American Politics: A Study in Political Dynamics* (New York: Harper & Brothers, 1938).

ism that was emerging was not primarily a debate about the reality of pluralism, but rather about the democratic implications of that reality.

When the *Review of Politics* began publication in 1939, it not only
brought a new kind of religious perspective to the theory of democracy,
and one that extended beyond its Catholic sponsorship, but allied itself
both with the new wave of émigré thought and the agenda of Hutchins
and his intellectual allies, such as John Nef, the head of the Committee on
Social Thought, and Mortimer Adler, the promoter of the Great Books
program, at the University of Chicago. In the lead article of the first issue,
Jacques Maritain set the tone for much of what would be published during the next few years when he called for a new Christian humanism as a
bulwark against totalitarianism and for a rejection of both "*anthropocentric*
rationalism" and the "*irrational* tidal wave" of modern political thought
that had given rise to "bourgeois civilization." Although Friedrich found
some of the recent literature, such as the work of Kolnai, "lurid" and almost
as bad as the Nazi condemnation of "Liberalism," he too worried about the
rise of secularism and the false god of the state created by Hobbes, and
concluded that, in fact, "*the state does not exist.*" Wilson, himself a Catholic,
also began to take a religious turn in his political theory and argued that
democracy must rest on a combination of Christian principle and Greek
rationalism. Elliott reprised his argument about the connection between
pragmatism and totalitarianism and argued that "a *real* religious cleavage
as to the ends of human life and society can not be sustained in a constitutional state" and that there must be limits to liberal toleration. His colleague at Harvard, the sociologist Pitrim Sorokin, argued that the modern
age had fallen away from the Sermon on the Mount and an "ideational"
culture and now embraced a "sensate" or materialist culture. All and all,
the message was that too much democracy, particularly as it had been construed by liberal social scientists, was not a good thing, and what was
needed, as individuals such as Yves Simon maintained, was more authority. Nef saw liberalism as at least complicit in the rise of totalitarianism
and called for a return to the ideas of the Middle Ages. The modern crisis, he claimed, was really moral rather than material, and "the western
world, including the United States, has been preparing a gift for the power
of evil" by denying transcendental truth and Christianity. Social science,
in his view, had undermined democracy and assisted totalitarianism by
undercutting Christian humanism. The time had come for focusing on
"beauty, truth, and virtue." Adler, in a series of articles on the "dialectic
of morals," argued that ethical skepticism had led to the modern crisis and
that the answer was the creation of a new kind of "inductive" Thomism

that would defeat positivism on its own ground and prove that there was such a thing as objective moral knowledge. Even the Harvard sociologist Talcott Parsons joined in to criticize modern secular rationalization.[69]

By the end of the decade, one defender of liberalism lamented that there seemed to be "unanimity of opinion on one thing, namely, that liberalism is essentially negative, paralytic and disintegrative. Its boasted open-mindedness is nothing more than axiological anemia." Although he noted that such an indictment might be overdrawn, he warned that liberalism could not afford to allow its principles to give rise to "illiberalism." And the political theorist Mulford Q. Sibley suggested that "much of so-called liberalism which boasts of its tolerance of all points of view really assumes the dogma that no philosophy matters." At this point, however, Sabine felt compelled to defend a besieged liberalism and to reassess its "historical position."[70] He had consistently taken the position that fact and value involved distinct and unbridgeable logical domains and that ultimately values were based on commitment, choice, and preference and were historically and causally relative to the contexts in which they were embedded. It was, he argued, precisely the transcendental and absolutist beliefs of individuals such as Hegel and Marx and of modern totalitarian ideologies that rendered them vulnerable to logical and scientific criticism. Although Sabine viewed history as progress and wrote the history of political theory as the story of the rise of liberalism, a story that in later editions of his textbook presented totalitarianism as an aberration doomed to failure, his image of progress was based on the pragmatic assumption that logically and scientifically unsupportable values would fall by the wayside. Although he found it difficult to formulate a definition, in terms of either philosophy or institutions, he claimed that the essence of the liberal persuasion, from Bacon to Dewey, had been a moral commitment to "intelligence" as the basis of ordering human affairs. This, he argued, was manifest both in pluralism, which allowed and propagated free discussion, and in the attempt to apply knowledge to the rational direction of political life.[71] Years later, shortly before Sabine retired from Cornell, an undergraduate student asked him, after listening to his account of so many political ideas, what ideas *he* believed. His answer was "none." It was precisely this kind of skepticism that animated the critique of liberalism.

69. See *Review of Politics* 1 (1939); 2 (1940); 3 (1941).

70. Leslie M. Page, "Liberalism, Dogma, and Negativism," *Journal of Social Philosophy* 5 (1940): 346; Mulford Q. Sibley, "Apology for Utopia," *Journal of Politics* 2 (1940): 57.

71. Sabine, "The Historical Position of Liberalism," *The American Scholar* 10 (1940–41): 49–59.

Much of the discussion of democracy reflected the international political ambience and the growing domestic emphasis on leadership and positive government by the end of the decade. As one reviewer of several books on democracy noted, the period of debunking democracy had ended. "Negativism is no good in an ideological war; affirmation is necessary," and Karl Mannheim's attempt to meld centralized planning with liberal values had been translated into English.[72] It was, many believed, time to provide a coherent statement and defense of liberal democracy. The most important statement about the nature of democracy, however, was that of Herring in *The Politics of Democracy*. He had continued to argue that the democratic state reflected and represented the interests of groups in society, but he now not only more fully elaborated the position enunciated in his earlier work, but gave new voice to sentiments that had been pervasive in the discipline for a decade. What he presented was a realist account of democratic politics that now carried with it a much more developed normative vision.

Herring announced that "we shall examine the factors which are commonly treated as grave dangers to democracy: machine control, pressure politics, propaganda, monied interests, patronage, and bureaucracy. This is the rogue's gallery of American politics. . . . Yet these factors are but the reverse side of the elements integral to the democratic process." He maintained that it was necessary to stop debating the "democratic dogma" and realize that "the ultimate evaluation of democracy is to be found in the procedures through which it works" and through its "extralegal implementation." Ideals and ideal types of democracy, he claimed, placed too heavy a burden on analysis and obscured the way politics actually worked. He maintained that "political analysis is one thing; political philosophy is another," that it was important not substitute "the philosopher for the politician," and that what was required was to "search for ideals that suit the interests and the institutions." Herring, like everyone from Tocqueville to Dahl, assumed that studying the United States was, ipso facto, studying democracy, and, he claimed, it was in this very "milieu" with its attitude of "toleration" that "a science of politics may be developed and intelligence may be applied to our common problems."[73]

72. Alex Daspit, *Journal of Politics 2* (1940): 456. See Eduard Benes, *Democracy Today and Tomorrow* (New York: Macmillan, 1939); Ordway Tweed, *New Adventures in Democracy* (New York: McGraw-Hill, 1939); Ernest S. Griffith, *The Impasse of Democracy* (New York: Harrison-Hilton, 1939); James Feibleman, *Positive Democracy* (Chapel Hill: University of North Carolina Press, 1940); Karl Mannheim, *Man and Society in an Age of Reconstruction* (New York: Harcourt Brace, 1940); Carl L. Becker, *Modern Democracy* (New Haven: Yale University Press, 1941).

73. Herring, *The Politics of Democracy* (New York: W. W. Norton, 1940), vii-ix, 26, 30, 36, 287. See also *Public Administration and the Public Interest* (New York: McGraw-Hill, 1936).

For Herring, the goal of the democratic process was "to seek a balance of interests," and "bargaining" was the essence of the process. Here, along with party integration and governmental accountability, political rationality could be found in the conflict and adjustment between interest groups. He argued that "the good citizen cannot act without allying himself with various interests," and "the time for traditional politics is past," since "power conflicts call for interest adjustment through the careful formulation of public policy." And in the end, "policy is the product of political compromise, dressed in the language of justification by the philosopher of the winning side," and "democratic government is not a set of principles which must be consistently followed but rather a method for compromising differences and for freely expressing disagreement according to generally accepted rules of procedure." He noted that although it might appear that governance is centralized, the authority of the state and law was only a "fiction," since power is diverse and dispersed.[74]

Herring was willing to "defend the myth of the public interest because by its very vagueness it permits the freest interplay of group interests. . . . The dominant combination at any one time can claim that its program expresses the public interest." This "core of faith" about "justice" and the public interest was part of the consensus that allowed the system to operate. Citing Elliott, he acknowledged that this faith was a myth, but one that helped ensure that despite the rough and tumble of pressure politics, the players would not "infringe the rules of the game." Compromise and "adjustment" were, nevertheless, the real goals of "democratic politics." "Adjustment" was the word, and concept, that dominated Herring's discussion, and he made little secret of his support of positive government. It was in the end leadership and effective parties that made it all work and produced a "balance" among "power groups." Public opinion, he argued, was another myth. "If we talk about what the 'people' want, we reify an abstraction and accord it a moral conscience." What public opinion really amounted to was "those conditions whereby special interests are free to seek a working compromise harmonious with the values prevailing in the community." He referred to Dickinson when he claimed that "the political process in a democracy lies not in the expression of a mythical popular will but in the freedom for the group wills that press for expression."[75] To work properly, the process required not only strong parties and leaders but such things as decentralized power, opportunities for competition, values that supported the pursuit of group interests, adequate access to govern-

74. Ibid., 40, 45.
75. Ibid., 56, 179, 309, 313, 325, 335.

ment by diverse interests, a type of "liberal" who was not a "true believer," and the acceptance of certain amounts of economic inequality. This account well summed up what had not been fully stated since the early part of the 1930s, and, as in the case of the earlier account, it left little that was new to be said by those who subscribed to pluralism in the 1950s.

E. E. Schattschneider noted, but without expressing direct agreement, that this book represented a "new mood" in which "the whole subject undergoes a substantial transformation," and he deemed it the "most thoroughgoing defense of American politics ever written by a reputable scholar." Odegard counted Herring's book as in a league with Tocqueville and praised it as "one of the most lucidly expressed and penetrating analyses of the theoretical assumptions upon which American democracy rests." Odegard was in tune with Herring with respect to both political ideology and the role of political scientists, as well as with respect to democratic theory. He stressed the book's "significance for those who believe in the perpetuity of free institutions and the democratic way of life."[76] Among American political scientists, there was little dissent from the image that Herring advanced. Some, such as the political theorist John Lewis, emphasized the need for "the existence in the democratic community of a common interest or common will as the basis of political action," but he admitted that there was not a natural harmony or organic unity as nineteenth-century theorists had argued and insisted that unity should not be imposed from above or created by propaganda. Since even totalitarian regimes were now claiming the title of "democracy," it was important to specify what it actually was, but the requirements, he suggested, were minimal—an opportunity for voters to express individual preferences coupled with representatives and skillful administrators who could create and implement policy.[77]

Smith once again affirmed his long-standing belief that compromise and accommodation, now with more "discipline" from above, were still the essence of democracy and the opposite of totalitarianism. As a response to arguments such as that of Maritain and the new concerns about grounding democracy on religion and faith, he pointed out that political pluralism was, in principle, not really different from "Christian forbearance."[78]

76. E. E. Schattschneider, review of *The Politics of Democracy,* by Herring, *American Political Science Review* 34 (1940): 789; Odegard, review of *The Politics of Democracy,* by Herring, *Political Science Quarterly* 55 (1940): 474; "The Political Scientist and the Democratic Service State," *Journal of Politics* 2 (1940).

77. John D. Lewis, "Elements of Democracy," *American Political Science Review* 34 (1940): 476.

78. Smith, *The Democratic Way of Life* (1926; reprint, Chicago: University of Chicago Press, 1939);

While Elliott agreed that tolerance was part of the democratic ethos, and noted once more that it should extend to capitalist economics, he again voiced concern about the dangers of pluralism for the theory and practice of democracy.[79] Majoritarian democracy was, from a number of perspectives, clearly out of favor, but concerns about the New Deal and the impending war, as well as the new challenge to liberalism from within the discipline, were instigating a reformulation of democratic, that is, pluralist, theory.[80]

In a remarkable article published in 1941, two political scientists raised, with a degree of sophistication that would not generally be in evidence for a generation, some important theoretical and empirical questions about the place of "private associations and autonomous groups" in constitutional democracy and "the role they are to play in the whole political process." They noted that although there was general agreement that the existence of such entities was one of the major distinctions between totalitarianism and democracy, individualists, they claimed, still wanted to think them away, while statists wanted to swallow them up. Although freedom of association was generally considered an element of democracy, it had, they claimed, been viewed from the perspective of the individual and not in terms of group freedom, the issue of group identity, and the place of groups in the constitutional structure with respect to such functions as representation. Although a focus on groups raised questions about the danger of corporativism and the delegation of power to quasi-public groups, which was often associated with fascism, they suggested that what was evolving in the United States was a "a new sort of 'free corporativism'" in which "autonomous groups, grown to maturity from below, and not thrown together by some dictatorial architect overnight, share with the government of the State, openly and constitutionally, the function of promoting the interests of the community in all their variegated aspects."[81] Heinz Eulau, an émigré whose views were more attuned to the American per-

---

The Legislative Way of Life (Chicago: University of Chicago Press, 1940). See also Jacques Maritain, *Scholasticism and Politics* (New York: Macmillan, 1940).

79. Elliott, review of *Leviathan and Democracy,* by MacIver, *American Political Science Review* 35 (1941).

80. See, for example, Wilmoore Kendall, *John Locke and the Doctrine of Majority Rule* (Urbana: University of Illinois Press, 1965); Merriam, *What is Democracy?* (Chicago: University of Chicago Press, 1941); *On the Agenda of Democracy* (Cambridge, Mass.: Harvard University Press, 1941); Avery Craven, *Democracy in American Life* (Chicago: University of Chicago Press, 1941); R. B. Huliman, ed., *Aspects of Democracy* (Baton Rouge: Louisiana State University Press, 1941).

81. James J. Robbins and Gunnar Heckscher, "The Constitutional Theory of Autonomous Groups," *Journal of Politics* 3 (1941): 28.

spective than some of those who were becoming vocal in the conversations of political theory, reprised the long debate about sovereignty, which had begun before the turn of the century. He concluded that it was necessary to regenerate the idea of popular sovereignty, but along the lines of Preuss's Gierkean critique of the centralized "inorganic" state and his defense of a theory of political society based an "organic" plurality of associations.[82]

By the time that Hutchins, Nef, Adler, and Sorokin had published extended versions of their animadversions on modernity (including positivist social science, relativism, pragmatism, and liberalism), Wilson noted that "a battle is shaping up among academic thinkers, the lines of which are still difficult to locate," even though it was apparent that the divide was in part along secular versus theological lines. Friedrich suggested, however, that this literature constituted a "conservative revolution."[83] While Wilson was guardedly sympathetic, Friedrich, although voicing a belief in universal moral principles, argued that democracy was based less on a moral consensus than on a belief in the need to live together in disagreement. He published a new edition of his text *Constitutional Government and Politics* as *Constitutional Government and Democracy* (1941), in which he continued his attack on the idea of the state and pressed the image of democracy as involving less agreement on principles than on constitutional methods. This kind of argument about democracy as a method, already articulated by Herring and others, was further reinforced by the publication of the influential work of their Harvard colleague, Joseph Schumpeter, which stressed giving up the idea of democracy as a search for the common good and as giving voice to the will of popular majorities and, instead, reformulating it as a method for circulating decision-making elites.[84]

In his presidential address to the APSA in 1942, Frederic A. Ogg noted that in light of the impending political crisis, this might be the last meeting for some time, but that it had become clear that changing social conditions as well as new philosophical challenges meant that after the war

82. Heinz Eulau, "The Depersonalization of the State," *Journal of Politics* 4 (1942).

83. See Robert M. Hutchins, *The Higher Learning in America* (New Haven: Yale University Press, 1936); *Education for Freedom* (Baton Rouge: Louisiana State University Press, 1943); John V. Nef, *The United States and Civilization* (Chicago: University of Chicago Press, 1942); Mortimer Adler, *A Dialectic of Morals—Toward the Foundation of Political Philosophy* (Notre Dame: Notre Dame University Press, 1941); Pitrim A. Sorokin, *The Crisis of Our Age—The Social and Cultural Outlook* (New York: E. P. Dutton, 1941). See also reviews of these books by Wilson and Friedrich, *Journal of Politics* 4 (1942).

84. Friedrich, *Constitutional Government and Democracy* (Boston: Little-Brown, 1941); Joseph Schumpeter, *Capitalism, Socialism, and Democracy* (New York: Harper & Brothers, 1942). For a thorough discussion of Schumpeter, see John Medearis, *Joseph Schumpeter's Two Theories of Democracy* (Cambridge, Mass.: Harvard University Press, 2001).

the question of what constituted democracy would have to be faced anew.[85] By the beginning of the war, however, the redemption of pressure groups was, despite some distinct opposition,[86] nearly complete among mainstream political scientists. Such groups were viewed as vehicles of public opinion and representation and as "the modern expression of democracy by the people and for the people." They were also seen as "particularly an American institution," which fit into the two-party system and should not be confused with such things as third parties, the proliferation of ideological parties characteristic of countries such as Germany, or mere lobbies and propaganda. But although the pluralist image of politics and democracy dominated the literature, political scientists were hardly entirely unanimous regarding the democratic implications of this image.

While Herring had suggested that parties and pressure groups fitted well together, V. O. Key recommended focusing less on parties than on pressure groups as the principal "contenders for power." Schattschneider, however, saw the latter as a "parasite" on the "sovereign majority" and as inhibiting parties, those "orphans of political philosophy," from exercising their democratizing functions of aggregating and universalizing public opinion. And Lasswell continued to maintain that democracy involved seeking justice through popular majorities, even if majority opinion might require purification though psychiatric therapy.[87] Even the defense of pluralism did not break along what, in American political terms, were conservative and liberal lines. The sociologist Robert Nisbet presented a conservative case for pluralism in his attack on majoritarian democracy, including Rousseau's philosophy and similar ideas, as destroying the natural fabric of society.[88] What was very clear, however, was a basic split between, on the one hand, the perspectives of liberalism and its "philosophy of American democracy," centered around the concept of pluralism and values such as compromise and which was widely embraced in the social sciences, and, on the other hand, a new mode of conservative European thought, rejecting liberalism and pluralism and its basic philosophical premises and generally set against the project of social science.[89]

85. Frederic A. Ogg, "Democracy After the War," *American Political Science Review* 36 (1942).

86. See, for example, J. A. C. Grant, "The Gild Returns to America," *Journal of Politics* 4 (1942); Stuart Chase, *Democracy Under Pressure* (New York: Twentieth Century Fund, 1945).

87. V. O. Key, *Politics, Parties, and Pressure Groups* (New York: Thomas Crowell, 1942); Schattschneider, *Party Government* (New York: Farrar and Rinehart, 1942); Lasswell, *Democracy Through Public Opinion* (Menasha, Wis.: George Banta, 1942).

88. Robert A. Nisbet, "Rousseau and Totalitarianism," *Journal of Politics* 5 (1943). See also Emil Lederer, *The State of the Masses* (New York: W. W. Norton, 1940).

89. See, for example, Charner Perry, ed., *The Philosophy of American Democracy* (Chicago: University

Just as political theorists had created an academic version of liberalism, conservatism as a political theory slowly came into being as its counterpoint. For example, in a series of articles, Wilson began to move still more explicitly toward what he termed a "conservative" political philosophy. This was not easy to specify in terms of contemporary literature, but he harked back to individuals and ideas such as Burke, T. H. Green, Hegel, and Chancellor Kent and a vision of organic society, and fastened on to characteristics such as incremental change, the importance of tradition and continuity with the past, the place of Christian morality in maintaining the social fabric, and a rejection of utopianism and radicalism.[90] During World War II, American political scientists, partly because of wartime occupations and foci, did little in the way of directly confronting issues in democratic theory, and they awoke after the war to find that their vision had been seriously challenged and even subverted.

More than anyone else during this period, John Hallowell, at Duke University, gave a unified voice to the claims that composed the growing critique of liberalism, and his work embodied themes that would later be more closely identified with individuals such as Strauss, Eric Voegelin, and others who would be associated with the conservative wing of political theory but that would eventually be embraced by a much wider range of academic ideologies within the subfield. Influenced by thinkers such as Kolnai and theologians such as Reinhold Niebuhr, Hallowell began to address the "decline of liberalism." He attributed the rise of Nazism to the acceptance of positivism and the separation of fact and value among German academics and jurists, and he interpreted scientism in American political science as a tributary of the development of European positivism and its attack on metaphysics. Hallowell claimed that liberalism had devolved from its original seventeenth-century form to its present "degenerate" condition, which was characterized by a trend toward intellectual nihilism, in turn culminating politically in anarchy and tyranny. Liberalism, internally weakened by its inability to defend transcendentally its own substantive values and convictions, collapsed, and Nazism developed as a practical "corollary." And "the spiritual crisis out of which totalitarianism emerged is a crisis, peculiar not to Germany, but to Western civilization." The reconstruction of liberalism could be effected, Hallowell argued, only by a religious and

---

of Chicago Press, 1943); Helmut Kuhn, *Freedom Forgotten and Remembered* (Chapel Hill: University of North Carolina, Press, 1943).

90. Wilson, "A Theory of Conservatism," *American Political Science Review* 35 (1941); "The Ethics of Political Conservatism," *Ethics* 53 (1942); "Tradition and Propaganda," *Journal of Politics* 5 (1943); "The Revival of Organic Theory," *American Political Science Review* 36 (1942).

philosophical grounding in modern theology. Voegelin considered Hallowell's critique as right on target in recognizing that "totalitarian ideas are not an event superceding liberalism, but the logical outcome of the internal inconsistencies of the liberal position." His only complaint was that Hallowell did "not quite go back far enough" in seeking the roots of Western decadence even though he recognized that liberalism today must be placed on "a more solid basis in the religious experiences and the metaphysics which lend vitality to its principal tenets."[91]

Hallowell most directly entered the conversation by responding to a challenge that the sociologist William Foote Whyte had presented to political scientists in the midst of the war. Whyte suggested that the contemporary ethical and philosophical turn in political science was a typical response to times of crisis, but that the unfortunate result was that political scientists were forgetting about "plain politics" and the description and analysis of political behavior. Hallowell took this article as an opening for discharging his animus toward political science for, paradoxically, doing what Whyte claimed it was not doing, and along the way he attributed to political scientists, as well as to Whyte, philosophical ideas such as positivism and nihilism and images of liberalism that were largely unknown to them. Hallowell had direct experience of the conditions in Germany during the rise of Hitler and of matters about which most Americans were yet only dimly aware, but in assessing and explaining the European situation, he not only adopted the émigré account of it as emanating from the decadence of Western philosophy, but applied it to a critique of democracy in the United States and to the premises of American political science.[92]

Although Hallowell's philosophical arguments had little to do with concrete domestic political issues, the link between academic and political discourse about liberalism that had characterized the 1930s was still manifest in work such as Frederick von Hayek's attack on collectivism and social planning as the "road to serfdom" and his attending condemnation of relativism, historicism, and scientism. Smith reflected the general mood of perplexity and irritation among many American thinkers in the face of these criticisms. Although his Keynesian position on economics was quite the opposite of von Hayek's philosophy, he considered von Hayek's arguments

91. John H. Hallowell, *The Decline of Liberalism. With Particular References to German Politico-Legal Thought* (Berkeley: University of California Press, 1943); Eric Voegelin, review of *The Decline of Liberalism,* by Hallowell, *Journal of Politics* 5 (1944), 108–9.

92. William Foote Whyte, "A Challenge to Political Scientists," *American Political Science Review* 37 (1943); Hallowell, "Politics and Ethics," *American Political Science Review* 38 (1944).

"hysterical" and claimed that they were "the inevitable result of a book written by a European who has fled bondage in one land . . . and carries his fears with him into the land which he does not intimately know." And political theorists such as Friedrich did not look upon the book favorably.[93]

Liberalism, as a form of political life, was largely identified by both its critics and defenders with pluralist politics, but for the émigrés on both the left and right, pluralism was viewed through the lens of Weimar and perceived as the political counterpart and consequence of a defective liberal philosophy and as the precursor of mass society and totalitarianism. Otto Kirchheimer, a member of the Frankfurt School and already a critic of pluralism in Weimar, took his bearings, paradoxically, from both Carl Schmitt and Karl Marx. He warned against the dismissal of the idea of the state and the acceptance of "group interests superseding the . . . sovereign community," and he claimed that the pluralist image of the state as a neutral "arbiter" only concealed the locus of real power and produced ad hoc justifications for government intervention. Kirchheimer's arguments for "bringing the state back in," to employ a phrase characteristic of a generation later, adumbrated those of later critics of pluralism within political science such as Theodore Lowi. Kirchheimer claimed that groups were, in fact, not internally democratic and that the process of group politics actually constrained rather than enhanced competition. It also produced a vacuum of authority in which, as in the case of the New Deal, sovereign power was parceled out to private or quasi-public groups.[94] Hallowell also began to turn his attention to more indigenous and specific accounts of pluralism such as those characteristic of the empirical work of Herring and the theory of political compromise advanced by Smith. The idea that conflict and compromise were at the heart of democracy was, Hallowell argued, a result of positivism, pluralism, and relativism, and reflected the denial of objective values and the rejection of moral absolutism.[95]

It was in part this incipient crisis in democratic theory near the end of the war that prompted a meeting of the Political Theory Research Committee of the APSA. Wilson, who chaired the Committee and planned and organized the meeting, once again noted that there was a "deep cleavage among political theorists in the area of primary ideas," but, despite the obvious divide between "theological" and "secular" points of view, he, as

93. Friedrich A. von Hayek, *The Road to Serfdom* (Chicago: University of Chicago Press, 1944); Smith, review of *The Road To Serfdom*, by Hayek, *Ethics* 55 (1945): 224; Friedrich, review of *The Road To Serfdom*, by Hayek, *American Political Science Review* 39 (1945).

94. Otto Kirchheimer, "In Quest of Sovereignty," *Journal of Politics* 3 (1944).

95. Hallowell, "Compromise as a Political Ideal," *Ethics* 54 (1944).

well as most of the participants, still had difficulty specifying the exact axis of the division. What was clearly involved, however, was the increasing distance, on several fronts, between the content and form of political theory as it had been practiced as part of political science and as it was now taking shape under the influence of the émigré perspective, and this included the growing controversy about what constituted democracy.[96] At this point, even Mannheim, whose work had seemed to many to sustain the relativistic ethic of American social science, was suggesting that maybe new Christian values should guide democratic planning in modern society, and Niebuhr rejected the traditional secular defense of democracy in favor of a new form of Christian "vindication."[97]

It was this kind of radical divergence about the basis of democratic values that prompted J. Roland Pennock to seek a middle ground by accepting the idea of democracy as a process of reconciling interests, along with the kind of relativism and skepticism that this entailed, while still holding to "a rational and empirical foundation for democratic theory" that would provide a certain universal standard of right and prevent a lapse into nihilism. In a similar vein, Herman Finer argued that while the democratic world was characterized by "bargaining and adjustment between interests," it was necessary to find a unity and a "faith" or "spiritual" basis in this modern relativistic age. The faith that he suggested was the pragmatic one of tolerance and accommodation, which, he admitted, really meant being "driven to embrace the faith that there is none, and therefore to draw the social conclusions of this." It was, however, just such a conclusion that concerned the critics of liberalism. While one might characterize Pennock's and Finer's position as a liberal contingent optimism, Wilson advanced his conservatism as representing a "contingent pessimism" in line with Christianity and ideas such as those of Hannah Arendt, Schmitt, Voegelin, and Niebuhr and as distinguished in part by a relinquishment of the idea of progress that had governed both nineteenth-century thought and subsequent liberalism.[98] It is not surprising that after

96. Wilson, "The Work of the Political Theory Panel," *American Political Science Review* 38 (1944).

97. Mannheim, *Diagnosis of Our Time* (New York: Oxford University Press, 1944); Reinhold Niebuhr, *The Children of Light and the Children of Darkness: A Vindication of Democracy and a Critique of its Traditional Defense* (New York: Charles Scribner's Sons, 1944). See also William Aylott Orton, *The Liberal Tradition: A Study of the Social and Spiritual Conditions of Freedom* (New Haven: Yale University Press, 1945); and Sabine's skeptical review of *The Liberal Tradition*, by Orton, *American Political Science Review* 40 (1946).

98. J. Roland Pennock, "Reason, Value Theory, and the Theory of Democracy," *American Political Science Review* 38 (1944); Herman Finer, "Toward a Democratic Theory," *American Political Science Review* 39 (1945): 255, 263; Wilson, "Pessimism in American Politics," *Journal of Politics* 7 (1945).

being long out of print, Tocqueville's ambivalent account of *Democracy in America* was republished in 1945.

While liberalism would maintain its dominance in both politics and political theory until the end of the decade, the academic critique of liberalism was gaining ground. Just as positive images of liberalism had, a generation earlier, been projected backward in telling the story of Western political thought and explaining the present, a negative view of liberalism and its history was fast becoming the basis of a new story that captured the imagination of much of political theory in the 1950s and 1960s. Although the general social and political environment may have been congenial to this development, the descent of liberalism, as in the case of biological evolution, was most essentially a matter of contingency coupled with the conceptual potential and the structural character of the disciplinary conversation. The émigrés were to liberalism as an image of American political identity what a meteorite may have been to dinosaurs. It was not liberalism's small brain, its large size, or the climate that brought it to the brink of extinction, but rather an unexpected and unpredictable incursion from an alien world. By the 1970s, varieties of liberalism would rise again, but, like birds, those vulnerable successors of the dinosaurs, they would never again be free of natural enemies.

PLURALISM REDUX

The word "pluralists" may be properly
applied to these investigators since
they deal with the plurality of observed
group forms.

—Earl Latham

Subsequent to World War II, it was a commitment neither to empirical science, on the part of behavioralists, nor to normative concerns, on the part of many political theorists, that most fundamentally precipitated the estrangement between these elements in the discourse of political science. Although the concept of science entered into the debate in various ways as a touchstone, the basic catalyst and axis of division, as in the case of the controversy about the direction of the discipline that characterized the 1920s, was a rupture in the consensus about democratic theory. The underlying tenets of mainstream political science's vision of liberal democracy were, at this point, once again sinking into the background, but the critique of liberalism drew them to the surface, just as the attack on the scientific study of politics initiated a more sophisticated philosophical articulation of scientism.[1] The philosopher Morris Cohen's testament to his

1. For a discussion of political science's involvement in the philosophy of science, see Gunnell, *Between Philosophy and Politics: The Alienation of Political Theory.*

faith in liberalism had hardly mentioned the concept except to indicate optimism about human nature and an attitude of openness to change and a rejection of the extreme attitudes that he associated with a conservative outlook,[2] but it was these general attributes that many of the émigrés called into question. Hans Morgenthau, for example, claimed that the fundamental "inability of our society to understand, and to cope with, the political problems which the age poses" was the consequence of a "general decay in the political thinking of the Western world" that was manifest in the evolution of liberalism and its naive embrace "of reason, of progress, and of peace." Liberals, he claimed, simply failed to recognize that fascism was not an anomaly but something rooted historically in the "bankrupt age that preceded it."[3]

While in effect conventional histories of political theory had been, and continued to be, histories of the development and progress of liberalism, what was emerging from the new wave of literature in political theory was an image of civilizational decline in which liberalism, and political science itself, was deeply implicated. By the late 1940s, the challenge was sufficiently focused that a more specific recovery and affirmation of the liberal tradition seemed necessary. Frederick Watkins, at Yale, noted that while "most people are aware that liberalism is in the throes of a major crisis," the "full significance" was not yet adequately understood. His goal was to "recapture" the meaning of liberalism and to make it "whole," and he set out to demonstrate that liberalism was not just a "policy" or even a single tradition, but "the modern embodiment of all the characteristic traditions of Western politics. If liberalism fails to survive, it will mean the end of the Western political tradition." In his view, the choice was a stark one— between liberalism and totalitarianism—and the essential feature of liberalism, as so many of his colleagues would soon affirm, was intellectual and political pluralism. He even interpreted Rousseau's general will as a pluralist consensus, and he suggested that the "hope of modern liberalism lies in the further development of private associations."[4]

The behavioral movement in political science, as it emerged in the 1950s, was certainly characterized by a renewed emphasis on science, but such an emphasis was hardly novel. The search for an authentic science of politics had, for a century, been a consistent and enduring dimension of American

2. Morris Cohen, *The Faith of a Liberal* (New York: Henry Holt, 1946).

3. Hans J. Morgenthau, *Scientific Man and Power Politics* (Chicago: University of Chicago Press, 1946), v, vi. 7.

4. Frederick Watkins, *The Political Tradition of the West: A Study of the Development of Modern Liberalism* (Cambridge, Mass.: Harvard University Press, 1948), ix, 118.

political science, and the commitment to science had never been disjoined
from the search for democracy. Political science had always been a science
of and for democracy, despite the changing concepts behind the word, and
the values of science and democracy had been viewed as complementary
and even identical.[5] Although by the 1960s, many critics of behavioralism
would charge that the pursuit of science had become an end in itself, the
recommitment to a scientific study of politics that began in the 1940s was
still informed by the purpose, at least latent, of gaining authority and control in political matters and enhancing democracy, and this recommitment
was in large measure a response to the attack on liberalism and on what
Lasswell had referred to as the "liberal science of politics" and the American
"science of democracy." Behavioralism was at its core an affirmation of liberalism, and the behavioral movement was less a revolution in attitudes
toward science than a counter-revolution or reformation in defense of a
long-standing commitment to science and, above all, a commitment to
liberalism qua pluralism.[6] Despite the overt emphasis on separating fact
and value, behavioralism was, as much of political science before it, in large
measure devoted to finding the values of democracy in the practice of
American politics, and it was at ease with the notion of a separation
between empirical and normative theory precisely in part because of the
assumption that the facts and values were, at bottom, one and the same.
It was in this context that a number of political scientists set themselves
the task of rearticulating the theory of pluralist democracy that had last
been given full and pointed expression by Herring on the eve of the war.
In speaking of this as a theory, I am not necessarily equating the term "theory" with its usage in political science at that time, but rather suggesting,
as in the case of the phrase "theory of the state," that it was an empirical
and normative account of social reality and of processes that they claimed
validated the United States as a democracy.

In 1951, David Truman offered a general systematic account of groups
and particularly of the role of pressure groups or, as he preferred to call
them, "interest groups" in American government. Truman had been a graduate student at Chicago in the 1930s, but it was not there, in the intellectual universe of Merriam and Lasswell, that he generated his pluralistic
perspective, even though he was first exposed to the work of Bentley in

---

5. For an insightful and comprehensive account, see Rogers M. Smith, "Still Blowing in the
Wind: The American Quest for a Democratic, Scientific Study of Politics," *Daedalus* 126 (1997).

6. For a fuller discussion of this period, and of the impact of émigré thought, see Gunnell, *The
Descent of Political Theory*, chapters 9 and 10.

Merriam's seminar and, like so many others of his generation, became dedicated to the idea that political science needed a general theoretical framework that would bring coherence to the discipline. Although he emphasized that Bentley "has been the principal benchmark for my thinking," he was far removed from Bentley's original philosophical and political perspective. Truman's focus on Bentley had been developed while teaching at Cornell, but it was his association with Herring and others that prompted him to adapt Bentley's thesis to the kind of empirical research that was beginning to emerge in the 1940s. Truman did not advance his work as a theory of "pluralism," a term he associated with the literature of the 1920s and that he believed had held promise but failed to contain a "real" theory. This conclusion was probably based on his lack of familiarity with much of the literature, but also on his idea of theory as a conceptual scheme for ordering empirical data. Although Truman drew on a wide range of material, his aim, like Herring's, was to transcend the persistent propensity among some to treat the presence of interest groups as a "pathology," as well as the tendency, even among his behavioral allies, to neglect them in favor of looking at the behavior of individuals. Although he claimed that groups were an essential part of any society and had always been central to the practice of American politics, they had, he argued, assumed an even larger place in modern life. He admitted that there might be reason for concern about the manner in which groups sometimes operated in a democratic political order, but it was first necessary to grasp accurately their actual and basic role in the governmental process. Although he suggested that his work was in the tradition of Madison as well as Bentley, it did not, apart from stressing Madison's image of the manner in which factions tended toward equilibrium, reflect Madison's concerns and attitude toward factions. It exemplified the theory that had emerged in the late 1920s and early 1930s, but where it did accord with Madison was in the assumption that it was possible to have a popular government without a people.

Truman concluded that the political process could not be understood apart from the behavior of groups and particularly those that he called "organized and potential interest groups."[7] The former had become as much a part of the political system as parties and the formal constitutional institutions, and the latter, or "unorganized" elements, represented an "ideological consensus" that determined the "rules of the game." Although Truman did not deny that there could be implications of group politics that were inimical to representative democracy, a "pathogenic" or "morbific"

7. David Truman, *The Governmental Process* (New York: Knopf, 1951), 502.

danger, his work was devoted primarily to describing and explaining how groups functioned in representative government, and he made it clear that his study was intended in part to demonstrate not only that there was no inclusive public and public interest, but there need not be one. His assessment was that government was a center of "interest-based" power to which groups sought "access" and thereby produced government decisions. As long as there were numerous points of entry and reasonable opportunities for group articulation, the process worked reasonably well in terms of the adequacy of both inputs and outputs. Balance or equilibrium was facilitated by "multiple or overlapping membership" and by the limits produced by consensus. "It is thus multiple memberships in potential groups based on widely held and accepted interests that serve as a balance wheel in a going political system like that of the United States."[8]

Earl Latham's work, published a year later, was explicitly an attempt to endorse empirical pluralist theory while disengaging it from its normative background. Latham claimed that he was "concerned less with prejudged progress of society and economic reform than with the correct investigation of the many phenomena connected with the activities of groups in society," or with what he called an "analytical" rather than a "philosophic" pluralism.[9] But at a point at which political science was still attempting to explain and defend its image of democracy, this distinction was difficult to maintain. Robert Dahl's earliest work also did not indicate any distinct attachment to the normative pluralist tradition, and he appeared to have only a vague sense of the literature of the 1920s. What he addressed was the difficulty of achieving rational foreign policy in the context of contemporary mass society "where decisions are arrived at as a result of bargaining among a great variety of different groups."[10] But by the early 1950s and his collaboration with Charles Lindblom, who maintained that a general theory was already implicit in the work of Herring, he had joined a growing chorus attesting to the American political and economic system as one of self-correcting "countervailing powers."[11] Dahl and Lindblom argued that the best approximation of democracy, which they defined in terms of the values of equality and majority rule, was achieved less by congressional checks or any formal institutional arrangements than by a process called "polyarchy" whereby power devolved to small groups. This solved

8. Ibid., 514.

9. Earl Latham, *The Group Basis of Politics* (Ithaca: Cornell University Press, 1952), 9.

10. Robert A. Dahl, *Congress and Foreign Policy* (New York: Harcourt Brace, 1950), 261–62.

11. See John Kenneth Galbraith, *American Capitalism: The Concept of Countervailing Powers* (Boston: Houghton-Mifflin, 1952).

what they designated as "the first problem of politics"—how to keep rulers from being tyrants—and they concluded that "polyarchy, not democracy, is the actual solution," that is, not "democracy" in what they took to be the traditional senses of that concept.[12] Building, in their view, on Madison, they wished to put the "democratic dogma" finally to rest.

Dahl and Lindblom's underlying contrast models were the United States and Russia, and they described the former as representing a political process whereby leaders or elites were forced to compete for support. Such a system, however, which critics would later call the theory of elitist democracy, required "social indoctrination and habituation" as well as agreement on the rules of the game by all participants. They stressed that polyarchy *"requires a considerable degree of social pluralism,"* and they claimed that it was the failure to grasp this that led utopian egalitarians like Rousseau astray. They argued that the dangers of mass society and control by a welfare state had been exaggerated and that "social pluralism was so great in the United States that, combined with the constitutional structure, the extent of bargaining among diverse social groups in making government policy is a dominant feature of our political system"—nothing less than a "social separation of powers."[13] They concluded that classical liberalism and socialism were dead ends, but that freedom and the fundamental elements of a rational society could be achieved through "incrementalism." Social pluralism and constant bargaining at every level among group leaders and politicians were the key features of democratic or polyarchal politics and more important than either constitutional structures or individual political participation. The form of American government and the nature of American society encouraged and provided opportunities for bargaining, but this required preserving small group life and creating personalities and democratic identities suited to polyarchy.

It would be difficult to specify anything in the work of Truman, Latham, Dahl, and Lindblom that theoretically exceeded the earlier literature, but this work was less a rediscovery of the wheel than an attempt to demonstrate that the United States in fact invented and possessed it and to affirm that there was substance to the theory and practice of liberal democracy that was, in a variety of ways, being denigrated in the recent literature of political theory.[14] Coker's reaction was typical of the response that the crit-

---

12. Dahl and Charles E. Lindblom, *Politics, Economics, and Welfare: Planning and Politico-Economic Systems Resolved into Basic Social Process* (New York: Harper & Brothers, 1953), 273, 275–76.

13. Ibid., 302, 307–8.

14. For a concise overview of the pluralist literature, see G. David Garson, *Group Theories of Politics* (Beverly Hills: Sage, 1978).

ical literature had engendered in the community of traditional political science. Although he had long been uneasy about certain elements of pluralist theory and hardly an enthusiastic advocate of the emerging behavioral persuasion, he was not sympathetic to the perspective represented in the work of individuals such as Niebuhr, Maritain, and Hallowell. Coker claimed that these thinkers were, as a matter of principle, distrustful of human nature and individualism, that they mistakenly wanted to absorb political theory into moral and theological discussions, and that it was ludicrous to suggest that conditions in Germany were a product of liberalism.[15] Although the émigrés, apart from Voegelin, who had visited the United States as a student supported by the Rockefeller foundation, probably were for the most part ignorant of the debates of the 1920s in American political science, their position on scientism, pluralism/liberalism, and pragmatism (or the contemporary version of that philosophy), was uncannily similar to that of Elliott.

It was somewhat difficult to find a label to represent the position that was often associated with these early critiques of liberalism, but just as liberalism in political theory had originally been an effervescence of liberalism in politics, conservatism was continuing to be infused with a theoretical or academic meaning. In 1950, Lionel Trilling, speaking of the "liberal imagination," had asserted that "in the United States at this time liberalism is not only the dominant but even the sole intellectual tradition,"[16] but the conservative "imagination" had already sprung into being. Hartz and others would note the absence of a conservative tradition in America, but like liberalism, conservatism in the discourse of political scientists and historians was largely an analytical construction. Once conservatism had become the antithesis of liberalism in politics, intellectuals and academicians began, as in the case of liberalism in the 1930s, to empty it of concrete political content and provide it not only with philosophical meaning but with a history of its own.[17] In both politics and political theory, there was a debate between liberalism and conservatism, but there was an increasing distance between the terms of these controversies that would never again be bridged. By the 1960s, it would be common for academicians to inform students that what they, as well as journalists and others,

15. Coker, "Some Present-Day Critics of Liberalism," *American Political Science Review* 47 (1953).
16. Lionel Trilling, *The Liberal Imagination* (New York: Viking, 1950), ix.
17. See, for example, Peter Viereck, *Conservatism Revisited* (Chicago: University of Chicago Press, 1949); Russell Kirk, *The Conservative Mind* (Chicago: H. Regnery, 1953); Lippmann, *The Public Philosophy* (Boston: Little-Brown, 1955); Hallowell, *The Moral Foundations of Democracy* (Chicago: University of Chicago Press, 1954); Clinton Rossiter, *Conservatism in America* (New York: Knopf, 1955).

took to be liberalism and conservatism in politics, was actually quite different from, if not the opposite of, the actual historical and philosophical meaning of these terms. This deeper meaning, however, was more an invention than a discovery.

The émigré critique of liberalism, which represented one strain of conservatism in political theory, peaked in mid-century in two series of Walgreen lectures delivered, respectively, by Leo Strauss (1949) and Voegelin (1951) at the University of Chicago.[18] Strauss claimed that the "unqualified relativism" that had taken over German philosophy a generation ago was now characteristic of Western thought in general and especially American social science and liberalism. It was not the first time, he suggested, that a victor had been defeated by the ideas of the vanquished. "Liberal relativism," historicism, and the triumph of natural science, with its emphasis on the heterogeneity of fact and value, led to a rejection of "natural right" and opened the door to nihilism and totalitarianism. To understand this crisis, a crisis of both ideas and politics, required the historical project of both tracing its evolution in modern political theory, an evolution that was in fact a decline since Machiavelli and Hobbes, and recovering the truth of classical political philosophy, as exemplified in the work of Plato and Aristotle, away from which the modern age had consciously turned.[19] For Voegelin, communism was only the "radical expression" of liberalism, and consequently an important issue was who was "soft" on liberalism. In reviewing Arendt's *Origins of Totalitarianism,* he had criticized her for still embracing certain liberal assumptions and failing to recognize the extent to which the "typically liberal, progressive, pragmatic attitude" was implicated in the decline of the West and how much "liberals and totalitarians have in common." Arendt responded by stating that "liberals are clearly not totalitarians," but she continued to emphasize "the fact that liberal or positivistic elements also lend themselves to totalitarian thinking."[20] Wilson hailed Voegelin as "one of the most distinguished interpreters to America of the non-liberal stream of European thought," as exposing the "presuppositions of liberalism," and as leading political science "away from the obsolescence of positivist liberalism."[21]

It was in the wake of these lectures that Daniel Boorstin, also speaking in the Walgreen series, offered his account of the "genius of American pol-

18. Voegelin, *The New Science of Politics* (Chicago: University of Chicago Press, 1952); Leo Strauss, *Natural Right and History* (Chicago: University of Chicago Press, 1953).

19. Strauss, *Natural Right and History.*

20. Hannah Arendt, *Review of Politics* 15 (1953): 68–85.

21. Wilson, review of *New Science of Politics,* by Voegelin, *American Political Science Review* 47 (1953), 542–43.

itics" as a kind of serendipitous consensual ignorance. His position might be called "conservatism," but it was of a very different sort. His argument was, in a peculiar way, a reprise of Hart's 1907 statement in the context of a similar failing faith in the ability to articulate the theoretical character of American democracy, but it was also an attempt to give credence to what had, from the beginning, been an essential element of the pluralist vision, that is, the existence of an underlying consensus. Boorstin set out to demonstrate that although there might not be an American people in any traditional republican sense, there was—in addition to the institutions that, like the structure of a kaleidoscope, held the fragments of society together—a historically rooted value consensus and tradition that both pointed toward an "end of ideology" and sustained and gave credence to a vision of *e pluribus unum*. Boorstin's image of the United States was likened to Machiavelli's assessment of Rome. Its genius and virtue came not from some political theory but from circumstances, history, and institutions. The lack of a feudal society and a felicitous environment made everyone effective pragmatists. There was an American "orthodoxy," but no democratic philosophy that could be specified, transformed into a set of principles, and disseminated.

Boorstin's image of American of "givenness" was perhaps the quintessential statement of the thesis of American exceptionalism among American historians and support for the "end of ideology" argument that emerged during this period. It was, he claimed, the untheoretical character of American politics that, from the time of the Puritans onward, successfully defused all forms of fanaticism and produced a kind of "natural conservatism" that encompassed what, politically, was construed as liberalism and conservatism. The American Revolution had not really been a revolution in European terms, but a rebellion in support of entrenched democratic norms, and the Civil War was less the product of conflicting ideologies than a sectional dispute against a background of common values and, in the end, an affirmation of underlying principles. Even religious differences were based on a fundamental nondenominational and pragmatic ethos that sustained tolerance. Although Americans in the 1950s may have believed that they needed a democratic faith and philosophy and a sense of identity and purpose, these had been there all along in the very practice of American politics, and Americans should be thankful that, in an age of "idolatry," unity was based on something, like the Holy of Holies in the temple of Solomon, that was invisible and intangible.[22]

22. Daniel J. Boorstin, *The Genius of American Politics* (Chicago: University of Chicago Press, 1953).

Although Louis Hartz was far from happy with what he believed were the consequences of the American consensus, his image of the liberal tradition was basically the same as that described by Boorstin—the lack of feudal past and the absence of a social revolution had given rise to an endemic set of values that overrode any ideological differences between political parties. While Boorstin had postulated a natural conservatism that circumscribed political differences, Hartz found a natural liberalism that functioned as the fundamental American *Weltanschauung* and explained the small difference between parties. Although a leitmotif of Hartz's book was an attack on an atmosphere induced by the Cold War, liberalism, paradoxically, was also being attacked, despite the difference in ideological perspective, by individuals such as Joseph McCarthy. But this only indicated the disjunction between the discourses of political science and politics and the extent to which Hartz was already constrained by the past of the academic image of liberalism. For other thinkers of the time such as historian Arthur Ekirch, the problem with liberalism was a "decline," in action and spirit, from its classical form. This decline, he claimed, was manifest in a variety of ideas including Rooseveltian collectivism, McCarthyism, and conservatism.[23] Hartz pointed to many of the same problems, but attributed them to the apotheosis of the liberal tradition in America, which prevented Americans from understanding others and, because of its unconscious character, understanding themselves. This tradition, he claimed, echoing Tocqueville's account of the American mind, was one that Americans did not know that they had embraced, even though the "American way of life" was the "liberal way of life." This "fixed, dogmatic liberalism" was not a "movement" or a "party," but a submerged and irrational "moral unity" and a kind of tyranny of the majority based on an attachment to the ideas of Locke. It was "not even recognized for what it is: liberalism," and it was an "articulation of Locke which usually does not know that Locke himself was involved." The significance of Bentley's work, Hartz suggested, was that it represented an implicit recognition that the "free and easy play of pressure groups was a real characteristic of the American liberal world and the moral settlement underlying it." It was not, however, that Hartz wished to jettison liberalism anymore than Tocqueville had wished to eliminate individualism and equality, but rather to demonstrate that, as if suffering from some autoimmune disease, the spirit of the body politic was attacking itself. Liberalism had been an escape from authoritarianism, but it carried its own genetic defects. After devoting an entire book to the dangers

23. Arthur Ekirch, *The Decline of American Liberalism* (New York: Longmans, Green, & Co., 1955).

of "liberal absolutism" and the inability of Americans to think and act out-side the liberal consensus, he concluded, paradoxically, that "the hope of the free world surely lies in the power for transcending itself inherent in American liberalism."[24]

Hartz's language and rationale were, despite the philosophical differ-ence, much like that of Strauss and others of this period who undertook a critique of liberal democracy, in response to a perceived "crisis" of con-temporary political ideas and institutions, by tracing its putative histori-cal roots. "So in fact," Hartz claimed, "it is the entire crisis of our time which compels us to make that journey to Europe and back which ends in the discovery of the American liberal world." If Hartz had omitted the concept of liberalism from his account of American political thought, the basic argument would not have been altered. His use of "liberalism" to stand for features he wished to emphasize indicates that his work was more an entry, couched in historical form, in a contemporary debate about lib-eralism than an account of any historical tradition. This tradition was a rhetorical construction, but although Hartz did not invent the idea of a liberal tradition, he, more than anyone else, contributed to the sedimen-tation of the idea that there was such a tradition.

Hartz admitted that liberalism was a vague term even if used in "the classic Lockean sense," but there was, ironically, no such sense.[25] He was one of the first to categorize Locke as a liberal, let alone as the founder of a liberal tradition. Hartz, coming to Harvard from Youngstown, Ohio, embraced the idea of such a tradition just as surely as Strauss and others had when they came to America from Germany and stumbled onto, or into, it. It was already there, largely a product of the academic culture of the 1930s, to be manipulated, re-formed, and infused with new meaning—a meaning that largely reversed the dominant story from one of progress to decline. In a later elaboration of his construction of American liberal-ism, Hartz revealed, but maybe inadvertently, that what he referred to as liberalism was not really any particular historical tradition at all, but sim-ply a tendency toward a "pervasive and unnatural attachment" to "sym-bols such as individualism, equality, competition, and opportunity."[26] As in Macpherson's account of "possessive individualism,"[27] the reader was

24. Louis Hartz, *The Liberal Tradition in America* (New York: Harcourt Brace, 1955), 9, 250, 309.

25. Ibid., 4–5.

26. Hartz, "The Coming of Age of America," *American Political Science Review* 51 (1957): 474.

27. Macpherson, *The Political Theory of Possessive Individualism* (Oxford: Oxford University Press, 1962).

invited to imagine the imprint of Locke on contemporary society. Subsequent scholars became so accustomed to calling Locke a liberal and designating him the founder of the liberal tradition that they neglected the fact that neither the term nor the concept were available to him. And, again, it was not until after 1950 that there was even any significant characterization of Locke as a liberal. Hartz had first announced his thesis about Locke and American liberalism two years after Hallowell incorporated Locke as a major actor in his synoptic story of the rise and decline of Western liberalism and his version of the "crisis of our times."[28]

The often cited conclusion to the 1954 study of voting in America, like so many earlier statements from the 1920s onward, stressed the disjunction between "democratic practice and democratic theory" and the need to bring them into accord with one another. Both Boorstin and Hartz had, in their own way, accomplished this, but in a largely evocative manner. Although, as in the case of Dahl, it was difficult to point, in political science, to any specific adherent of what the authors took to be "traditional normative theory," they quoted Lindsay's and Alfred Cobban's complaints about the gulf between the theory of politics in political science and the actual facts of politics and pointed to the manner in which the results of their study might be used to "temper some of the requirements" of "traditional" theory. Robust theories of democracy were, in their view, not only unrealistic but dangerous. They concluded that despite the lack among voters of interest, knowledge, and motivation, the "system" worked and that it was, after all, the "collective properties" of the system that mattered. "Virtue" was, as Madison had suggested, in the system rather than in individuals. While the "classical" requirements were "more appropriate for opinion leaders" or elites, citizen apathy, they suggested, might actually be perfectly functional as well as a sign of public content. Consequently, they argued, democratic theory should be revised to conform to democratic practice, that is, the practice of politics in the United States. Of course, in fact, this had largely been the story of democratic theory in the United States—a continual process of revision to fit what it construed as the realities of politics. The essence of the system, they found, was the symbiotic relationship between "cleavage" and "consensus"—a pluralistic social organization "moved" the system, while "a basic consensus" served to "hold it together."[29] Dahl's *Preface to Democratic Theory* was, among other

28. Hallowell, *Main Currents in Modern Political Thought* (New York: Holt, Rinehart, and Winston, 1950).

29. Bernard R. Berelson, Paul F. Lazarsfeld, and William N. McPhee, eds., *Voting* (Chicago: University of Chicago Press, 1954), 306, 312–13, 318, 322.

things, an explicit attempt to formalize this "new" theory and to incorporate the results of research that supported it. But it was, in fact, less a preface than a coda.

Just as the original formulation of pluralist democracy in the early part of the century was part of the Americanization of political science and a response to the breakdown of the theory of the state, Dahl's work was an attempt to articulate and provide a basis for the faith in liberal democracy, but now in the context of perceptions of the Cold War and as a response to internal attacks on the integrity of pluralist theory. It was in part an answer to charges of political elitism in American politics advanced by sociologists such as C. Wright Mills, who argued that the "theory of balance" advanced by accounts such as that of Truman falsified the structure and processes of political decision-making. It is ironic, but maybe not surprising, that the *Preface* was published in the same year as *The Power Elite*,[30] but Dahl's book was also an attempt to codify in a full and formal manner the theory of democracy, and of America as a democracy, that had become so deeply embedded in the discourse of political science. Not only had the theory been left somewhat elliptical in recent literature, including the work of Truman, on the assumption that democracy could be equated with the practices of American institutions and politics, but this image of liberal democracy was being severely attacked by the émigré scholars and by those educated under their auspices. While pluralism in the 1920s was in part a flight from past involvement with German philosophy, German philosophy was now pursuing pluralism on its home turf. Finally, and more broadly, Dahl attempted to address once again the perennial paradox of democracy in American political theory and to provide a systematic answer to the question of how democracy could exist without a democratic public. The book, which had originated in a graduate seminar at Yale, had not yet fully reappropriated the term "pluralism," and it eschewed any extended discussion of "group theory." Dahl also avoided "liberalism," which was becoming less than a term of approbation in both politics and political theory, and, instead, reached all the way back to Laski and Barker for the word "polyarchy." As in the case of Strauss, Voegelin, and Boorstin, Dahl's book was the product of his lectures at the invitation of the Charles R. Walgreen Foundation for the Study of American institutions. The Foundation Chair, Jerome G. Kerwin, noted that this organization had recently sponsored "works on democracy from the point of view of the philosopher and moralist," but it now welcomed Dahl as a "representative

30. C. Wright Mills, *The Power Elite* (New York: Oxford University Press, 1956).

of the empirical school" of political theory, which focused on "testing democratic ideas empirically." The irony was that this work was as much the
product of a moralist as any of the previous lectures.[31]

As in his earlier work, Dahl once again defined democratic theory as
concerned with how citizens controlled leaders, but he claimed that
"despite centuries of speculation," the theory continued to be "rather unsat-
isfactory." He suggested that there was not so much one democratic theory as a number of theories, but he argued that what dominated American
culture was both the vision of Madison and an ethical image he labeled
"populist democracy." Although, unlike Truman, he took pains to distance
himself from Madison's account, he developed a thesis that, in general
terms, was nearly indistinguishable. While there is room for interpretive
differences, Dahl's account of Madison was too egregiously selective in its
emphasis to be accidental. Dahl criticized what he claimed to be Madison's
excessive focus on constitutional and intragovernmental structures, such
as the separation of powers, as a way of preventing tyranny and his failure
to stress the "the inherent social checks and balances existing in every pluralistic society." This rendition of Madison, so obviously at odds with what
Madison said in *Federalist 10,* and even *51,* reflected the emerging emphasis on rejecting formal institutional analysis in favor of a focus on political behavior and the social and economic bases of politics, but Dahl also
wanted to defend and recapture the majoritarian dimension of democratic
governance, which had suffered from Madison's strictures. Probably Dahl's
own political leanings inclined him toward the majoritarian politics of the
New Deal and against a range of minorities from economic elites to seg-
regationists. He viewed Madison's theory as a "convenient rationalization"
for minorities that wished to veto social policies and as representing a position that was reflected in various ways in the ideas of "aristocratic elites"
as well as "political adventurers, fanatics, and totalitarians of all kinds"
including "Plato and Lenin." While Dahl believed that Madisonianism
would persist as an American ideology, and properly so, it was, in the end,
an inadequate theory for "political science."[32]

It was surely somewhat off the mark to treat Madison's account of the
American polity as a "theory" of twentieth-century politics, rather than
the piece of rhetorical imagination that it represented, but Dahl was no

31. Dahl, *A Preface to Democratic Theory* (Chicago: University of Chicago Press, 1956).

32. Dahl, *A Preface to Democratic Theory,* 22, 30–32, 51. For a perceptive and systematic analy-
sis of this point, see Richard Krouse, "Robert Dahl: The Theory of Polyarchial Democracy," in *The
Constitutional Polity: Essays on the Founding Principles of American Politics,* ed. Sidney A. Pearson Jr.
(Lanham, Md.: University Press of America, 1983).

happier with "populist democracy," which he took to be a contending element of the American ideology that focused on maximizing equality and achieving popular sovereignty. This principle, he claimed, also tended toward fanaticism and threatened democracy. If Dahl's account of Madison was skewed to provide a setting for his thesis about American democracy, his formulation of populism was a straw man that did not refer to any particular contemporary theorist or regime. Based on maximizing equality and popular sovereignty, it largely represented the vague image of popular government that the previous generation had referred to as the "democratic dogma." One of Dahl's principal criticisms was that it was an "ethical" position rather than an "empirical system" and said nothing about the "real world," but apart from a passing reference to Rousseau, Dahl did not specify the locus of this abstract theory, which seemed to have no definite existence outside of his presentation.[33] Dahl was confronting shadowy opponents both in politics and in political theory, but the basic purpose was to set up his own account of democracy and of how the United States epitomized it. Instead of postulating general goals to be maximized, Dahl advocated what he called a "descriptive method" for creating a democratic theory. This involved taking "all those nation states and social organizations that are commonly called democratic by political scientists" and determining their characteristics and requirements. Although no actual political system might fully exemplify all of these attributes, Dahl claimed that factors such as "competitive politics" or the "bribery of the electorate by politicians" were what, in the end, distinguished democracies from totalitarian regimes. Such countries were "polyarchies" and were characterized by processes such as elections, but particularly by "social prerequisites" such as a multiplicity of associations supported by a consensus about the rules of the game. For Dahl, the "American hybrid" was the paradigm case. Here were all the necessary "social variables." Both the interaction of interest groups and the constraining matrix of a crucial "underlying consensus" of social values were so important that more visible everyday dimensions of politics and government could be considered as "merely the chaff." Noting in passing the work of Bentley, Truman, and Latham, Dahl claimed that "we can only distinguish groups of various types and sizes, all seeking in various ways to advance their goals, usually at the expense, at least in part, of others." Substantive majorities, those defined by either a distinct value or interest, were in fact neither a problem nor a possibility. Elections were devices for aggregating individual preference and the

33. Ibid., 22.

diverse sources from which it sprung, as well as for making leaders responsive and holding them responsible, but the real stuff of politics consisted of "minorities ruling" or "government by minorities" with the acquiescence or indifference of a numerical "apathetic majority." But this, he maintained, was far from minority rule in any traditional sense. Both in government and society, the process was one of "endless bargaining" and competition that produced a virtual majority. There was a "steady appeasement of relatively small groups," but in this context, there was "a high probability that an active and legitimate group in the population can make itself heard effectively at some crucial stage in the process of decision" and that government would be responsive. The "manifold specialized groups become vested interests" and "part of the fundamental warp and woof of the society."[34]

Dahl, as in the case of many political scientists of this era, such as Gabriel Almond and Sidney Verba (*The Civic Culture,* 1963), argued that we should begin by examining the character of those countries that we know, in our hearts and minds, as both citizens and political scientists, to be democracies, and by extracting an empirical basis for a normative vision. This accomodationist approach had always informed the vision of democracy in political science, and the elements of Dahl's "hybrid" were precisely those that constituted the theory of pluralism in the late 1920s and the liberalism of the 1930s, which were later advanced as the essence of "pluralist democracy." The question that cannot be avoided is whether Dahl was really unfamiliar with the details of the earlier literature and his formulation was simply his attempt to make explicit what was endemic in the discourse of political science or whether he consciously decided not to acknowledge that he was repeating an already systematically articulated position. The weight of evidence would seem to favor the first interpretation. Thirty years later, Dahl acknowledged that he had not viewed democratic theory as a well-defined subject and that he had not seen himself as primarily working in that area. He also indicated that he had little grasp of the earlier literature and that he entered the discussion in terms of his perception of a vague notion of a tradition reaching from Rousseau's "monistic" democracy, via Tocqueville as a "bridge," to Madison who, despite the limitations of his formulation, represented "the elements of a new vision, that of a *pluralist* democracy on the large scale of a country."[35]

34. Ibid., 63, 68, 71 131–32, 145, 150.

35. Dahl, *Toward Democracy: A Journey of Reflection: 1940–1997* (Berkeley: Institute of Governmental Studies, 1997), 34, 279–80.

Pluralist theory, as taught at Yale by Dahl and individuals such as Robert Lane in the late 1950s and early 1960s, was not a doctrinaire position with any clear sense of its connections to the past, and it was challenged internally by some of Dahl's students at various points in the course of its evolution.[36] In some respects, the idea of pluralism as a distinct theory was a creation of its critics. It was at first simply part of the folklore of political science that informed the discipline after the war, and then it was a rather pragmatic response to general images of participatory democracy, elitist theories of society, and the émigré literature that questioned the underlying pluralist/liberal vision in the discipline, and it took on much of its growing solidarity in response to such criticism in the course of being transformed into a more self-conscious orthodoxy by students of Dahl such as Nelson Polsby and Aaron Wildavsky. But Dahl's "hyrid," whatever the exact story of its gestation may have involved, very clearly reflected the persistent theoretical paradox of democracy first fully visible in the *Federalist*. While he could not let go of the majoritarian dimension of democracy and its egalitarian implications, his political ontology destroyed any substantive sense of republican imagery by disaggregating majorities into individuals and a collection of minorities.

Critics of mainstream political science continued to attack liberalism and pluralism as based on "philosophical relativism,"[37] but by 1960, the old images of pressure politics as a democratic pathology that Herring and Truman had attempted to counter had been reasserted in a new wave of criticism that, unlike the arguments of the elite and stratification theorists, aimed at challenging less the reality of pluralism than the norm and at criticizing the actual and probable consequences of this norm for both politics and, once again, for "the political."[38] But some "conservative" sociologists had joined in equating pluralism with democracy and defending it as a hedge against mass society and totalitarianism, and some political scientists believed that it provided a general "theory of stable democracy" applicable beyond American borders.[39] Although both Boorstin and Hartz

36. Richard M. Merelman, *Pluralism at Yale: The Culture of Political Science in America* (Madison: University of Wisconsin Press, 2003).

37. See, for example, John Livingston, "Liberalism, Conservatism, and the Role of Reason," *Western Political Quarterly* 9 (September 1956).

38. Grant McConnell, "The Spirit of Private Government," *American Political Science Review* 52 (1958); David Spitz, *Democracy and the Challenge of Power* (New York: Columbia University Press, 1958); Wolin, *Politics and Vision* (Boston: Little-Brown, 1960).

39. Nisbet, *The Quest for Community: A Study in the Ethics of Order and Freedom* (New York: Oxford University Press, 1953); William Kornhauser, *The Politics of Mass Society* (New York: Free Press, 1959); Harry Eckstein, *A Theory of Stable Democracy* (Princeton: Princeton University Press, 1961).

had warned against attempts to transplant American democracy, mainstream political scientists were considerably more confident that it could provide both a framework of analysis and an ethical and institutional export, and many advanced this belief on both theoretical and practical fronts.

The idea of a general theory of groups gained ground—despite the efforts of some persistent detractors—and Bentley became both hero and villain. The publication of successive editions of Bentley's book (1935, 1949, 1955) had culminated in a *Festschrift* (1957) in which the political science contributor suggested that group theory would do for political science what supply and demand theory had done for economics, since "values are authoritatively allocated in society through the process of the conflict of groups."[40] It would be a mistake, however, to assume that the pluralist paradigm was accepted by all behavioralists. Easton, who introduced the definition of politics as the "authoritative allocation of values" and who probably more than anyone else gave voice to the meaning of the behavioral movement as a scientific project, never endorsed the core theory of pluralist democracy, even though many found it tempting to read such a theory into his account of the "political system." Dedicated to creating a general theory of politics, Easton viewed the empirical theory of pluralism both as limited to certain regimes and as an example of the limitations of equilibrium theory. As a normative theory he found it inadequate, because it did not maximize equality and popular rule and concealed the real uses of power.[41] Some of those who had contributed to the original constitution of the group paradigm, such as Odegard, did not appear to grasp fully the terms of the contemporary discussion, but Odegard also took issue with some of the premises of the literature. The group idea was, he claimed, hardly new. It was part of a tradition of political theory stretching from Plato to Marx, but current theories were at best ambiguous about key concepts such as group and equilibrium. Even more problematical, he argued, was the failure to make room for the individual, values, and other factors in the process of democratic government. In its present form, group theory, he concluded, had "all but banished reason, knowledge, and intelligence from the governmental process" in its pursuit of the absolution of what had formerly been called "invisible government."[42] What was dif-

---

40. Charles B. Hagan, "The Group in Political Science," in *Life, Language, Law: Essays in Honor of Arthur Bentley,* ed. Richard Taylor (Yellow Springs, Ohio: Antioch Press, 1957), 110.

41. For a discussion of the implications of Easton's work for democratic theory, see Henrik P. Bang, "David Easton's Postmodern Images," *Political Theory* 26 (1998).

42. Odegard, "A Group Basis of Politics: Notes on Analysis and Development," *Western Political Science Quarterly* 11 (1958): 699.

ferent was not the theory but the context. What Odegard sensed was the extent to which pluralist theory was becoming an apology for American politics. In 1960, the *APSR* published four articles on Bentley and group theory, three of which were in a symposium titled "Bentley Revisited." Although one defended the approach and argued for building on Bentley's work, the others attacked the theory as parochial, a methodological failure, and a conservative "sanctification of the actual."[43] As the rearticulation of pluralism took form, so did the critique of this theory. In some cases, the critique was a product of new persuasions in political theory influenced by the émigrés, but it was also grounded in the more indigenous discourse of the field.

Wolin's *Politics and Vision* was a study of the history of political theory that closely reflected the emerging image of that history as one of decline in which the degeneration of the "political" was manifest in a liberal tradition beginning with Locke and culminating in contemporary pluralism and its underwriting by behavioral political science. By this point, the tradition of liberalism that was a creation of disciplinary discourse had, as in the case of Crick's account in the *American Science of Politics,* been retrospectively projected as a historical context for explaining that discourse. Wolin's account was closely related to the new literature of political theory, but, despite his ideological divergence from Elliott, the resonance of images from *The Pragmatic Revolt Against Politics* was evident—just as the progressive students of Burgess did not escape some of the fundamental structures of his perspective. The criticism of pluralism was also rooted in a tradition within the discipline that hearkened back to the ideas of Dewey and other Progressives of the early part of the century. There is no doubt that the conversation that dominated the field was a response both to immediate issues internal to the discipline and to perceptions of and concerns about contemporary politics, but it is necessary to recognize the extent to which the form and content of the conversation was also a legacy from the past.

Pluralist theory was closely tied to arguments such as that of Daniel Bell and Lane announcing the "end of ideology," but while the sociologist Seymour Martin Lipset, maybe the contemporary counterpart of Harry Elmer Barnes, concurred and maintained that the essence of democracy

---

43. Myron Q. Hale, "The Cosmology of Arthur F. Bentley," *American Political Science Review* 54 (1960): 957; in the same issue, see also R. E. Dowling, "Pressure Group Theory: Its Methodological Range"; Robert T. Golembiewski, "The Group Basis of Politics: Notes on Analysis and Development"; Stanley Rothman, "Systematic Political Theory: Observations on the Group Approach."

was to be found in a system in which "different groups can attain their ends,"[44] Schattschneider's earlier reservations about pluralism once again surfaced. He claimed that pluralism as a form of political practice tended to privatize and localize conflict rather than socializing, nationalizing, and democratizing it. While parties, and the ascendancy of presidential politics, contributed to the latter, pressure groups reinforced the former. He argued that "the business or upper-class bias of the pressure system shows up everywhere" and that "the flaw in the pluralist heaven is that the heavenly chorus sings with a strong upper-class accent." Although he never mentioned Dahl, Schattschneider argued that an empirical or "realist" examination of American politics actually revealed that "the notion that the pressure system is automatically representative of the whole community is a myth fostered by the universalizing tendency of modern group theories." He claimed that "the system is skewed, loaded, and unbalanced in favor of a fraction of a minority."[45]

H. B. Mayo's *An Introduction to Democratic* Theory (1960) did not recognize pluralism as a theory, but although Dahl would claim that *Who Governs?* "was not written to advance a general 'pluralist theory of politics,'" the concept of polyarchy gave way to that of pluralism and to a distinction between "oligarchy" and "pluralism."[46] This book, based on a study of New Haven, Connecticut, can be reasonably construed as an attempt to validate empirically the theory of democracy laid down in the *Preface,* but the purpose was also to undercut by empirical evidence the idea advanced by Vilfredo Pareto and Gaetano Mosca, and more recently by sociologists such as Floyd Hunter and Mills, that behind the facade of politics is always an economic elite, as well as the idea that American politics could be conceived as a mass society manipulated by remote leaders.[47] It was also designed to demonstrate once again that democracy need not be conceived along populist participatory lines.

Dahl had already challenged the "ruling elite model,"[48] and by 1961,

44. Daniel Bell, *The End of Ideology* (Glencoe, Ill.: Free Press, 1960); Robert Lane, "The Politics of Consensus in an Age of Affluence," *American Political Science Review* 59 (1965); Seymour Martin Lipset, *Political Man* (New York: Doubleday, 1960), 403.

45. Schattschneider, *The Semisovereign People: A Realist's View of Democracy in America* (New York: Holt, Rinehart, and Winston, 1960), 31, 35.

46. Dahl, *Who Governs?* (New Haven: Yale University Press, 1961); "Polyarchy, Pluralism, and Scale," *Scandinavian Political Studies* 7 (1984). See Grant Jordan, "The Pluralism of Pluralism: An Anti-Theory?" *Political Studies* 38 (1990).

47. Floyd Hunter, *Community Power Structure: A Study of Decision-Makers* (Chapel Hill: University of North Carolina Press, 1953); *Top Leadership U.S.A.* (Chapel Hill: University of North Carolina Press, 1959).

48. Dahl, "A Critique of the Ruling Elite Model," *American Political Science Review* 52 (1958).

he sought to give definitive empirical substance to his theory of democracy. He argued that in New Haven there had been a long historical development from rule by a hierarchical patrician oligarchy to a "pluralist system" of *"noncumulative"* and *"dispersed inequalities,"* which, in its operation, was the best approximation of a stable "democratic system." Dahl clearly wished to extrapolate from New Haven to a more general claim about American politics. He asked, "who, then, rules in a pluralist democracy?" and the answer, essentially, was no one in particular.[49] Different issues brought into action different groups and aggregations of interests. The catalyst, however, of both stability and instability was a "political stratum," leaders working within the constraints of consensus and beliefs about the rules of the game, while "most citizens are not engaged very much in politics." Dahl reiterated his claims in the *Preface* and emphasized what he called the "myth" of the "primacy of politics" and of the "concern of citizens with the life of the democratic polis."[50] In an extended study entitled *The Republic of New Haven,* written seventy-five years earlier, Charles H. Levermore, a student of Herbert Adams, had suggested, much as Dahl would, that it might "reveal and explain some of those minor activities which New Haven, as one town among thousands, has added to the great sum of national well-being." Even then, however, he noted that "citizens of all parties and all shades of respectability ignore the Town-Meeting and School-Meeting alike" and "hardly know when it is held."[51] Maybe not much had changed in New Haven—or maybe the way in which some political scientists conceived politics had not altered significantly.

In the same year that Dahl published his study of New Haven, Henry Kariel described what he called the "decline of American pluralism." What he referred to was the emergence of large "power blocs" that had, in turn, given rise to a "new public order" and overshadowed the "conglomeration of little groups" and "voluntary associations" that had so long been identified with "Americanism."[52] According to Kariel, it was not simply that the conditions of pluralist society had changed. He had little sympathy for the basic claims of pluralist theory, which he noted had been imported during the debates of the 1920s but which made little sense in the American context where the problem was one of creating a state in a situation where the fact of social and governmental pluralism had been assumed. Even Madison, he argued, was mistaken about pluralism as a self-correcting

49. Dahl, *Who Governs?,* 85–86.

50. Ibid., 281–82, 311.

51. Charles H. Levermore, *The Republic of New Haven* (Baltimore: Johns Hopkins University Press, 1886), iv, 290.

52. Henry Kariel, *The Decline of American Pluralism* (Stanford: Stanford University Press, 1961), 2.

mechanism. Although Kariel addressed the ideas of Bentley and Truman as a part of a tradition in which social scientists had assimilated ideology and political description, oddly, he did not mention Dahl. Pluralism, Kariel argued, had "defined a state without a government" and had assumed a situation in which there was a "plurality of voluntary associations so guided by an unseen procedure that their interaction constituted the public good." Even if this doctrine had some merit, the contemporary answer, he claimed, could no longer be a reinvigoration of pluralism by strengthening centers of "organized private power." The problem was to "control them by some means short of establishing an illiberal political order." Kariel argued that the "theory of pluralism under conditions of large-scale technology con-flicts with the principles of constitutional democracy" and must give way to a more egalitarian society that would be achieved in part by state inter-vention.[53] There was, he argued, precedent for such an answer in the non-pluralist tradition of "American statism" that ran from Hamilton through Progressives such as Croly to aspects of contemporary liberal political the-ory that advocated governmental centralization and public regulation through such devices as increased presidential power and leadership. Constitutionalism must rise up above groups that claim to be private but that are really public in both character and function, threatening the "aes-thetic, intellectual, moral, or spiritual good of the individual."[54]

Kariel's book represented the kind of criticism of the theory and prac-tice of pluralism from within political science itself that sometimes found itself in an uneasy alliance with the critique that originated with the émi-grés and those who followed their lead.[55] His work returned to one ver-sion of the fundamental alternative answer to the paradox of democracy—to the idea that democracy required a public and that the task of government was to represent that public. The irony, however, was that most of this lit-erature, including arguments such as Kariel's, had come to accept essen-tial elements of the empirical thesis of pluralism. Increasingly, it was less pluralism as representing an account of society and politics that came under attack than its status as a normative theory of democracy and the alleged pathological implications of the practice of pluralist politics. In an impor-tant sense, pluralism had become everyone's reality despite different accounts of exactly how the pluralist process worked and its implications for democracy.

53. Ibid., 2, 4, 68.

54. Ibid., 271, 274.

55. For a compendium of Straussian assessments of the classic figures in the American science of politics, see Herbert J. Storing, ed., *Essays on the Scientific Study of Politics* (New York: Holt, Rinehart, and Winston, 1962).

Associates and students of Dahl such as Polsby continued to pursue the form and substance of the "pluralist alternative," as both a tentative "theory" and an entailed method of research, to account for community power and to criticize the "stratificationists." Polsby more explicitly, but as somewhat of an afterthought, tried to link this approach to a tradition that began with Madison and Tocqueville and ran through the work of Herring, Truman, and Key.[56] Lindblom also saw his work as completing the "unfinished business of pluralist thought" in a tradition that included Figgis, Maitland, Laski, Bentley, Latham, Herring, and Truman, and he argued that this amounted to demonstrating how "people can coordinate with each other without anyone's coordinating them, without a dominant common purpose, and without rules that fully prescribe their relations to each other." Dahl also continued to elaborate the theory, but there was still no indication that any of these individuals were deeply immersed in, or often even conscious of, the details of the theory that had evolved during the late 1920s and had been so fully integrated into the discourse of the field during the 1930s.[57] They were the propagators of a tradition, but, like many who perpetuate a tradition, were actors within it rather than creators. Like the behavioral movement itself, it was as much a rearguard action as the opening of a new front.

As the pluralist image of American politics and society reached its zenith,[58] so did the criticism of this doctrine. In his discussion of pluralism in the new *Encyclopedia of the Social Sciences,* Kariel continued to recount the twentieth-century history of the theory and to criticize the practice of pluralist politics. He argued that pluralism "as an ideology has lost most of its explicit apologists and only lingers quietly as a submerged, inarticulate ingredient of Western liberalism."[59] Pluralism, as both theory and practice, was now and would continue to be attacked on many fronts: as ultimately elitist in its implications; as concealing the effect of non-decisions and the power of ideology and socialization; as creating a vacuum of authority filled by experts; as producing governmental deadlock; and as a

56. Nelson W. Polsby, *Community Power and Political Theory* (New Haven: Yale University Press, 1963).

57. Lindblom, *The Intelligence of Democracy* (New York: Free Press, 1965), 3, 12. See also "The Science of Muddling Through," *Public Administration Review* 19 (1959); Dahl, "Further Reflections on the 'Elitist Theory of Democracy,'" *American Political Science Review* 60 (1966); *Pluralist Democracy in the United States: Conflict and Consent* (Chicago: Rand-McNally, 1967).

58. See, for example, Avery Leiserson and Oliver Garceau, eds., *Political Research and Political Theory* (Cambridge, Mass.: Harvard University Press, 1968); Charles F. Cnudde and Deane E. Neubauer, *Empirical Democratic Theory* (Chicago: Markam, 1969).

59. Kariel, "Pluralism," in *The International Encyclopedia of the Social Sciences,* vol. 12, ed. David Sills (New York: Macmillan, 1968).

form of "pure tolerance" that invited the demise of its own principles.[60] The 1969 volume of the *NOMOS* series was devoted to the issue of the place of what Elliott had called "voluntary associations" and by which the editors, wishing to avoid the now ambiguous word "private," meant "political pluralism." They claimed that pluralist thought was a tradition reaching from Aristotle to Hegel but that in the twentieth century, there had been a coming together of "descriptive" and "normative" pluralism.[61] But by the end of the 1960s, the critics of pluralist theory as well as its proponents had largely lost sight of its, and their, past. An anthology of critical essays on the "bias of pluralism" and political science described the pluralist tradition as represented by the work of Aristotle, Madison, Tocqueville, and Dahl.[62]

There are many ways to explain the intense debate about pluralism during the 1960s: as academic reflections of different political ideologies; as a function of the professional controversy over behavioral approaches to political analysis that were historically tied to pluralist theory; as part of the growing concern about the relevance of political science to a critical understanding of public issues; and as an outgrowth of new ideas in political theory that had been generated outside the context of American political life. But whatever the immediate influences may have been, both within and outside the discipline and profession, it is necessary to recognize the extent to which the discussion was bound by the terms of a conversation that had taken shape a generation earlier. By the end of the 1960s, however, pluralism and liberalism had largely become like Venus and the evening star. Robert Paul Wolff's account of the "poverty of liberalism" was really a critique of pluralism, and when Theodore Lowi, the dissident

60. See, for example, Graeme Duncan and Stephen Lukes, "The New Democracy," *Political Studies* 11 (1963); Peter Bachrach and Morton Baratz, "Decisions and Nondecisions: An Analytical Framework," *American Political Science Review* 57 (1963); Lane Davis, "The Costs of Realism," *Western Political Quarterly* 17 (1964); Robert Paul Wolff, Herbert Marcuse, and Barrington Moore Jr., eds., *A Critique of Pure Tolerance* (Boston: Beacon Press, 1965); Christian Bay, "Politics and Pseudo-Politics," *American Political Science Review* 69 (1965); Jack Walker, "A Critique of the Elitist Theory of Democracy," *American Political Science Review* 60 (1966); G. William Dumhoff, *Who Rules America?* (Englewood Cliffs: Prentice-Hall, 1967); Peter Bachrach, *The Theory of Democratic Elitism: A Critique* (Boston: Little-Brown, 1967); Charles A. McCoy and John Playford, eds., *Apolitical Politics: A Critique of Behavioralism* (New York: Thomas Y. Crowell, 1967); Stephen Lukes, *Power: A Radical View* (Bristol: British Sociological Association, 1974); Mark Kesselman, "The Conflictual Evolution of American Political Science: From Apologetic Pluralism to Trilateralism and Marxism," in *Public Values and Private Power in American Politics,* ed. J. David Greenstone (Chicago: University of Chicago Press, 1982).

61. Pennock and John W. Chapman, eds., *Voluntary Associations,* Nomos, 11 (New York: Atherton Press, 1969).

62. William E. Connolly, ed., *The Bias of Pluralism* (New York: Atherton Press, 1969).

from Yale, spoke at the end of the 1960s of the "end of liberalism," he was talking about the pathologies of pluralism or "interest-group politics."[63] While someone such as Wolin held liberalism and pluralism up to the standard of an image of participatory democracy,[64] Lowi, like Kariel, returned to the Progressive/statist tradition rooted in the work of Merriam, Dewey, Lippmann, and Croly, which had always been hesitant about the idea of a great society that was not a great community, and had clung to the notion of giving substance to the concept of public interest, which contemporary pluralists had deemed as devoid of meaning,[65] and to the idea that in a democratic society the government could or should represent a public.

Lowi's work was preceded not only by Kariel's book but by the arguments of Grant McConnell. McConnell criticized what he claimed was the manner in which pluralist politics blurred the line between the public and private spheres and led to a delegation of public authority to various groups that bypassed the formal constitutional structure of government. Despite the belief that the activity of groups produced public good, the fact was, he claimed, that well-organized interests prevailed and subverted popular sovereignty.[66] Lowi developed these themes in detail as well as presenting a critical alternative that he labeled "juridical democracy." Lowi characterized his work as a "polemic" directed at the "modern liberal state" as well as at "academic political science," which, he claimed, acted as a apologist for that state and which had created a theory by "borrowing" the "pluralist notion." Lowi labeled the public philosophy of the modern American state as "interest-group liberalism," which, he claimed, was an "amalgam of capitalism, statism, and pluralism." The old public philosophy had been based on capitalist ideology, but when its image of the "automatic society" and "unseen hand" gave way to the demands of "positive government" in the era of the New Deal, pluralism arose as a new account of a self-regulating society that tended toward equilibrium. This became a "potent American ideology" and "the principal intellectual member" of the new public philosophy that now encompassed both what was commonly called liberalism and conservatism. Lowi claimed that the "pluralist model is overwhelmingly superior" as a description of American society,

63. Robert Paul Wolff, *The Poverty of Liberalism* (Boston: Beacon Press, 1968); Theodore Lowi, *The End of Liberalism* (New York: W. W. Norton, 1969).

64. Wolin, "The Liberal-Democratic Divide: On Rawls's *Political Liberalism*," *Political Theory* 24 (1996).

65. See, for example, Glendon A. Schubert, *The Public Interest, A Critique of the Theory of a Political Concept* (Glencoe, Ill.: Free Press, 1960). See also Friedrich, ed., *The Public Interest*, Nomos, 5 (New York: Atherton, 1962).

66. McConnell, *Private Power and American Democracy* (New York: Alfred Knopf, 1966).

but he took up the task of demonstrating how the politics of pluralism, and the modern liberal state, undermined democracy and the idea of separate government and displaced government as a representative of the public interest.

Lowi went into great detail in describing and explaining the pathological consequences of pluralism. Rather than providing access to various groups, the process, he argued, favored the powerful and organized and tended toward elitism rather than wider participation, as well as introducing subtle forms of coercion by abandoning individuals to the power of groups. Under these conditions of dispersed power, government failed to gain confidence in its legitimacy or authority to make public policy and parceled power out to private venues. In the end, government became incapable of achieving justice and the vacuum of authority was filled in ad hoc ways by experts and the most powerful elements of civil society. For Lowi, the solution, juridical democracy, represented a call for a return to the rule of law and to democratic constitutionalism based on majority rule. It would require more public deliberation and the articulation of national purpose and would encourage more citizen participation, while at the same time subjecting citizens to public standards of law that embodied and produced fairness.

Although Lowi presented a very convincing and trenchant critique of American politics, it is necessary to step back and consider exactly what he was saying. First of all, unlike many of the critics of pluralism in the 1920s, Lowi did not question the image of pluralism as either a political state of affairs or the dominant public philosophy, that is, as the core of American political thought and action. His criticisms resembled less the arguments of someone such as Elliott, who claimed that pluralism was counterfactual, than the concerns of individuals such as Lippmann, Dewey, and Merriam, who sought to transcend it. Second, although Lowi characterized contemporary mainstream political science and individuals such as Truman and Dahl as apologists for pluralism, pluralism was a reconstruction and interpretation of American politics to which they had added the latest endorsement and which Lowi himself had learned as a student at Yale . Lowi, like many of the advocates of pluralism, seemed relatively unclear about the evolution of pluralist theory, which had, in fact, been formulated far in advance of what he designated as the liberal state and its commitment to positive government. Lowi not only accepted this empirical theory of the structure of politics, despite his disagreement with accounts of how the process actually worked, but went on to provide the image it projected with a history, thus in a peculiar way reinforcing the sense of reality attaching to it as well as the implicit identity between liberalism and pluralism that had developed during the previous generation. Lowi suggested that the pluralist theory of politics in political science was a principal source of contemporary public philosophy as well as a justification for it, but he, like so many others, did little more than juxtapose the two and left the actual historical connections quite ambiguous. But again, the greatest conceptual problem was that his "description" of American politics as pluralistic was in large measure informed by a construction produced by political science—and by the same political scientists that he criticized. Finally, the latent premise behind Lowi's recommendation for separate government and juridical democracy was not unlike that which was at the heart of both nineteenth-century state theory and its Progressive successors. It required a kind of social homogeneity and civic virtue that was belied by an acceptance of pluralism as a description of American politics. In effect, Lowi, somewhat like the *Federalist,* presented an ambivalent political ontology, or at least offered an account of politics that disrupted the normative image of democracy that he championed. What seemed to be required, and maybe was implied, was what individuals such as Merriam had deemed necessary—a creation or reconstitution of an American people or its functional equivalent.

The close of the 1960s was a watershed. In the same year that Lowi declared the end of liberalism, and, in effect, the end of the prevailing democratic vision in mainstream political science, Easton announced a "new revolution" in political science that would temper its pursuit of science and redirect its efforts toward political relevance. At the very same moment, however, Wolin proclaimed that any reconciliation between political theory and the dominant persuasion in the discipline was impossible and that the "vocation of political theory" was, and really always had been, a separate endeavor.[67] Wolin's statement was a rallying cry for an emerging intellectual cohort in search of identity, but mainstream political science did not significantly challenge the decision of this subfield to go its own way as long as it remained professionally attached, and political theory was content to be professionally attached as long as it could pursue its own intellectual path. In this new division of labor, often understood as the difference between empirical and normative concerns, democratic theory largely became the province of the subfield of political theory. By this point, the literature of political theory had almost become defined by a

---

67. David Easton, "The New Revolution in Political Science"; Wolin, "The Vocation of Political Theory," *American Political Science Review* 63 (1969).

dedication to a critique of liberalism as positions such as Arendt's elevation of "the political" or the public realm were joined to the importation
of Habermas's neo-Marxist critique of liberalism and his own valorization
of the public sphere. But despite much talk during the 1960s about the
death of both political theory and liberalism, they, together, found new life
in John Rawls's philosophical rehabilitation of liberalism as well as in the
work of individuals such as Robert Nozick. This, however, was a liberalism from which pluralism had largely been eliminated, and it had limited
immediacy for the study of American politics. Among the models of
democracy in Macpherson's *Life and Times of Liberal Democracy* (1977), pluralism appeared as part of a discussion of equilibrium images and the work
of Schumpeter, and Pennock's *Democratic Political Theory* (1979) scarcely
mentioned pluralism. Similarly, for example, pluralism as anything other
than a reference to Weber and Schumpeter, a repetition of Macpherson's
critical perspective, and a discussion of Dahl also received short shrift in
David Held's *Models of Democracy* (1987). For Held, Truman and Dahl represented the "classic pluralist position." Although pluralism had gained
wide acceptance in fields such as comparative politics as a way of general-
izing about polyarchy and democracy beyond the borders of the United
States, it was attacked on this front as well. Philippe Schmitter recast pluralism as "corporatism" or the dominance of elite groups that have a special relationship to the state.[68] By the middle of the 1980s, pluralism had
receded as the centerpiece of democratic theory, but in the 1990s, it quite
suddenly once again sprung onto the scene in various but pervasive forms
and in the midst of what had for so long been a hostile ambience—the discourse of academic political theory.[69]

68. See, for example, Philippe Schmitter, "Still the Century of Corporatism?" in *The New
Corporativism,* ed. F. B. Pike and T. Stritch (Notre Dame: Notre Dame University Press, 1974); *Patterns
of Corporatist Policy-Making* (Beverly Hills: Sage, 1982).

69. The emphasis on pluralism was evident as early as Michael Walzer's *Spheres of Justice: A Defense
of Pluralism and* Equality (New York: Basic Books, 1983); in addition to references in other notes,
see, for example, Will Kymlicka, *Liberalism, Community, and Culture* (New York: Oxford University
Press, 1989); *Multicultural Citizenship* (New York: Oxford University Press, 1995); Iris Marion Young,
Justice and the Politics of Difference (Princeton: Princeton University Press, 1990); Stephen K. White,
Political Theory and Postmodernism (Cambridge: Cambridge University Press, 1991); Charles Taylor,
Multiculturalism and the Politics of Recognition, ed. Amy Guttmann (Princeton: Princeton University
Press, 1993); Chantal Mouffe, ed., *Dimensions of Radical Democracy: Pluralism, Citizenship, and
Community* (London: Verso, 1992); idem, *The Return of the Political* (London: Verso, 1993); Jean L.
Cohen and Andrew Arato, *Civil Society and Political* Theory (Cambridge: MIT Press, 1992); Nicolas
Rescher, *Pluralism: Against the Demand for Consensus* (Oxford: Oxford University Press, 1993); J.
Donald Moon, *Constructing Community: Moral Pluralism and Tragic Conflicts* (Princeton: Princeton
University Press, 1993); Anne Phillips, *Democracy and Difference,* (University Park: The Pennsylvania
State University Press, 1993); Paul Hirst, *Associative Democracy* (Amherst: University of Massachusetts

One might suggest that part of what turned the conversation around was Rawls's conclusion that his original formulation of a theory of justice did not adequately take into account the need for a "reasonable pluralism" within the context of an "overlapping consensus," which, he claimed, "political liberalism" logically and practically implied. But this work was probably more a symptom than a cause of the redistribution of emphasis. Already, Richard Rorty, attacked for his philosophical relativism by a wide variety of political theorists who were, in various ways, sentimental about the transcendental, found himself defending a kind of reconstituted version of the 1930s version of liberal democracy. The implications of Rawls's first book were distinctly antipluralist and universalist, but now, Rawls decided, the "facts" of social life dictated that social unity would have to be based on a "political conception" that could gain the support of "a diversity of comprehensive doctrines" embraced by various groups and that liberalism itself could not be such a doctrine.[70] This kind of claim was, as a general position, almost indistinguishable from the arguments of someone such as T. V. Smith in the 1920s and 1930s, and by the early 1990s, pluralism was once again at the heart of the democratic imagination whether the brand of democratic theory was overtly pluralistic or conceived as primarily deliberative, associative, or agonistic. It is not that the new pluralism springs from the same philosophical source as the old, and in many instances it contradicts the assumptions and values that characterized the pluralism of political science during the 1950s and 1960s—and would be quick to challenge any such association. But notwithstanding all the discriminations that might be made between the two, the similarities and continuities are neither analytically negligible nor historically accidental.

Press, 1994); *From Statism to Pluralism* (London: UCL Press, 1997); William E. Connolly, *The Ethos of Pluralization* (Minneapolis: University of Minnesota Press, 1995); Avigail Eisenberg, *Reconstructing Political Pluralism* (Albany: State University of New York Press, 1995); Gregor McLennan, *Pluralism* (Minneapolis: University of Minnesota Press, 1995); James Bohman, *Public Deliberation: Pluralism, Complexity, and Democracy* (Cambridge: MIT Press, 1996); Jürgen Habermas, *Between Facts and Norms* (Cambridge: MIT Press, 1996); Seyla Benhabib, ed., *Democracy and Difference: Contesting the Boundaries of the Political* (Princeton: Princeton University Press, 1996); John Dryzek, *Democracy in Capitalist Times* (Cambridge: Cambridge University Press, 1996); Charles Larmore, *The Morals of Modernity* (Cambridge: Cambridge University Press, 1996); A. Grillo, *Pluralism and the Politics of Difference* (Oxford: Clarendon Press,1998); Amy Guttman, ed., *Freedom of Association* (Princeton: Princeton University Press, 1998) Nancy Rosenblum, *Membership and Morals* (Princeton: Princeton University Press, 1998); Jon Elster, ed., *Deliberative Democracy* (New York: Cambridge University Press, 1998); Richard Bellamy, *Liberalism and Pluralism* (London: Routledge, 1999); Mark Warren, *Democracy and Association* (Princeton: Princeton University Press, 2001).

70. John Rawls, *Political Liberalism* (New York: Columbia University Press, 1993); "The Domain of the Political and Overlapping Consensus," in *The Idea of Democracy,* ed. David Copp, Jean Hampton, and John E. Roemer (Cambridge: Cambridge University Press, 1993).

What is most striking is the manner in which many of the contemporary participants seem oblivious to both the existence and character of the earlier dialogue as well as the extent to which they are bound to the form and substance of the discursive past that they are "resurrecting."[71] And there has been little attempt to reconcile the new enthusiasm for pluralism with the calumny that up until so recently had been heaped upon it. In a recent issue of the journal *Political Theory* commemorating the thirtieth anniversary of the journal as well as Isaiah Berlin's 1961 announcement that, despite rumors to the contrary, political theory was alive and would remain so in a world where "ends collide," the editor noted that Rawls's acceptance of the "fact of pluralism" indicated that "the overall point seems undeniable: we are constrained to an even deeper and more extensive engagement with pluralism."[72] Not only did political theory advocate pluralism as a theory of democracy, but the "fact of pluralism" was perceived as giving vitality to the enterprise of political theory itself, which, like mainstream political science before it, seemed to bask in its own liberal diversity and its mutual tolerance of the multifarious perspectives that composed what was now construed by many, and somewhat warily by Wolin, as the "vocations" of political theory.[73] But if the vocation was difficult to pin down, what Wolin now referred to as "fugitive democracy" was still more elusive. If it was not an epiphany, it seemed, like the Holy Spirit, to inhabit the world in a pantheistic manner.

There are a number of ways in which one might account contextually for the return of pluralism in political theory during the last decade of the twentieth century. The end of the Cold War and the collapse of communism were construed by some as a validation of and victory for what had for so long been advanced as the heart of democratic society. The pluralism of civil society had been defended theoretically, even by some Marxists, as a source of democratic values, and, in a practical sense, it seemed that both economic and political liberalism were part of the future of the former Eastern bloc. The long-standing debate between Marxist and pluralist theorists seemed, historically, as in the case of politics itself, to be resolved in favor of the latter. Maybe more important, however, was the transformation in the intellectual environment occasioned by the embrace

---

71. For insightful discussions of the connections between the old and new pluralism, see David Schlossberg, "Resurrecting the Pluralist Universe," *Political Research Quarterly* 51 (1998); Eisenberg, *Reconstructing Political Pluralism.*

72. Stephen K. White, "What is Political Theory?" *Political Theory* 30 (2002): 474–75.

73. See, for example, Jason A. Frank and John Tambornino, eds., *Vocations of Political Theory* (Minneapolis: University of Minnesota Press, 2000).

of philosophies such as postpositivism, neopragmatism, poststructuralism, postmodernism, and multiculturalism. For political theorists, these ideas and the intellectual forum were more attractive than the theory and practices of collective action. In various ways, the work of individuals such as Thomas Kuhn, Michel Foucault, Jacques Derrida, Jean-François Lyotard, and Rorty provided a renewed basis and enticement for a pluralist vision, and this trend was accentuated by the focus on feminist political theory and various kinds of identity politics that brought the idea of group autonomy and primacy back into currency.

One less obvious explanation for the pluralist turn in political theory was that despite all the criticism to which pluralism had been subjected, a pluralist bias had been, in various forms since at least the 1920s, deeply infused and diffused in the discourse of both political science and political theory. This bias was not only represented in the work of icons of American political thought, such as Madison and Tocqueville, but in the discipline itself, from Lieber to Dahl. Even those such as Dewey and Elliott who wished to transcend pluralism and achieve a more organic society, or who continued to view authentic democracy as an association writ large, did not reject plurality and localism as an essential characteristic of democracy.[74] For many of the theorists who, quite surprisingly it might have seemed, embraced pluralism in the 1990s, it was really a matter of concluding, or accepting the fact, that there was no place like home. Not only were they in the grip of the discursive heritage of political science, but they were, when push came to shove, for the most part culturally and intellectually liberals and pluralists. Despite all the pathological tendencies they had found in pluralism, it was, in the end, the reality they perceived and in an important sense the ineluctable foundation upon which they believed democracy must be erected.

Like the old pluralism, however, the new pluralism is accomodationist and has been in part a response to what may seem to be the inevitable realities of modern societies and particularly liberal democracies. In many ways, however, the new pluralism has been quicker than the old to valorize the sociology of diversity but, at the same time, less inclined to examine closely that sociology and the modes of economic and political power that characterize it. It is evident that it is responding to perceptions of events and conditions in the political and social world, but the response is mediated through the language of the academy and the terms of abstract democratic

74. See Aryeh Botwinick and William Connolly, eds., *Democracy and Vision: Sheldon Wolin and the Vicissitudes of the Political* (Princeton: Princeton University Press, 2001).

theory, in a manner that makes it difficult to relate it directly to what may
have occasioned it. More significant, however, is that it does not constitute an attempt to engage concretely the issue of what constitutes democracy in America. While the old pluralism attempted to distill a theory of
democracy from a description of practices that, by many criteria, were not
very democratic, the new pluralism often begins with an abstract image
of democracy, involving features such as deliberation, which it attempts to
validate by reference to various social processes and structures that often,
if examined carefully, are questionable exemplifications of democratic practice. But although the new pluralism has in some instances recognized the
limitations that principal characteristics of contemporary society and the
economic enterprise place on the realization of democratic values such as
freedom and equality, it has not confronted fully the constraints of pluralist practice on those values.

It is ironic that at the same time that many political theorists who had
been critical of pluralist liberalism for its failure to achieve equality and
had taken Dahl's work as the paradigm instance of this position began to
embrace pluralism, Dahl and Lindblom increasing became concerned with
the manner in which the economics and sociology of pluralist society, particularly in the United States, inhibited the achievement of equality—and
democracy.[75] Although the new pluralism tended, at least in the beginning, to distance itself from the old pluralism and arguments such as
Dahl's, many of the same criticisms that had been directed at the old pluralism still appear to be relevant in assessing the new versions. Few of the
alleged pathologies of pluralist politics seem to be eliminated, in either
theory or practice. Dahl had taken it as proper that in a polyarchal society, no one governs or that minorities govern, but the problem had been,
and continues to be, that if this is the case then democracy as the media-
tion of public decisions through a general citizenry does not exist, and, at
worst, elites of various kinds rise to the surface. Some even suggest that
since liberalism is congenitally universalistic, "pluralism and liberalism
are rival doctrines,"[76] but while plurality, one might argue, is surely a necessary condition of any realistic concept of democracy in contemporary soci-

75. See, for example, Dahl, *A Preface to Economic Democracy* (Berkeley and Los Angeles: University
of California Press, 1985); *After the Revolution?: Authority in a Good Society* (New Haven: Yale
University Press, 1970); *On Democracy* (New Haven: Yale University Press, 1998); Lindblom, *Politics
and Markets* (New York: Basic Books, 1977); "Another State of Mind," *American Political Science Review*
72 (1986).

76. John Gray, in *Pluralism: The Philosophy and Politics of Diversity,* ed. Maria Baghramian and
Attracta Ingram (London: Routledge, 2000), 101.

ety, it may not be a sufficient condition of authentic democracy. If the bottom line of democratic theory is that there is no natural right to domination, and consequently equality in decision-making is an entailed norm, it seems that passing off the problem by devolving authority and democratic identity to groups will not suffice. The paradox of democracy once again reasserts itself, and the response is not surprising.

Just as in the 1920s and in earlier eras, the claim that democracy demands community, and maybe a national community, has paralleled and at least implicitly challenged the advocacy of pluralism. So-called communitarian liberals such as Michael Sandel and William Galston have emphasized a civic republican tradition and returned to political virtue as an antidote to the extremes of individualism, or emphasis on personal autonomy, that they detected in Rawls's ideas and other versions of liberalism, and they worry about an abstract image of justice detached from tradition and community. Similarly, Robert Bellah and Robert Putnam have suggested that ironically, what unites Americans, as Tocqueville had noted, is an ethics of individualism and group identity that in the end drives citizens apart and destroys the trust and other attributes that encourage civic participation and engender "social capital" on a large scale.[77] These theorists with a communitarian or neorepublican bent, however, somewhat like Hartz more than a generation earlier, see resources for transformation within the American liberal tradition and within American society and, in the end, are as accomodationist as the new pluralists. Yet it seems increasingly difficult to find the requisites of this image of democracy within many of the dominant existing social and political practices. Attempts to propagate a theory of democratic community, and to discover a republican tradition to support it, seem as romantic and fanciful as the nineteenth-century vision of the state as the invisible public behind the constitution and government. But they, like the pluralists, remain bound to the terms of the paradox of democracy. This persuasion, however, is no more antipluralist in the manner of Rousseau than its ancestral manifestations, but rather seeks, like Dewey, a larger and more integrated sense

---

77. See, for example, Michael Sandel, *Liberalism and the Limits of Justice* (New York: Cambridge University Press, 1982); "The Procedural Republic and the Unencumbered Self," *Political Theory* 12 (1984); *Democracy's Discontent: America's Search for a Public Philosophy* (Cambridge: Belknap Press, 1996); Robert Bellah et al., *Habits of the Heart* (Berkeley and Los Angeles: University of California Press, 1985); *The Good Society* (New York: Knopf, 1991); Cass Sustein, "Beyond the Republican Revival," *Yale Law Journal* 97 (1988); William A. Galston, *Liberal Purposes* (Cambridge: Cambridge University Press, 1991); *Liberal Pluralism: The Implications of Value Pluralism for Political Theory and Practice* (New York: Cambridge University Press, 2002); Robert D. Putnam, *Bowling Alone* (New York: Simon and Schuster, 2000).

of the whole with its parts. Yet, unlike Dewey's formulation, it seems to hold little relevant critical purchase in its contemporary context.

A typical academic response to the persistent tension between the latest versions of pluralism and monism is to seek, as has been the case since Lieber, some conceptual compromise, such as that between deliberative and associative democracy, but this tends to be an analytical exercise that only suspends the issue. As the philosopher J. L. Austin suggested, when faced with a dichotomy the answer is not to find a middle ground but to abolish it. What the present situation may suggest is the ultimate exhaustion of the original terms of the dialogue revolving around the paradox of democracy. It may be time to think in a fundamentally different way about the democratic concept, but to make any such effort relevant to American democratic hopes will also require coming to grips with the persistently repressed and displaced problem of the cognitive and practical relationship between political theory and its subject matter.

APPENDIX:
TELLING THE STORY OF POLITICAL SCIENCE

I know that there is high contempt
on the part of many persons for
the pursuit of learning that does
not end in the vindication of their
preconceptions.

—*Charles A. Beard*

From the beginning, American political science has had a built-in understanding of its past. The classic texts of political philosophy were not only
part of the subject matter of the discipline, but were increasingly construed
as the elements of a tradition that represented the history of the field. Many
early studies in the history of political theory were explicitly presented as
accounts of the development of political science and as establishing an
ancestry rooted in ancient Greece and extending to modern times.[1] This
image, whether celebrated or in some manner criticized, would never be
entirely jettisoned, and it contributed to inhibiting close attention to the
actual history of the discipline. Prior to the so-called behavioral revolution
and controversies surrounding the behavioral movement, there was a general and persistent consensus about the progress of political science, or at
least about what would constitute such progress. This sense of well-being

1. See, for example, Frederick Pollock, *An Introduction to the History of the Science of Politics* (London:
Macmillan, 1890); Murray, *The History of Political Science from Plato to the Present* (New York: Appleton,
1925); Shepard, "Political Science," in *The History and Prospects of the Social Sciences,* ed. Barnes (New
York: Knopf, 1925).

did not encourage detailed historical reflection, and when such reflection did occur, it was usually in the service of furthering some particular research program as in the case of Merriam's account of the development of political science as passing through the a priori deductive stage (up to the mid-1800s), the historical comparative period (until the turn of the century), and the contemporary tendencies to employ quantification and empirical observation, moving eventually toward a psychological treatment of politics.[2]

The first piece of scholarship that was more than an element of a rhetoric of inquiry and could qualify as a systematic study of an aspect of the history of the discipline was Anna Haddow's still very useful compilation of the literature and curricula of the early years of the field.[3] However, beginning with some of what might be taken as the prototypes of the behavioral and antibehavioral literature of the 1940s, there emerged a kind of work that had a significant impact on images of the field's past. The medium was historical even if the historicity of the message can be questioned. Between 1940 and 1950, internal challenges to the values attached to the American vision of a science of politics, largely mounted by political theorists, as well as a growing sense of a failure to realize—theoretically, practically, and reputationally—the traditional scientific and liberal democratic promise of the field, prompted a more critical view of the history and current state of political science.[4] This line of argument was continued in many of the early claims associated with the behavioral revolution such as David Easton's historical overview and his account of the field's deficiencies and possibilities.[5] The arguments of behavioralists in favor of what they claimed was the creation of a truly scientific study of politics, which would fundamentally break with what they claimed was the institutional emphasis of the past, were countered by attacks, often by émigré political theorists, on the very idea of this initiative and by alternative views of the past of political science and less than favorable references to

2. Merriam, *New Aspects of Politics* (Chicago: University of Chicago Press, 1925).

3. Haddow, *Political Science in American Colleges and Universities, 1636–1900*. New York: Appleton-Century, 1939).

4. Benjamin Lippincott, "The Bias of American Political Science," *Journal of Politics* 21 (1940); William Anderson, "Political Science North and South," *Journal of Politics* 11 (1949); Lasswell and Abraham Kaplan, *Power and Society* (New Haven: Yale University Press, 1950); Leonard White, "Political Science, Mid-Century," *Journal of Politics* 12 (1950).

5. Easton, "The Decline of Political Theory," *Journal of Politics* 13 (1951); *The Political System: An Inquiry into the State of Political Science* (New York: Knopf, 1953); Dahl, "The Behavioral Approach in Political Science: Epitaph for a Monument to a Successful Protest," *American Political Science Review* 55 (1961).

the pedigree of the discipline and the legitimacy of contemporary political thought in general.[6]

By the early 1960s, behavioralists had declared victory and were typically assessing the history of political science from that standpoint.[7] In a series of APSA presidential addresses during this decade, the cumulative progress of the discipline was proclaimed, often in the increasingly popular terms of Thomas Kuhn's framework.[8] This was somewhat ironic, since Kuhn's work would provide much of the philosophical basis for a critique of the behavioralist account of scientific explanation, and his argument questioned the extent to which one could speak meaningfully about some general concept of scientific progress. By the end of the decade, however, the view of behavioralism was less sanguine—even on the part of some of its strongest advocates. Easton, for example, had scarcely finished an account of the development of the discipline in which he stressed its culmination in the successes of the behavioral movement when, in this era of volatility, both in the discipline and its political context, he prescribed a "new revolution" in political science.[9] As the postbehavioral era was ushered in during the 1970s, new images of the evolution of the discipline began to emerge as political scientists struggled to keep ahead of their past. While these general accounts of the history of the discipline served to make political scientists aware of their past, they also tended to cloud that past. They now deserve attention primarily as events *in* the history of political science and as examples of the uses of history in disciplinary debates. But during this period, there was also the beginning of historical studies of a more comprehensive and autonomous character even though the initiating motivation derived from the context of disciplinary controversy.

6. See, for example, Morgenthau, "Reflections on the State of Political Science," *Review of Politics* 17 (1955); Leo Strauss, *What is Political Philosophy?* (Glencoe, Ill.: Free Press, 1959) "Epilogue," in *Essays in the Scientific Study of Politics,* ed. Storing (New York: Holt, Rinehart, and Winston, 1962).

7. Heinz Eulau, "Tradition and Innovation: On the Tension Between Ancient and Modern Ways in the Study of Politics," in *Behavioralism in Political Science,* ed. Eulau (New York: Atherton, 1969); Marion Irish, ed., *Political Science: The Advance of a Discipline* (Englewood Cliffs: Prentice-Hall, 1968); Evron Kirkpatrick, "The Impact of the Behavioral Movement on Traditional Political Science," in *Essays in the Behavioral Study of Politics,* ed. Austin Ranney (Urbana: University of Illinois Press, 1962).

8. Emmet Redford, "Reflections on a Discipline," *American Political Science Review* 55 (1961); David Truman, "Disillusion and Regeneration: The Quest for a Discipline," *American Political Science Review* 59 (1965); Gabriel Almond, "Political Theory and Political Action," *American Political Science Review* 60 (1966).

9. Easton, "Political Science," in *International Encyclopedia of the Social Sciences,* ed. David Sills, vol. 12 (New York: Macmillan, 1968); "The New Revolution in Political Science," *American Political Science Review* 68 (1969).

Bernard Crick's *The American Science of Politics* profoundly affected writing about the history of American political science—structurally, substantively, and thematically. Its impact is apparent in much of the subsequent literature, and it became a point of reference for both those who sympathized and those who disagreed with his thesis. It was originally presented as a doctoral dissertation at the London School of Economics, largely conceived and drafted on the threshold of the 1960s while he was a visiting scholar in the political science departments at the University of California at Berkeley and Harvard. It looked backward from the early years of the behavioral movement and the height of the Cold War. Although Crick expressly demurred with respect to an intention to write a history of the discipline and profession of political science, and claimed that it was more the history of an "idea," the book was the closest thing to such a history that was available, and it forced its readers to come to grips with many obscure names such as Lieber and Burgess that were already hardly known or remembered by either faculty or graduate students. Crick's purpose was to demonstrate the degree to which the idea of a scientific study of politics was a uniquely American invention that, from its earliest beginnings in citizenship training to the methodological claims characteristic of behavioralism, must be understood in the context of the tradition of American liberalism, which it both reflected and abetted. Despite its pretensions to an objective, value-free study of politics, American political science, Crick maintained, manifested submerged but "strong assertions of political doctrine." Embedded in its "facts" were presuppositions associated with an "intense democratic moralism" that made it more an example of American political thought than a science.[10] There is no doubt that Crick was less than sympathetic to the philosophical assumptions that had informed the dominant ideas about science in the American discipline, but he was more concerned to point out what he believed was the often paradoxical relationship between the commitments to science and democracy—especially in the case of Merriam and the Chicago school. A belief in the need for social control eventuated in what Crick suggested was the "direct totalitarian implication in Lasswell's manner of thought" and reflected "a deeper derangement in the wider thought of American liberalism" that "confused science with technology." This, he claimed, was "profoundly at odds with almost all that is best in American political experience and expression" and threatened the integrity of the

10. Crick, *The American Science of Politics* (Berkeley and Los Angeles: University of California Press, 1959), v–vi.

very realm of politics itself. A secondary but important theme in Crick's book, however, was the extent to which the pursuit of a scientific knowledge of politics was rooted in an underlying antipathy toward its own subject. It was, Crick argued, not only those political scientists of the Progressive era who, as advocates of political reform, were "emotionally and philosophically . . . in revolt against politics itself." The goal, from early progenitors of American disciplines of social science such as Ward to Lasswell, had been a mode of social control that, although seeking to serve democratic values, would "take the politics out of politics." Less prominent, but also implicit, was Crick's suggestion that it was not simply the passion for scientific certainty that distanced political scientists from politics but the demands and allure of the profession and discipline that both required a posture of objectivity and detachment and demanded its own vocational commitment.[11]

The brand of liberalism reflected in American political science was, Crick claimed, as writers such as Hartz had already emphasized, a conservative ideology that was in itself in many ways as inimical as scientism to the "Western tradition of constitutional politics" and its emphasis on the "application of experience to the creative conciliation of differing interests" and ethical perspectives. The American liberal ethic of individualism produced, ironically, as Tocqueville had noted, social uniformity and conformity and, in its attachment to the image of American exceptionalism, a kind of "traditional antitraditionalism." Crick argued that American political science both reinforced and reflected these values and that the "dreams of the social scientist" in some ways paralleled the "practice" of totalitarianism in its search for a way to overcome the uncertainty, inconvenience, and limitations of politics. Crick claimed that American political science's liberal ideology was manifest in the attempt of some of its founders to turn politics into administration and law and in a tendency to forget tradition and the need for human judgment. Crick was writing at a time when, he believed, "the preservation of the political is challenged." Although, as he noted, his original concern in exploring the literature of American political science was with overcoming some of the skepticism about the possibility of political philosophy that had been engendered by positivism, his investigation of political science, he claimed, revealed a tendency more to "narrow" than "explain" the political realm.[12] Crick, like earlier and more famous commentators on the American scene, such as

11. Ibid., 208–9, 233–34.
12. Ibid., 213, 221.

Tocqueville and Laski, was in part imposing his concerns about his home country on his observations of American political science, and, just as Tocqueville was concerned about American democracy becoming the fate of the world, Crick was concerned about the spread of American political science in the postwar era. Also, as in the case of Tocqueville and Laski, Crick's analysis was shaped by the source of his information.

Among his American "mentors and friends," Crick counted Harvard professors, Hartz, Elliott, and Friedrich, and the imprint of their ideas was obvious, but the Berkeley ambience was even more important. The mid-1950s marked the beginnings of what might be called the Berkeley school in political theory, which would, along with and sometimes in competition with the work of Strauss and his students, become one of the principal voices of opposition to behavioralism in political science during the 1960s. Behavioralism represented the zenith of the trends that Crick had critically analyzed in his account of the work of individuals such as Lasswell. Crick indicated his debt to Dwight Waldo, who had been an early critic of the emphasis on value-freedom and the attempt to emulate the methods of natural science, as well as to Odegard, who, in his reverence for everyday politics and his advocacy of a common sense approach to political studies, was something of a scientific skeptic. He also acknowledged Norman Jacobson, who offered a continuing seminar critically examining the dominant assumptions about science in American political science, which Crick attended. Jacobson specialized in American political thought and had argued strongly against the tendency in contemporary political science and political theory to sacrifice the autonomy of politics and political thinking to the extremes of moralism and scientism.[13] Arendt, whose *Origins of Totalitarianism* was noted sympathetically by Crick, was a visitor at Berkeley during this period and was completing *The Human Condition* (1958), which would be the most important theoretical defense of "the political" in the face of its putative modern demise as a consequence of the rise of society, modern technology, and other forces of modernity. This theme, albeit in a more prosaic form, would be manifest in the successive editions of Crick's *In Defence of Politics* (1964). Finally, Wolin had recently joined the Berkeley faculty and was in the process of writing his influential *Politics and Vision* (1960), a study of the history of political theory that sought, in part, to rescue traditional political theory from its devaluation by behavioralism, but that also embraced the new image of the history of political thought as suffering a modern decline, in this case from the point

13. See Norman Jacobson, "The Unity of Political Theory: Science, Morals, and Politics," in *Approaches to the Study of Politics,* ed. Roland Young, (Evanston: Northwestern University Press, 1958).

of Locke and the beginning of the liberal tradition. In his concluding chapter, Crick found hope for the restoration of political thought and the reformation of political science in the work of scholars such as Strauss, Voegelin, and other critics of scientism and liberalism who were introducing arguments about the decline of politics and political theory into the literature of political science. Although Crick may have been too close to the events of the early 1950s and the emergence of behavioralism to gain much perspective on the period, his work was an insightful rendering of a rapidly ingested and digested corpus of material, ranging from Lieber to Lasswell, that had receded from the view of most political scientists.

A study that has received relatively little attention, but deserves more, is Albert Lepawsky's monograph, "The Politics of Epistemology." Given the concerns voiced in this study, the Berkeley context is once again relevant. Lepawsky's organizing premise was derived from the intellectual climate created by the debate between the growing hegemony of "devout political scientists" seeking a science of "universal validity" and those "more skeptical" members of the profession who "suspect that the criteria and methods of their discipline, and even its intrinsic content, are shaped by the values and politics of the culture in which they operate." Lepawsky wished to pursue the approach of the sociology of knowledge and explore the "reciprocity between politics and epistemology," by which he meant political concerns as opposed to concerns about science, through what he designated the five basic periods in the history of the discipline, to some extent following Haddow's classification. With respect to the main theme of the study, the crucial division he posited was between the years before the APSA was "firmly established" and the subsequent development of the field during which political science became "clearly recognized as a distinct scientific discipline." The first part of Lepawsky's project (a second was planned but never completed) was limited largely to an analysis of the first era when "political science was somewhat more noticeably influenced by the politics of the day," which included what he labeled as the "Classical" (1785–1825), "Transitional" (1825–65), and "Romantic" (1865–1905) periods. He claimed that the "Eclectic" and "Current" periods of the twentieth century were marked by "the dominance of the epistemological influence over the political circumstances"—when the "politics of epistemology" prevailed over the "epistemology of politics." And Lepawsky asked the reader to keep in mind the question of whether the discipline was "more 'productive'" before or after it became a "science."[14]

14. Albert Lepawsky, "The Politics of Epistemology," *Western Political Quarterly*, supplement (1964), 21–23.

Lepawsky's essay is significant in several respects. First, although limited in scope, it was probably the most careful and detailed piece of research on the intellectual history of the discipline that had appeared. Second, it raised, even more pointedly than Crick's work, the important question of the impact of professionalism and specialization on the discipline and the implications for the relationship between academic and public discourse. Finally, it pointed at issues regarding the relationship between "internal" and "external" history. If, for example, the development of the discipline was after the turn of the century shaped more by internal "epistemological" concerns, broad contextual explanations of its development after that period might be less significant.

Something of the nature of the Albert Somit and Joseph Tanenhaus volume, *The Development of American Political Science: From Burgess to Behavioralism,* might be extrapolated, particularly in view of Crick's argument, from the fact that in the original printing of the first edition the word "American" was not present in the title. The book was written at the height of American political science's aspiration to scientific universalism, but although the story told was very much, at least structurally, a tale of the rise of the profession and the evolution of political science from its earliest American origins to behavioralism, it was far from merely a historical apology. The two authors were of somewhat different minds about behavioralism, and although hardly a critique, the book was not a celebration. It was, however, a discussion in which the authors decided to limit their "attention to those aspects of the past that they believed bore directly on the present 'state of the discipline,'" and it was a story told from the perspective of the current mainstream image of the identity of the profession. The project had begun as a prospective textbook chapter, but the subject increasingly seemed too complex to be encompassed within that scope. The authors did not pretend to be historians, and their intention was not to offer "a full-blown history of political science" or even a "short survey" of such a history, but rather an overview of how political scientists had defined their professional responsibilities and goals and viewed the scope and method of their enterprise.[15] They were probably too modest in assessing their success, since they produced something that was more than a short systematic account of the development of the discipline and profession. The work provided much useful information for a field that, in general, was vague about the details of its past. The study was divided into

15. Albert Somit and Joseph Tanenhaus, *The Development of American Political Science: From Burgess to Behavioralism* (1967; reprint, Boston: Allyn and Bacon, 1982).

five periods: the pre-history of the field (up until 1880), 1880–1903, 1903–21, 1921–45, and 19–1965. And the second edition (1982) provided a short epilogue covering the period from 1965 to 1980. The focus on behavioralism was evident, and it was designated as "the paramount development in the discipline's entire intellectual history" and as a manifestation of one of the discipline's cycles of enchantment with the "idea of a scientific study of politics" and as something that could be treated, in Kuhnian terms, "as an attempt to move political science from a pre-paradigmatic (or literally non-scientific) condition to a paradigmatic stage." They believed that behavioralism had not yet become a "predominant paradigm," and they predicted, probably quite accurately, that although the discipline would become "more behavioral in tempo," its "'scientistic aspirations' would become more modest."[16]

In 1975, Waldo, who two decades earlier had addressed the state of political science in the United States, in *Political Science in the United States of America: A Trend Report* presented what he referred to as a "historical-interpretive" analysis and overview of political science. This was a comprehensive and balanced account, appropriate for the "handbook" to which it contributed, but its point of view was explicitly that of the contemporary situation of political science in the United States. Even though Waldo claimed that, in some general sense, political knowledge was cumulative and although he recognized the presence of a "strict interpretation" that viewed the discipline in terms of the methods of natural science, he followed what he referred to as an "ecumenical approach." This reflected the pluralism he discerned in the practice and sentiments of the field during the emerging postbehavioral era, and he assumed that "there is no unquestionable 'objective' perspective" from which to describe the discipline's history.[17]

Waldo's conclusion that "probably by the mid-sixties there was decreasing tension and controversy" in the discipline was, in fact, misplaced by at least a decade, but he raised the issue of whether, "from the vantage point of 1980," the events of the late 1960s and "the proclamation of a 'postbehavioral sensibility' will appear but a temporary aberration, another detour in a march toward a more scientific politics" or whether "a new balance of forces will emerge" in which science is less an end in itself than a means to achieve certain values. Waldo treated postbehavioralism as

16. Ibid., 173, 175, 205, 208, 210.
17. Dwight Waldo, *Political Science in the United States of America: A Trend Report* (Paris: UNESCO, 1956); "Political Science: Tradition, Discipline, Profession, Science, Enterprise," in *Handbook of Political Science*, ed. Fred Greenstein and Nelson Polsby, vol. 1 (Reading: Addison-Wesley, 1975), 3.

basically a phenomenon involving the influence of the "New Left" and the "Counterculture" on the discipline rather than as a philosophical and methodological position involving serious claims about the nature of political inquiry. And the general tenor of his essay reflected a new "policy-turn," as political science sought a postbehavioral identity that would validate it as a science that was politically relevant. Waldo claimed that although there might be a sense in which political science could be construed as a natural science, it was surely a "cultural science," in that it was shaped by its historical and social environment. At the most general level, he claimed, it had been "carried on in a particular tradition" of "political thought" that, while manifest in particular institutional settings, had constituted a "Great Dialogue" with "a degree of independence" stretching from ancient Athens through the nineteenth century. He suggested that, for a variety of reasons, it was the United States that had taken the lead in this tradition in the twentieth century and developed what Crick called something "unique in Western intellectual history," which culminated in contemporary political science.[18]

Although Waldo offered a general and perspicuous account of the history of American political science from the standpoint of the mid-1970s, he still assumed that the past of political science was to be found in the great tradition of political thought. Nonetheless, his work was a masterful synthesis and commentary by a senior practitioner even if it presented little that was distinctly new in the way of information or conception about the history of field. It was nearly a decade before a new wave of historical concern about the discipline emerged, even though thorough studies of particular individuals such as Merriam and Bentley had been undertaken.[19] During the 1980s, however, there was the beginning of renewed attention to the "state of the discipline" and its history, and this revolved around both the issue of the relationship of political theory to mainstream political science and a continued concern about the discipline's general identity in the postbehavioral era.[20] By mid-decade, there were two major general works on the history of political science in the United States. David Ricci's *The Tragedy of Political Science* and Raymond Seidelman's *Disenchanted*

18. Ibid., 115, 4, 8, 19.

19. Paul Kress, *Social Science and the Idea of Process: The Ambiguous Legacy of Arthur F. Bentley* (Urbana: University of Illinois Press, 1973); Barry Karl, *Charles Merriam and the Study of Politics* (Chicago: University of Chicago Press, 1975).

20. See Ada Finifter, ed., *Political Science: The State of the Discipline* (Washington, D.C.: American Political Science Association, 1983), especially Gunnell, "Political Theory: The Evolution of a Subfield."

Realists did much to galvanize discussion about the history of political science, but despite their contribution to knowledge of the field, they were distinct examples of history as a form of disciplinary critique. These works were in many ways thematically quite similar even though they were structurally and ideologically different. Following Crick's lead, the narrative plot of each focused on the issue of the relationship between political science and politics and, more specifically, on the connection, and tension, between the discipline's scientific aims and pretensions and its commitment to democratic values and their implementation.

Ricci's account of the history of political science was still rooted in the 1960s controversy between behavioralism and its critics. He posited, following the rhetoric surrounding the study of the history of political theory during this era, a fundamental break between the "great tradition" from Plato to Marx, on the one hand, and modern empirical political science, on the other hand. Relying on recent literature on the rise of professionalism and the development of the modern university, Ricci suggested that it was more than a coincidence that "the line of first-rate thinkers in the Western tradition came to an end" with university-based professional social science and its emphasis on "a scientific approach to natural and social affairs." He claimed, much like Strauss, that the "old tradition of political thought" and the "aggregate wisdom of the ages" were replaced by the inferior learning of modern political science.[21] What might be considered the subplot, the story of the "tragedy" of political science, involved a claim very much like that of Crick with respect to the interpenetration of political science and American liberalism. Ricci defined the issue by claiming that "the discipline is committed to two ends which, from time to time, turn out to be incompatible": "the study of public life in scientific fashion" and "devotion to democratic politics. . . . It is between these two commitments of the discipline—acceptance of scientific techniques and attachment to democratic ideals—that trouble begins." The attempt to plot the story of the development of the discipline, quite literally, as a tragic tale with the protagonist's flaw in its "stubborn insistence on studying politics scientifically, even though inquiry in that mode cannot insure the health of a democratic society," was a strategy in support of what was by then a long-standing complaint within and about the field.[22]

Seidelman recounted the history of the field by focusing on pairs of prominent political scientists, and he provided concise and compelling

21. David M. Ricci, *The Tragedy of Political Science: Politics, Scholarship, and Democracy* (New Haven: Yale University Press, 1984), x.

22. Ibid., 23–25.

intellectual portraits of Wilson, Bentley, Beard, Merriam, and Lasswell as well as a group who he suggested were their most legitimate heirs—Key, Lowi, and Walter Dean Burnham. Both Seidelman and his collaborator, Edward Harpham, were students of Lowi when they conceived and began this project, and the moral of the story was that running through the history of professional political science was a "tradition" of liberal scientific realists who, nevertheless, had been disenchanted with conventional liberal politics and whose work constituted "a consistent and critical perspective," or "third tradition," which stood between the conservative "institutionalist" approach and certain *radical democratic* tendencies. This tradition, Seidelman claimed, had "blended scholarship and political advocacy" and embraced "political science as a non-revolutionary alternative to outdated ideologies and practices."[23] Like Ricci, Seidelman argued that professionalism had obscured deep structural problems in the American liberal tradition and that the democratic aspirations of political scientists "have always excluded and feared a future beyond liberalism." He argued that today, however, the third tradition, and its peculiarly American vision of political science with its commitment to achieving social harmony through scientific state-building, had finally petered out as political science and political reality went their separate ways.[24]

During the 1970s, something of a revolution had occurred in studies of the history of social science as these disciplines became a distinct subject matter for intellectual historians,[25] and this work, along with that of Crick, fundamentally informed the narratives of both Ricci and Seidelman. Much of this scholarship, such as that by Robert Wiebe and Burton Bledstein, focused on the rise of professionalism in the United States and its implications for the American academy, and Thomas Haskell and Mary Furner directed their attention to the professionalization of social science. In their

23. Raymond Seidelman with the assistance of Edward Harpham, *Disenchanted Realists: Political Science and the American Crises, 1884–1984* (Albany: State University of New York Press, 1985), 2.

24. Ibid., 12–13, 241.

25. See, for example, Wiebe, *The Search for Order, 1877–1920* (New York: Hill and Wang, 1967); Edward A. Purcell Jr., *The Crisis of Democratic Theory: Scientific Naturalism and the Problem of Value* (Lexington: University of Kentucky Press, 1973); Mary O. Furner, *Advocacy and Objectivity: A Crisis in the Professionalization of American Social Science, 1865–1905* (Lexington: University of Kentucky Press, 1975); Burton J. Bledstein, *The Culture of Professionalism: The Middle Class and the Development of Higher Education in America* (New York: W. W. Norton, 1976); Thomas Haskell, *The Emergence of Professional Social Science: The American Social Science Association and the Nineteenth Century Crisis of Authority* (Urbana: University of Illinois Press, 1977); Alexandra Oleson and John Voss, eds., *The Origins of Knowledge in Modern America, 1860–1920* (Baltimore: Johns Hopkins University Press, 1979); John Higham and Paul Conkin, eds., *New Directions in American Intellectual History* (Baltimore: Johns Hopkins University Press, 1979).

TELLING THE STORY OF POLITICAL SCIENCE   265

focus on the tension between professional and political commitments and demands, Furner and Haskell opened up an important window on the history of the discipline that no scholar of this subject matter can ignore. This inquiry, however, attempted to explain these developments by reference to general accounts of the historical and social context, which were largely constructed from other secondary literature and more juxtaposed than concretely connected to the events in question, and by explaining them in terms of certain sociological theories. Haskell and Furner, as well as Bledstein, were deeply influenced by Wiebe's work, which in turn drew heavily upon certain models of social evolution and earlier historical research.

Furner's account certainly had something of a tragic plot about it. The story was one in which the movement from amateur to professional social science was not the great development often celebrated by the disciplines and their Whiggish attitudes. Instead, it was one in which a basic commitment to social reform on the part of early social scientists was transformed into a commitment to science, alienating it from its original purpose. In order to gain authority for their demands, social advocates found it necessary to define themselves as scientists and, in turn, to depoliticize themselves in order to gain legitimate professional university status. The demands of the academy, as well as the search for professional security, were, however, ultimately incompatible with effective, or at least radical, political advocacy. This tale of the fate of reform-oriented social scientists remains compelling as a general image of a certain dimension of this era, but it gave little attention to either the actual arguments of the individuals discussed or to the structure and internal development of the discursive practices in which they were engaged.

Haskell's work was a good deal more complicated, but the same virtues and problems were manifest. He set out to explain the "emergence" of professional social science in terms of the important transition represented in the demise of the American Social Science Association (ASSA) and its particular goals and outlook. This story had been told before, but in much more Whiggish terms.[26] Professional social science, Haskell argued, had evolved out of the ASSA and survived because it was functionally better adapted to the social and political context. Traditional society, he claimed, had been breaking down, and differentiation in the face of modernity and factors such as urbanization and industrialization created a "crisis of authority" that led to a demand for a new form of authority and integration,

---

26. L. L. Bernard and Jessie Bernard, *The Origins of American Sociology: The Social Science Movement in the United States* (New York: Russell and Russell, 1943).

which was based on what Haskell termed "interdependence" and which, he claimed, was characteristic of modern capitalism. The agenda of those associated with the ASSA fell apart slowly, like the gentry class they represented, as they clung to notions of individual autonomy and efficacy and old ideas of moral authority in an age of specialization in which scientific experts constituted a "community of the competent." The old reform social science spawned the new, but the latter siphoned the vitality of the former and left it a hollow shell.

Another work by a guild historian that was relevant to the history of political science was that of Edward Purcell. He noted that his study of democratic theory and the social sciences grew out of his concern with social activism in the 1960s and the problem of finding "rational foundations" for "ethical propositions." This, he stated, led him to examine the period of the 1930s and the American confrontation with totalitarianism, which had produced an earlier but similar perplexity about the validity of democratic principles. He claimed that while "the democratic ideal" was unquestioned during the nineteenth century, pragmatic philosophy, in the twentieth century, introduced the doctrine of "scientific naturalism," which held that there was "no absolute or *a priori* truth." Although this position was resisted in certain quarters, it "helped expose major weaknesses in traditional democratic theory." The problem of establishing the validity of democracy brought about a new attack on scientific naturalism, but by the 1950s, a relativistic/naturalistic theory of pluralist democracy, largely situated in political science, won out as an answer to authoritarian politics. This theory, which equated facts and norms, was, according to Purcell, in part a reflection of events such as the New Deal, McCarthyism, and the Cold War, but it also helped shape the history of the period and became an unreflective ideology, ultimately serving to justify the status quo. In Purcell's work, the story of political science once again became a tale of the triumph of science over the ethic of democracy, but also, once again, the plot was carried by a cast of abstract protagonists such as "naturalism" and supported more by intimations than demonstrations of contextual influence.[27]

What constitutes proper historical analysis is indeed, and deservedly, a contentious issue, but no matter how one might choose to define it, a case can be made without taking an unduly puritanical stance that much of the literature that had appeared by the mid-1970s was historical primarily still in the broad sense that it talked about the past. It was not simply that it

27. Purcell, *The Crisis of Democratic Theory*, ix, 6, 11.

was to a large extent written from what Michael Oakeshott had termed the "practical" rather than "historical" perspective where the principal concern was to say something about the present.[28] It was still tightly enmeshed in the "politics of epistemology." But at least innocence of the difference between the discourse *of* political science and discourse *about* political science had been lost. Where political science and its history represent two different orders of discourse, questions of the integrity of the latter and its relationship to the former cannot be avoided. In the first volume of the *Journal of the History of the Behavioral Sciences,* George Stocking, one of the founders of the journal and an anthropologist, wrote an editorial, "On the Limits of 'Presentism' and 'Historicism' in the Historiography of the Behavioral Sciences," which sought to raise certain "questions of motive and method." Although noting the vagaries of historical study, he stressed that "history remains a discipline of sorts" after all, and its practice requires self-consciousness about the endeavor. In the case of the history of the social sciences, the choice between the (admittedly overdrawn) poles of presentism (the study of the past for the sake of the present—what Herbert Butterfield had dubbed "Whig history") and historicism (the study of the past for the sake of the past) was, he argued, particularly salient.[29]

Although Stocking noted that the choices could in practice never be posed so starkly, he believed that there was a difference in distribution of emphasis worth considering. Was it possible to study the history of social science from a perspective that was not primarily informed by "normative commitment" but rather from a concern with understanding the past for its own sake? For Stocking, these ideal typical attitudes tended to be reflected in disciplinary distinctions. He suggested that since presentism was "virtually built into . . . the history of the behavioral sciences," the practicing scientist was likely to be Whiggish, while the historian, "in the spirit of the mountain climber attacking Everest," pursues the past simply "because it is there." Stocking was not advocating some purist position, but only urging a more "enlightened" perspective and a realization of the need to throw off the assumption of cumulative progress, which, despite the work of Kuhn and others, he believed still governed the social scientist's vision of history. He suggested that because social science was still largely preparadigmatic, its "historiography is more open to certain vices of presentism." The manifold "sins of history written 'for the sake of

28. Michael Oakeshott, *Rationalism in Politics* (London: Methuen, 1962).
29. George Stocking, "On the Limits of 'Presentism' and 'Historicism' in the Historiography of the Behavioral Sciences," *Journal of the History of the Behavioral Sciences* 1 (1965) 211.

the present' insinuate themselves" and must to some degree be repressed, he argued, if we are to achieve a realistic understanding of the history of these disciplines—even for present purposes.[30]

In 1988, John Dryzek and Stephen Leonard wrote a provocative article arguing that there can and should be an important link between research on disciplinary history and the practice of political inquiry—that appropriate histories could, in fact, contribute to the "progress" of political science.[31] However, they claimed that this would require moving beyond what they labeled the typical "Whig" and "skeptical" histories devoted to defending or criticizing the present state of the field. Although they maintained that there could not be a truly "neutral" history of political science, they argued that it was possible, even for disciplinary practitioners, to write histories that were attentive to past contexts and that could contribute to the development and rational assessment of research programs. Dryzek and Leonard claimed that because of the plurality of research orientations and competitive intellectual identities in political and social science, and because of the changing character of social phenomena and the fact that they are open to interpretation by both actors and investigators, disciplinary histories in these fields were even more important than in the case of natural science. Not only might different histories contribute to competition and development but, since different research programs might be found to be more appropriate in different situations, histories that were relatively objective could determine the contexts in which certain research strategies might be most appropriate. This article raised a number of contentious issues about such matters as the relationship between disciplinary history and disciplinary practice, the possibility of neutral history, the comparability of the history of natural science and the history of social science, and the role of contexts in historical inquiry.[32] The question of whether disciplinary history would continue to be a kind of dislocated rhetoric or whether it would become a credible practice of knowledge was not resolved. What was evident, however, was that at a point where individuals such as Quentin Skinner and J. G. A. Pocock were raising questions about the nature of intellectual history in general and about what constituted an

---

30. Ibid., 215.

31. John S. Dryzek and Stephen T. Leonard, "History and Discipline in Political Science," *American Political Science Review* 82 (1988). See also Dryzek, "The Progress of Political Science," *Journal of Politics* 31 (1987); Gunnell, "Continuity and Innovation in the History of Political Science: The Case of Charles Merriam," *Journal of the History of the Behavioral Sciences* 28 (1992).

32. See Farr, Raymond Seidelman, Gunnell, Leonard, and Dryzek, "Can Political Science History be Neutral?" *American Political Science Review* 84 (1990).

authentic recovery of the past and a truly historical approach, and the study of academic disciplines was being examined in this light, one could no longer be methodologically innocent in making claims about the history of political science.[33] It was not evident, however, as Stocking had implied, that the answer to achieving a more authentic account of the past of the discipline was to turn to professional historians who, as Purcell's book exemplified, often had very distinct disciplinary and ideological agendas of their own.

In 1991, Dorothy Ross, who had written several important pieces on the history of the social sciences focusing on professionalism and the image of experts and on the traditions of liberalism and republicanism, presented a comprehensive and detailed account of the origin and early development of economics, political science, and sociology in the United States.[34] This work may well remain close to definitive for a single project of this scope, and it provided a valuable background for more specialized studies. While Ross had carefully consulted many primary sources, she noted that she was "aided by a rich body of secondary studies," and her treatment of political science was heavily indebted to the imagery initiated by Crick and his successors. Ross made it clear that while she defended a version of the long-standing thesis of "American exceptionalism," which has played such a large role in historical scholarship, her work was a "critique" and not an "endorsement" of the manner in which this perspective had operated in American public life and in social science. Although she claimed that "American social science owes its distinctive character to its involvement with the national ideology of American exceptionalism," she maintained that this was also the source of much its difficulty, and her goal was to "render it less effective in the future." The exceptionalist character of American political thought to which Ross referred and which she spoke of as an "ideology," was, however, really a variously defined and evaluated, and controversial, concept constructed by academic historians rather than any distinct

33. See, for example, Pocock, *Politics, Language, and Time* (New York: Atheneum, 1971); *The Machiavellian Moment* (Princeton: Princeton University Press, 1975); James Tully, ed., *Meaning and Context: Quentin Skinner and his Critics* (Cambridge: Cambridge University Press, 1988); Stefan Collini, Donald Winch, and John Barrows, *That Noble Science of Politics: A Study in Nineteenth-Century Intellectual History* (Cambridge: Cambridge University Press, 1983).

34. Dorothy Ross, "Professionalism and the Transformation of American Social Thought," *The Journal of Economic History* 38 (1978); "The Development of the Social Sciences," in *The Origins of Knowledge in Modern America, 1860–1920,* ed. Oleson and Voss (Baltimore: Johns Hopkins University Press, 1979); "American Social Science and the Idea of Progress," in *The Authority of Experts,* ed. Thomas Haskell (Bloomington: Indiana University Press,1979); *The Origins of American Social Science* (New York: Cambridge University Press, 1991).

historical datum. One might suggest that social science represented an example of exceptionalism, but to say that exceptionalism was a "national ideology" reflected in social science was a more problematical claim.

Ross's work was a move in the long-standing critique of liberalism and scientism that had been so much a part of the discourse of political science itself as well as of historical accounts of the field. She claimed that "social science is a characteristic product of modern American culture" and "its liberal values, practical bent, shallow historical vision, and technocratic confidence," and that, in turn, it has had a detrimental but "profound effect on social practice and social thought in the United States." These disciplines, she claimed, were not only a product of American exceptionalist thinking, but were also "modeled on the natural rather than the historical sciences and embedded in the classical ideology of liberal individualism." Her narrative of the origins of American social science was the story of a struggle between the forces of republican historicism and liberal scientism with the latter finally, but sadly, emerging triumphant. Ross absolved the field of history, as a whole, from committing the sin of "social science." While historical thinking, she argued, encouraged humanistic ideas and critical analysis, "ahistorical" American social science dedicated itself "to a natural process" understanding of behavior and institutions, for the purpose of a "quantitative and technocratic manipulation of nature and an idealized liberal vision which suppressed earlier republican values."[35] Ross's work was not only cast against the background of the image of exceptionalism, but was part of the continuing debate about whether the American political founding and the subsequent development of American political ideas and institutions were basically "liberal" or "republican."[36] And her exemption of academic history from the category of social science seemed to reflect some disciplinary rivalry as well as tension within historical practice between the more traditional approaches and the incursion of social scientific techniques. Ross explicitly identified her approach with the methodological assumptions of Pocock and with the substance of his account of a republican tradition of political thought reaching from the early sixteenth century to the American founding. She stated that this was the "largest single intellectual stimulus for this book" and that "I recognize in *The Machiavellian Moment* the origins of my social scientists." This approach to intellectual history was not, however, uncontentious.[37]

35. Ross, *The Origins of American Social Science*, xiii–xiv.

36. For a critical examination of the use of the concept of exceptionalism in historical scholarship, see Daniel Rogers, "Exceptionalism," in *Imagined Histories: American Historians Interpret the Past*, ed. Anthony Molho and Gordon S. Wood (Princeton: Princeton University Press, 1998).

37. See, for example, Gunnell, "Method, Methodology, and the Search for Traditions in Political

In the specific case of political science, Ross claimed that its development after the turn of the century was characterized by a turn away "from historico-politics." And, as Haskell had claimed, "the scientific impulse in political science resulted in direct attempts" by a new generation who challenged the nineteenth-century "gentry conception" of American political values to transform the study of politics into an "independent science" and achieve a revision of American exceptionalism through naturalistic realism. This was an attempt to look "beneath" history to find the "self-interested motives of liberal, interest-group politics" that would in turn overcome history, as well as historical thinking, and achieve an "idealized liberal vision of modern American society." For Ross, these trends in political science persisted and finally gave rise to contemporary "instrumental positivism and neoclassical economics, with its offshoot of social and public choice theory, the paradigms that most clearly embody the individualistic and ahistorical premises of liberal exceptionalism." She noted that there were challenges to this "daunting scientism" from within social science, but without a "critical understanding of their own history, it was impossible for social scientists to grasp the predicaments of their contemporary situation and extricate themselves."[38]

Ross claimed that her approach involved an attempt "to reconstruct the discourses within which social scientists worked," emphasizing "the re-creation of the contextual experience of the past" and the existence of a "conversation, developed over time." She avowed a focus on the thinkers most responsible for moving the conversation forward while at the same time isolating "the problem that provoked the conversation," and aimed to demonstrate that "the intentions they pursued in that conversation arose from the disciplinary and historical contexts in which they lived."[39] The issues and concepts in terms of which she defined these conversations, however, were largely retrospective constructions, and the contexts in which they were situated were also primarily composites derived from a variety of secondary sources that reflected diverse intellectual and ideological agendas. The contexts within which she situated the development of social science and to which she interpreted social scientists as responding, such as "a crisis in the ideology of American exceptionalism" and the "discovery of modernity," were reifications. Ross claimed that "the discovery of modernity remains to this day the fundamental context in which to understand

Theory: A Reply to Pocock's Salute," *Annals of Scholarship* 1 (1980); "Interpretation and the History of Political Theory: Apology and Epistemology," *American Political Science Review* 76 (1982).

38. Ross, *The Origins of American Social Science,* 288, 298, 387–88, 471–74.

39. Ibid., xix, xxi, 474.

the social sciences," but in her work modernity turned out to be less any actually specifiable historical context than a retrospectively identified collation of attributes. Although she claimed that "what galvanized social scientific practitioners into self-consciousness and gave the new disciplines their American shape was a crisis in the national ideology of American exceptionalism," exactly in what manner exceptionalism was an intellectual context was far from clear.[40]

Notwithstanding the undeniable value of this work, it not only raised a number of historiographical problems but manifested the difficulty involved in extracting the practice of the history of social science from the rhetorical milieu in which it originated even when written by a professional historian.[41] It may be possible to suggest that Ross's story of the great conflict between historicism and scientism and between liberalism and republicanism was what was *really* going on in that it was the ultimate significance of or explanation for what social scientists were saying and doing, but Ross, like her predecessors, tended to neglect the more immediate discursive contexts even though such an exploration may very well have supported her critical premises. And the imposition of categories such as "Whig historico-politics," "liberal historicism," and "scientism" onto the alleged intellectual positions and intentions of actors obscured the actual conversations and arguments. Ross's work, however, prompted greater interest among both professional historians and political scientists in the history of the discipline, even though accounts of that history still tended to be part of general assessments of the field and did not generate much new information.[42]

The kinds of problems that I have pointed to in Purcell's and Ross's work were perpetuated in Mark Smith's account of early twentieth-century social science in terms of a "debate" between "objectivists" and "purposivists," his treatment of Beard and Merriam as examples of the latter, and his discussion of academic intellectuals who were devoted to public concerns and who escaped "the false choice between a mindless empiricism and an uncontrolled subjectivism."[43] Although it might not be untoward

---

40. Ibid., 8, 53.

41. See Ross, "An Historian's View of American Social Science," *Journal of the History of the Behavioral Sciences* 29 (1993).

42. See, for example, Donald M. Freeman, "The Making of a Discipline," in *Political Science: Looking to the Future,* vol. 1 of *The Theory and Practice of Political Science,* ed. William Crotty (Evanston: Northwestern University Press, 1991).

43. Mark C. Smith, *Social Science in the Crucible: The American Debate Over Objectivity and Purpose, 1918–41* (Durham: Duke University Press, 1994), 5, 7, 269.

to characterize in this manner the controversies in which Merriam and Beard were engaged, there was, in fact, no such debate, and a great deal of what they were saying and doing was lost in this description. But by the beginning of the 1990s, the study of the history of political science by both intra- and extra-disciplinary historians had become a recognizable endeavor.[44] James Farr had undertaken detailed studies of Francis Lieber and nineteenth-century political science as well as writing several essays on the general field, and Farr and Seidelman edited a valuable compilation of documents from the history of the field along with some major commentaries on that history, which included extensive and comprehensive bibliographies of both primary and secondary literature.[45] A dormant oral history project of the APSA was resurrected, and other work by Farr, Terence Ball, and others dealing with the development of specific concepts, issues, research traditions in political science, and the work of particular individuals attested to the fact that summary accounts were giving way to more detailed, focused, and methodologically reflective investigations.[46] Since, as Crick had emphasized, political science among all the social sciences was in many ways a uniquely American invention, it is not surprising that work on the history of the discipline has centered on American political science. Yet beginning in the late 1980s, a significant comparative dimension emerged, and by the mid-1990s, there were four collections of comparative studies on the history of political science, which had emanated from conferences and panels sponsored by a research committee of the International Political Science Association.[47] These studies focused

44. See Farr, "The History of Political Science," *American Journal of Political Science* 82 (1988).

45. Farr, "Political Science and the Enlightenment of Enthusiasm," *American Political Science Review* 82 (1988); Farr and Seidelman, *Discipline and History: Political Science in the United States* (Ann Arbor: University of Michigan Press, 1993).

46. James F. Ward, *Language, Form, and Inquiry: Arthur F. Bentley's Philosophy of Social Science* (Amherst: University of Massachusetts Press, 1984); Terence Ball, ed., *Idioms of Inquiry: Critique and Renewal in Political Science* (Albany: State University of New York Press, 1987); Ball, Farr, and Hanson, eds., *Political Innovation and Conceptual Change* (New York: Cambridge University Press, 1989); Michael Baer and Malcolm Jewell, eds., *Political Science: Oral Histories of a Discipline* (Lexington: University of Kentucky Press, 1991); Farr, Dryzek, and Leonard, eds., *Political Science and its History: Research Programs and Political Traditions* (New York: Cambridge University Press, 1995); Brian Schmidt, *The Political Discourse of Anarchy: A Disciplinary History of International Relations* (Albany: State University of New York Press, 1998); Helene Silverberg, ed., *Gender and American Social Science: The Formative Years* (Princeton: Princeton University Press, 1998); Clyde Barrow, *More Than a Historian: The Political Thought of Charles A. Beard* (New Brunswick: Transaction, 2000); Ido Oren, *Our Enemies and Us: America's Rivalries and the Making of Political Science* (Ithaca: Cornell University Press, 2002).

47. Dag Anckar and Erkki Berndtson, eds., "The Evolution of Political Science: Selected Case Studies," *International Political Science Review* 8 (1987); *Political Science: Between the Past and the Future*

on particular countries and confronted general historiographical issues involved in disciplinary history. At the meetings of both the American Political Science Association and the International Political Science Association, panels on the history of the discipline had become common, but this growing body of research made some of the methodological issues surrounding such work increasingly salient and raised further questions about the relationship between disciplinary history and disciplinary practice.

There is, however, still too often a tendency to revert to rhetorical histories designed to support various claims about unity or disunity in the field or to support some methodological persuasion. A few years ago, Gabriel Almond claimed that "whoever controls the interpretation of the past in our professional history writing has gone a long way toward controlling the future."[48] Almond subsequently criticized recent research on the history of the field for producing a far too pluralistic image of the field that failed to underscore what he claimed was really, overall, a linear story of scientific progress. Subsequently, in a volume devoted to assessing the state of the discipline of political science from an international perspective, he presented an account of the history of political science that not only was written from an exclusively American standpoint, but was a quintessential example of using history in the service of legitimation and the propagation of a particular methodological persuasion.[49] One might still expect this kind of exercise in presidential addresses and similar forums, but once the study of the history of the discipline, whether by professional historians or by political scientists, has moved beyond history as rhetoric, serious scholarship will be more effective than the kind of potted accounts typically advanced by disciplinary partisans. There is little evidence that the basic direction of the discipline is determined by images of its history, but the history of the field remains an important dimension of identity and critical reflection on the theory and practice of political science.

Just as the academic study of the history of political thought originated as a kind of dislocated rhetoric justifying American ideas and institutions, accounts of the history of political science began as a legitimating discourse

---

(Helsinki: Finnish Political Science Association, 1988); Easton, Gunnell, and Luigi Graziano, eds., *The Development of Political Science: A Comparative Survey* (London: Routledge, 1991); Easton, Gunnell, and Michael Stein, eds., *Regime and Discipline: Democracy and the Development of Political Science* (Ann Arbor: University of Michigan Press, 1995).

48. Gabriel A. Almond, "Separate Tables: Schools and Sects in Political Science," *PS* (1988): 835.

49. See Almond, "Political Science: The History of the Discipline," in *A New Handbook of Political Science,* ed. Robert Goodin and Hans-Dieter Klingemann (Oxford: Oxford University Press, 1996); for a critical discussion of this kind of literature see Gunnell, "Is It Still the American Science of Politics?: Handbooks and History," *International Political Science Review* (Fall 2002).

or rhetoric of inquiry, and both were eventually transfigured as stories of declination and vehicles of disciplinary critique. The question is whether or not such rhetorics can be successfully transformed into a practice of knowledge. There are also still some surprising examples of the neglect or suppression of the history of the field. The second decennial volume of the APSA on the "state of the discipline" (1993) was distinctly ahistorical, and the third volume, based on the 2000 annual meeting theme of political science at "century's end," did not include any section on the history of the field. In the same year, the journal *Political Theory* devoted a special issue— "What is Political Theory?"—to this perennial concern and anxiety, but there was hardly any notice of the history of this professional and intellectual subspecies. And although two contributions addressed dimensions of the general issue of the relationship between political theory and political science, the uninitiated would have been able to gain little grasp of what that relationship actually was or had been.[50]

Part of the continuing reluctance in some quarters to engage the past of the discipline in any detail stems from fear about the product of historical investigation. Some worry that such investigation will reveal a lack of unity, while others worry that it may reveal a less than acceptable form of unity. And many sense the possibility of a danger to the values they wish to advocate and to the beliefs they wish to sustain. There are, of course, always particular issues and problems that govern the perspective from which history is written, but there is also an important distinction between the purpose for which history is written and its status as a historical account. The purpose may, for example, be critical, and may even be designed to persuade with respect to perceptions of the present character of the field and its future direction, but since persuasive force can no longer be detached from issues of scholarly validity, the kind of strategic histories that have dominated the discussion for so many years can no longer suffice.

50. Ira Katznelson and Helen V. Milner, eds., *Political Science: The State of the Discipline* (Washington: APSA, 2002); *Political Theory* 30 (2002).

INDEX

academics, role in government of, 17–26, 150, 188–89
accomodationist democracy: emergence of, 15; pluralism and, 249–50
Adams, Brooks, 118
Adams, Henry, 67, 118, 132
Adams, Herbert Baxter, 17, 52, 58, 79–80, 239
Adams, John, 1, 27, 40
Addams, Jane, 115
Adler, Mortimer, 205–6, 211
Adorno, Theodor, 202
Agassiz, Louis, 68
Almond, Gabriel, 4, 234, 274
"Americanism," criticism of, 118
American Political Science Association (APSA), 111; Beard as president, 163; Bryce as president, 108–9; Coker as president, 189; Committee on Political Research, 136; founding and establishment of, 91, 94, 97–98; history of political science and, 116–18, 255, 259, 273–75; Munro as president, 164; National Conferences on the Science of Politics, 136; Ogg as president of, 211–12; oral history project of, 273–74; Political Theory Research Committee, 215–16; role of government discussed by,

187; Shepard as president, 188; Willoughby as president, 116
American Political Science Review (APSR), 96–97, 109, 139; articles on Bentley in, 237; liberalism discussed in, 198; pluralism discussed in, 163
American Republic, The, 66
American Revolution: "end of ideology" argument concerning, 227; Laski's discussion of, 126; rhetoric and ideology of, 31–56
American Science of Politics, The, 237, 256
American Social Science Association, 90, 265–66
An Economic Interpretation of the Constitution of the United States, 106
Anti-Federalists: concepts of democracy of, 16; popular sovereignty and, 32–33, 35–56
antimodernism, political theory and, 25
Anti-Saloon League, 172
Appleby, Joyce, 29–30
Arendt, Hannah, 216, 226, 246, 258
Aristotle, 79; democratic theory and, 145, 176, 226; pluralism and, 242; political theory and, 4, 162, 194; state theory and, 59, 69, 125
Arnold, Thurman, 203